Club Manitou

How to Plan, Build, and Operate a Gangster Speakeasy

[and Motown Laboratory]

2nd Edition

Mark Huck & Judith Landis

Copyright © 2022, 2023 by Mark M. Huck

All rights reserved. No part of this publication may be reproduced, distributed, or transmitted in any form or by any means, including photocopying, recording, or other electronic or mechanical methods, without the prior written permission of the author, except in the case of brief quotations embodied in critical reviews and certain other noncommercial uses permitted by copyright law. For permission requests, write to the author at mark@depth.network.

Acknowledgements

The first author is deeply indebted to the research provided by the second author, Judith Mallen Landis, as well as to her unimpeded access to the building once known as Club Manitou.

Photographs were supplied to Ms. Landis by Wendy Morris. Photographs, still or moving, more than anything presently known transport us back in time.

The work of Petoskey resident and college researcher Richard Wiles has also been invaluable, as has been the support of the Harbor Springs Area Historical Society. The Geology Department and, in particular, Stephanie Georgevich at Lake Superior State University have contributed valuable insights and data.

A special thanks to Jacqueline Frank, residing in Colombia after political turmoil in her native Honduras, who painstakingly reverse-engineered the various features of the club, giving a vivid impression of their designs and functions.

The 2nd Edition also benefits from the artistry of Hunter Finch, its cover designer.

Contents

Dedication		11
Preface to the 2nd Edition		13
Preface to the 1st Edition		15
Timeline		20
PLAN		23
1	Prologue to Slim and Club Manitou	25
2	Detroit Slim	37
	Growing up in Reading, Pennsylvania	37
	From Reading to Detroit	40
	From Detroit to Harbor Springs	51
3	Harbor Springs, Petoskey, and vicinity	59
	Emmet County	63
	Waterways	64
4	Motive	69
	Markets and profits	70
	Investment	74
BUILD		77
5	Risk Management	79
	Steel and concrete barriers	81
	Roller locks	90
	Exits	97
6	Construction	117
OPERATE		121
7	Operations	123
8	Guests at Club Manitou	129
9	Slim's Lounge	143
	Dance (west) room	147
	Fireplace	150

	Gaming	153
	Bar (east) room	158
	Kitchen	167
10	Personnel	171
11	Competition	175
12	Business interruption	179
13	Expansion and threats	183
14	Disruptive technology	189
	Colonial Club near the Greenbrier	192
15	The road not taken	197
16	Law un-enforcement	201
17	Unintended consequences	205

TRANSMOGRIFY — 209

18	Songs of Freedom	211
	Wilson	211
	Gordy	213
19	Baby Boom	216
20	Vinyl	218
21	Radio	219
22	Transistor Radio	220
23	Television	222
24	Motown	223
	Wilson	223
	Gordy	223
25	The Club transmogrifies	225
26	Late 1961	227
27	1962	229
	Race relations	230
	Adolescent wave	231
28	Music	231

		Motown	231
29		The Stage: 1962	238
30		The Stage: 1963	240
31		The Stage: 1964	250
32		The Stage: 1965	253
33		The Stage: 1966	266
34		The Stage: 1967	277
35		The Stage: 1968	280
36		The Stage: 1969	284
37		Other performers	289
38		Top artists and songs	300
39		Competition	305
		Local	305
		National	308
40		Demise	309
41		Club Ponytail's place in history	311
42		Golden Horseshoe Supper Club	312
43		Epilogue	317

Appendix A: 1970s plans — 319
Appendix B: Exterior photos — 321
Appendix C: 2022 Exhibit — 324
Appendix D: Miniaturization — 326
Index — 333
Notes — 339

Club Manitou, 2nd Edition

Dedication

To Keehn Landis:

Husband, Father, and Keeper of Club Manitou, 1974-2013

Club Manitou, 2nd Edition

Preface to the 2nd Edition

Around 2015 it became well known in Harbor Springs that a strikingly beautiful, willful, 80-something-year-old lady, about 5'5" and 110 pounds, was buying up 80-pound bags of concrete at the local hardware store and hauling them back to her home. No doubt quizzical eyes peered down on the diminutive woman pulling out a stack of $20 bills from her wallet to pay for her latest project.

The tunnels of Club Manitou were collapsing, but the woman needed to traverse their topsides. In fact, her whole house sat atop a vast cavern of steel-reinforced concrete-walled rooms and tunnels. The parts of that formidable bunker that were exposed to dripping water from above had started to crumble, and with that decay history was slipping away.

A few years later, she would succumb to the temptation of hiring young men to do the work of filling the collapsing tunnels. But it was a difficult decision and one, no doubt, that caused her many nights of sleeplessness as she considered delegating such important work.

The woman, Judith Mallen Landis, had been repairing Club Manitou for decades, but now its underbelly was collapsing. So, true to anyone born into the Depression, she applied what is known as "self-help": she filled the tunnels with concrete herself.

Because of her perseverance at keeping Club Manitou intact, we all today enjoy a lens into the history of Harbor Springs and Petoskey – and indeed the entire mob world of the early 20th century – that otherwise might not exist. For that we must thank this woman who weighed hardly more than the concrete sacks she dragged onto the Club's grounds, then dumped into its manmade sinkholes.

Judith Landis passed away peacefully at Club Manitou on August 20, 2023. She was 92. She will be greatly missed by all who passed through its rooms.

Mark Huck

August 26, 2023

Club Manitou, 2nd Edition

Preface to the 1st Edition

On August 19, 1918, Colonel Reed Landis, flying for the Royal Air Force above Vitry-en-Artois in France, shot down his 12th German aircraft, three months after Prohibition had gone into effect in Michigan. For his bravery in World War I, he received both the American Distinguished Service Cross and the British Distinguished Flying Cross. Those medals were passed on to his son, Keehn Landis, a pilot in World War II 22 years later.

Distinguished Flying Cross

On July 26, 1974 – 30 years after crash-landing out of World War II – the younger Landis purchased an old run-down home on the eastern edge of Harbor Springs, Michigan for the price of the land and proceeded to fix up the intriguing home. The house had a fortified basement with escape tunnels disappearing into its yards. Local children regularly broke into the basement to explore the subterranean labyrinth. Inevitably, soon after Keehn and his wife had moved into the house, one of the trespassers found the way through an opening in the basement ceiling – probably the dumb waiter – onto the main floor and swiped the medals. Keehn and Judy Landis had not touched alcohol in dozens of years, but alcohol was what facilitated the theft: the bootlegging tunnels always provided a thoroughfare for the shifty.

This is the story of those tunnels – why and how they came to be – and the house, people, and world inextricably linked to them.

It is also a story about two mobsters: Abe Bernstein, infamous Detroit mob boss, and Al "Slim" Gerhart, Abe's young protégé. Abe always in the background and Slim the protagonist of this story. Their paths in history absorbed the times into which they were born as well as their family histories. The reader should keep their two vectors in mind as this narrative unfolds: it is not a simple story; the world was not simple at the start of the 20th century.

Abe Bernstein was born in 1894 Russia into a world of privation and violence. His family landed in New York with little more than some clothing and the father's shoemaking skills.

Allah Schwendner, later known as "Al Gerhart" or "Slim", was born in Reading, Pennsylvania 11 years later. His world swirled with technology and promise. Yet, their paths collided on the violent streets of Detroit as Prohibition and the Spanish Flu took grip on the country.

Reed Landis had been awarded his Distinguished Service Cross in 1934 "For conspicuous gallantry and devotion to duty. He has carried out offensive patrols with marked determination and dash, and he has on all occasions engaged the enemy with marked skill and an entire disregard of personal danger." Prohibition had been repealed a year earlier, on March 22, 1933. By the time the medal was awarded to Reed, the business that had required those fortified tunnels – Club Manitou – had been running profitably for five years, likely repurposing some surplus airplanes from World War I.

Club Manitou is a monument to the colossal Constitutional failure known as the 18th Amendment.[1] Both the Club and the Amendment attest to the twisted side-effects that emerge when political power is brought to bear on normal social behavior. Both also belie attempts to gloss over the underlying social ills brought on by the Industrial Revolution and reflected today in the torrid pace of innovation and its unequal benefits as the final remnants of the industrial era became overgrown with weeds throughout the coal and rust belts.

There is a fair amount of conjecture in the following narrative, attempting to connect dots that may be several steps away from each other. Often, our claims have substantial but only circumstantial evidence. When this speculation enters the picture, we alert the reader to it with the following clues: "may", "possibly", "perhaps". If the evidence is stronger, look for "likely" and "probably". Unless there are better theories, the one with the preponderance of evidence wins. It's a low historical bar but not unusual. Without this best-efforts attempt to make sense of Club Manitou, its history and significance disappear into the dustbins of time.

As the lion in Aesop said to the Man, "There are many statues of men slaying lions, but if only the lions were sculptors there might be quite a different set of statues."[2] The best evidence is that which lays at our feet and is nearly incontrovertible: the place itself. And so we have tried to preserve for posterity the things and people that actually existed through measurement, photograph, and quotation. Hopefully, together, these will bring the past to life, speaking as lions.

> If the historian will submit himself *to* his material instead of trying to impose himself *on* his material, then the material will ultimately speak to him and supply the answers.[3]

Mark Huck and Judith Landis

February 1, 2022

Club Manitou, 2nd Edition

Timeline

1858	Eliza Mae, mother of Jackie Wilson, born in in Mississippi
1873	Railroad reaches Petoskey, Michigan
1876	Caster with offset pivot patented
1877	Schwendner family migrates to Reading, Pennsylvania from Germany
1881	Anti-Jewish pograms in Ukraine; Village of Harbor Springs formed
1882	May laws in Russia
1888	Berry Gordy II born in Georgia
1893	Formation of the Anti-Saloon League
1894	Abe Bernstein, eventual leader of the Purple Gang, born in Russia
1902	Bernstein family moves from New York City to Detroit's east side
1903	Ford Motor Company incorporated in Dearborn
1906	**Allah Schwendner (later changed to Al Gerhart a/k/a Slim) born in Reading, Pennsylvania**
1908	Jersey City, New Jersey becomes first U.S. city to disinfect city water; Model T introduced by Ford
1913	Federal Reserve Act creates a national banking system
1914	First federal note issued in the form of a ten-dollar bill
1916	Michigan referendum to go dry passes
1918	Michigan goes dry; Reed Landis downs 12th German aircraft over France
1919	World War I ends; Slim, age 13½, likely moves to Detroit from Reading to join his brothers in the auto industry
1920	U.S. Prohibition begins; Purple Gang ascends to power in Detroit gangland
1924	Slim turns 18; Slim's father, Max Schwendner, dies
1926	Slim convicted of bastardy
1928	Slim turns 22; Construction of Club Manitou begins
1929	**Club Manitou opens**; Slim linked to murder south of Detroit; Stock Market crash; Berry Gordy III born

1933	Prohibition ends
1935	Slim in the State Penitentiary for gun charges; Electro String Instrument Corporation reaches commercial success with its electric guitar
1936	Slim released from jail; Purple Gang implodes; Slim buys the Ramona Club Casino, then tears it down
1940	Slim marries Jeannette Kenich
1945	World War II ends
1946	Club Manitou triples in size
1948	First vinyl record arrives
1950	Color TV debuts
1953	Club Manitou closes
1954	Regency TR-1 transistor radio released
1959	Club Manitou sold to Jean and Stanley Douglas
1960	Slim opens the Colonial Club in White Sulphur Springs
1962	**Club Ponytail opens at Club Manitou location**
1963	FBI raids the Colonial Club, shutting it down; Beach Boys play at Club Ponytail
1967	Golden Horseshoe Supper Club opens a hundred yards north of the Club Manitou property
1969	Club Ponytail burns to the ground; original Club Manitou building survives
1972	Golden Horseshoe Supper Club closes
1974	Keehn Landis purchases former Club Manitou property
1987	Slim dies, age 81

Club Manitou, 2nd Edition

PLAN

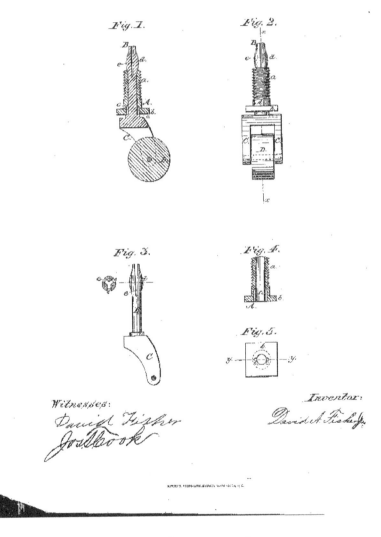

Patent 174,794.[4]

1   Prologue to Slim and Club Manitou

The answer to the business planning question of "when?" is usually "immediately." High priority and urgent business requirements regularly demand attention, now. Capital needs to be allocated to its best use so that managers meet the demands of the owners – and the owners can live the lifestyles to which they would like to become accustomed.

But this "when" is also the endpoint of all the events propelling the business to its starting line. Thus, understanding a business start requires a view into the world at international, national, state, and local levels leading up to that point; this macroscopic view informs the here-and-now.

The world at the close of the 19th century – as the characters of this book appear on our stage – continued that century's massive industrialization. Huge dislocations throughout the social, political, and economic world were underway. Invention responded to and in turn compelled this change; alcohol blunted the impacts of relentlessly seismic social and economic shifts.

Consider the lowly caster.

A case of whiskey weighs 34 lbs. Those twelve bottles, with 16 shots in each, might keep 24 people well served at a raucous summer party. To keep a party of 300 people going 6 hours might take 12 cases. So, the weekly needs for a never-ending summer party might be 100 cases, plus or minus. Keeping an entire community happy might take 10 or 20 times that number of cases. Heavy stuff needs to move. Illegal heavy stuff in the early 20th century needed to move in secret underground spaces with little wiggle room.

Casters – wheels attached to frames – have been around since ancient Egypt, when material handling needs were acute. Pyramids were large but the labor supply limited. Casters of this age eased the movement of stone and got the edifices built. But these casters were fixed: they did not pivot, turn, or steer.[5]

Steering fixed casters on a wagon with four wheels was complex and expensive, for thousands of years. Depending on how sharply you could turn two front wheels determined how much space or "turning radius" it required to change direction. Not a problem when you are in the Egyptian desert or driving a Conestoga wagon across a prairie. But a crowded manufacturing plant or hospital meant that space was valuable, and a big turning radius was a problem. The Industrial Revolution magnified the need to move heavy materials more efficiently using the least amount of floor space: the caster needed to pivot.

Working in the furniture industry in the middle of the 19th century, David Fisher understood the manpower needed to move a single piece of furniture in a factory. He discovered a way for a single person to do the work of several. In 1876, he patented offsetting the "kingpin" or "pivot point" of the caster from the axle. What this minor adjustment did was revolutionize material handling. The center of the caster frame pivot point was offset from the center of the axle. By trailing the center of the axle behind the pivot point, any friction on the side of the wheel causes the wheel to pivot and follow the path of least resistance. It rolls in the direction it is pushed. In fact, the caster allows the cart to spin 360 degrees without any travel.

The application of the caster was extensive, particularly in tight spaces with little room for movement (such as tunnels) where heavy loads (such as cases of liquor) were moved. Tight corners were easily negotiated, and the compact size of the casters allowed for low ceilings.

The inventions wrought by the Industrial Revolution gave bootleggers many of their best tools, but eventually their worst nightmares.

Alcohol has been a part of the human experience for all of recorded history. Discovery of late Stone Age jugs suggests that intentionally fermented beverages existed at least as early as the Neolithic period (c. 10,000 BC): traces of a wheat-and-barley-based alcohol were found in stone mortars carved into a cave floor.[6] Some have proposed that alcoholic drinks predated agriculture and it was the desire for alcoholic drinks that led to agriculture and civilization.[7]

Simultaneously, the abuse of alcohol began.

At the close of the 19th century in the U.S., alcohol continued its troublesome sway on human behavior. The country was in the midst of rapid industrialization, luring workers into the cities in search of steady income, despite the attendant hardships. Given that the water quality in the tenements of these burgeoning cities was non-existent, drinking alcohol in the form of beer was a health necessity. It was not until 1908 that the first city in the U.S. (Jersey City, New Jersey) routinely disinfected community drinking water.[8] Federal water quality standards did not arrive until 1914.[9] Want to stay alive? Drink beer. Whiskey was just as cheap – abundant corn on the western frontier encouraged its widespread production – and the hard stuff blunted the day's difficulties measurably better than beer.

The great land rushes of the 19th century subsided as the railroads saturated the West with immigrants. The availability of free or near-free homesteading land was largely gone by the end of the century. Newly arriving immigrants from Europe were given few options to subsist. They crowded into cities and scratched out a living by selling what they could on the streets in front of their tenements. Life was worse than hard: it was nasty, brutish, and short. Anger in all its forms, including violence, burst onto the streets, alcohol the accelerant.

Consumption of hard alcohol was nearly triple that of the early 21st century, averaging 1.7 bottles per week per person.[10] That was simply the average. Given a population teeming with children, the average for each *adult* was likely near 4 high octane bottles per week, supplemented with prodigious quantities of beer. Given the variances between adult tastes, a third of the population was sloshed. It was a very large social problem.

As cities compressed this social problem into ever tighter spaces, inevitably a countervailing force appeared. While the Temperance movement had its American beginnings in Benjamin Rush's 1784 tract, "An Inquiry Into the Effects of Ardent Spirits Upon the Human Body and Mind",[11] the formation of the Anti-Saloon League (ASL) in 1893 was pivotal for our story. The League successfully pushed for national prohibition after many earlier victories at the state level.

The alcohol problem had become so bad that, in 1887, members of the National Prohibition Party purchased 5,100 acres in Staten Island, New York, with the specification that no consumption of alcohol would be permitted in the area. The area became known as Prohibition Park.

The ASL's motto was "the Church in action against the saloon" and, energized by anti-German sentiment during World War I, it mobilized its religious coalition to get a referendum before the Michigan voters in 1916. The measure passed. On May 1, 1918, Michigan went dry, two years before national prohibition. But organized crime had over a year to prepare.

Prohibition begat workarounds.

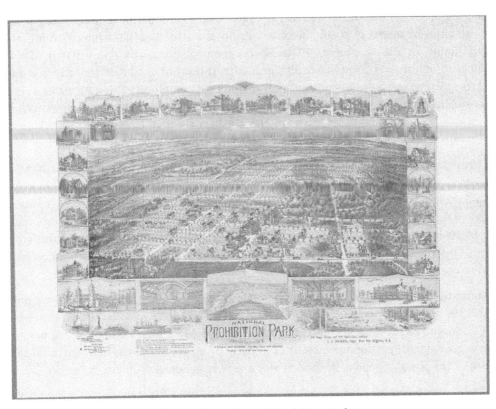

Prohibition Park, Staten Island, New York.[12]

At the close of the 19th century as well, but half a world away, Russia was exterminating or expelling its Jewish citizens. A large-scale wave of anti-Jewish pogroms swept Ukraine in 1881, after Jews were scapegoated for the assassination of Alexander II. In 1886, an Edict of Expulsion was enforced on the historic Jewish population of Kiev. Most Jews were expelled from Moscow in 1891 (except those deemed useful) and a newly built synagogue was closed by the city's authorities headed by the Tsar's brother. Tsar Alexander III refused to curtail repressive practices, remarking: "we must never forget that the Jews have crucified our Master and have shed his precious blood." Faith was twisted to political ends, again.

Between 1880 and 1920, more than two million Russian Jewish immigrants fled to the United States.[13] To uncover the reasons behind this mass exodus, the U.S. Government sent Philip Cowen, an immigration inspector, to Russia in 1906. What he found was relentless persecution.

Russia's May Laws of 1882 forced Jews from their homes and ordered them to live in the Pale of Settlement. Along with this displacement, which put Russian Jews into a confined areas where they struggled to survive, were the pogroms. While by broad definition pogroms are organized massacres of a certain ethnic group, the term is most particularly applied to Jews in Russia or Eastern Europe. In a comprehensive report, compiled from 1906 to 1907, Cowen detailed 637 pogroms. In his description of the Kalarash pogrom of 1905, Cowen wrote[14]:

> 550 homes representing 2,300 persons, were burned or plundered and the loss was over a million rubles. As the immediate result of the pogrom 100 families went of themselves to the United States, and 31 to Argentine and Canada, 150 houses were burnt, representing the best in the place, 75 were directly killed, 200 wounded, of whom 25 died subsequently, and 70 were rendered incapable of self-support. The only non-Jew hurt was a German who had sought to defend the Jews. For his pains his home, one of the finest in the place, was burnt to the ground. He was given a little financial relief by the Jewish committee, but is ruined and cannot rebuild.

He went on:

> [There was] a group of houses where 17 were burned to death. Not seeing a single store of any ambitious appearance I questioned if there had been any large business places there, when some of the above facts were given me and I was told that there were many fine ones. They had all been on one side of the street. These were plundered and burned. The other side was simply wrecked, even the stock of an iron merchant being destroyed, for the men came armed with powerful crowbars and other instruments. The only decent store in sight was the apothecary shop.

These desperate Russian Jews set out on foot, bound for port cities further east where many sailed to the United States. Almost half of the newcomers put down roots in New York City, Boston, and Chicago. Among those arriving was the Bernstein family. The families arrived fleeing violent persecution, a violence witnessed by the young and which surely burned in their memories.

Their experiences taught these children that life was cheap.

Home to Russian immigrants, New York City's Lower East Side became one of the most densely populated neighborhoods on earth. About 1900, Lower East Side, New York City. Credit: Hulton Archive/Getty Images

Life in the New York City tenements was rough for the new arrivals from the increasingly oppressive Europe and Russia. The immigrants faced not only blatant prejudice but also a language completely unknown and difficult to learn. They needed to work hard to find the next meal. As parents strove to make ends meet, their children played in the streets. Gangs were quick to arise as children fought to protect what little they had. But those with skills useful to the emerging automobile industry had different prospects.

In Germany, both Catholics and Jews were being pushed out by political and economic forces. For the Catholics:

> Laws enacted in the state of Prussia and in the empire in the early 1870s discriminated against Catholics. These laws were resisted by the Church, leading to heated public debates in the media and in the parliaments, during which the term "Kulturkampf" gained widespread currency. Diplomatic ties

with the Vatican were cut and additional laws were passed to quell Catholic opposition. This only resulted in more support by the Catholic population and more resistance by the Church. During the Kulturkampf, four bishops and 185 priests in defiance of the laws were tried and imprisoned and many more were fined or went into exile.[15]

Baden and Württemberg passed the legislation that gave the Jews complete equality before the law in 1861-64. The newly formed German Empire did the same in 1871. However,

> The modernization of the economies of much of Central Europe severely undermined the basis of the traditional Jewish economy, particularly that of the poorer classes. Industrialization and improvements in production and transportation wiped out much of the need for the classic Jewish occupations of peddling and eliminated the businesses of other Jews who served as intermediaries between the rural peasantry and the rest of society. As such, the daughters and sons of the less-well-off Jews had to find other options for themselves. Thousands of young Jewish women and men migrated to America because they could not make a living in Europe or marry.[16]

Toward the end of the German immigrations, the Schwendner family made its way from Bavaria to New York and then continued on to Reading, Pennsylvania, where the father used his mechanical engineering expertise in enterprises related to the nascent auto industry. Unlike the Bernstein experience, the Schwendner family immigration was not that of desperation; it was one of opportunity.

In 1891, 28-year-old Henry Ford became an engineer with the Edison Illuminating Company of Detroit. After his promotion to Chief Engineer in 1893, he had enough time and money to devote attention to his experiments on gasoline engines. Backed by the capital of Detroit lumber baron William H. Murphy, Ford resigned from the Edison Company and founded the Detroit Automobile Company on August 5, 1899. However, the automobiles produced were of a lower quality and higher price than Ford wanted. Ultimately, the company was not successful and was dissolved in January 1901.

Undeterred, Ford's next iteration of his company eventually become Ford Motor Company, incorporated on June 16, 1903. The Model T debuted on October 1, 1908. Sales skyrocketed for the $825 ($23,760 in 2020 dollars) vehicle and soared further as the price dropped to $360 in 1916.

Capitalism relentlessly widened the rift between haves and have-nots. With unions and worker protection laws still in the future – the National Labor Relations Act would not arrive until 1935 – workers were nearly always compensated at subsistence levels. Entire families, including the young, worked to make ends meet.

But Detroit provided opportunities for those who combined muscle with mechanic skills. The demand for labor among the competing auto manufacturers soared along with the fast-selling cars. Ford astonished the world in 1914 by offering a $5 per day wage ($130 today), which more than doubled the rate of most of his workers.[17] A Cleveland, Ohio, newspaper editorialized that the announcement "shot like a blinding rocket through the dark clouds of the present industrial depression". The move proved extremely profitable; instead of constant employee turnover, the best mechanics in the country flocked to Ford, bringing their human capital and expertise, raising productivity, and lowering training costs. Families seeking fortunes – or at least a better life – set out for Detroit from the tenements of New York.

The Ford assembly line in 1913.

The new auto industry concentrated wealth in and near Detroit. Together with their counterparts in Chicago and other Midwestern cities, the newly minted millionaire industrialists sought refuge from the Heartland's stifling summer heat, nasty mosquitos, and hay fever. The Wrigleys, Swifts, and Armours from Chicago were joined by the Fords and Dodges from Detroit in an annual summer pilgrimage to the cooler climes of Little Traverse Bay.

The Grand Rapids and Indiana Railroad had extended its line to Petoskey on November 25, 1873.[18] The Little Traverse ferry "Skater" plied between Petoskey, Harbor Springs, Roaring Brook, and Bay View from 1900 to 1910. Transportation systems were catching up with the demands of the wealthy. Eventually, at the height of the resort season as many as 5,000 passengers took the ferries every day to Harbor Springs from Chicago and other cities. The pathways for the rich to reach Harbor Springs were also well paved as the automobile world erupted at the beginning of the 20th century.

The Silver Spray entered the Little Traverse Bay area in 1903. Harbor Springs Historical Society.

Harry Bernstein, forced out of Russia around 1896, took his family to Detroit from New York in 1902[19], most likely to escape the rat race of the New York ghetto but also likely in anticipation of work for his eldest son, Abe, who was 9 at the time, and any future children. News of the nascent automobile industry had certainly reached all parts of the United States, including the Jewish ghetto in New York City.

The family moved into Detroit's east side to a neighborhood known as "little Jerusalem". Although conditions were not as bad as the lower east side of New York City, the east side of Detroit was one of the least desirable areas; it continually lagged other areas in the city by the number of water pipes laid, sewers installed, streets paved and streetcar lines extended. The district was more crowded and had higher rents and higher disease and death rates than other parts of the city.[20]

The norms of New York ghetto life had migrated to the Detroit ghetto. The young boys banded together to protect against other ethnic gangs, and to dominate them. Abe grew up violent, and pulled his brothers with him. From stealing candy and then rolling drunks, the young gang emboldened. Soon, merchants were shaken down.

By the time the 1916 Michigan referendum meant Michigan would go dry in 1918, Abe was 23 years old and firmly in control of an extremely violent gang others referred to as the "Purple Gang." It was then that the gang focused on controlling the increasingly lucrative illegal saloons – known and "blind pigs" – as well as gambling houses and brothels.[21] The gang was ruthlessly violent, likely involved in 500 murders.[22] Three years later, new arrival to Detroit, Allah Schwendner (later known as Al Gerhart), was recruited by this notorious gang.

All these forces – from international down to the local level – led to the arrival of Club Manitou. But "when?" is only the first planning question: "Who?" is perhaps the most critical question to answer in that plan.

Club Manitou, 2nd Edition

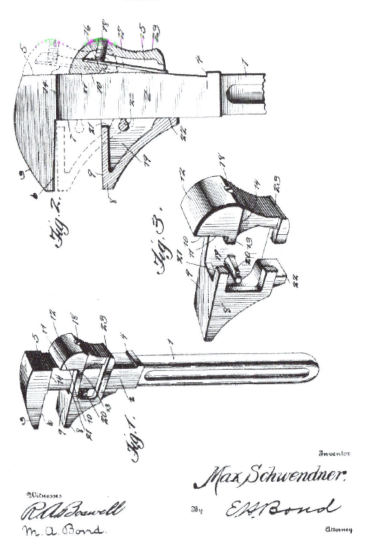

Patent issued to Max Schwendner in 1907[23]

2 Detroit Slim

Growing up in Reading, Pennsylvania

In 1877, the Schwendner[24] family joined the immense migrations out of Europe – escaping persecution of Catholics – beginning their journey from Munich in German Bavaria[25] and finally reaching Reading, Pennsylvania.[26] The father, Max Schwendner[27], born in 1854[28], was a mechanic. He had studied design at an art school in Bavaria and, after reaching the U.S. at age 19, "followed his profession as a designer in New York City and later in New England states."[29] In Reading, he invented a wrench, or brought its design with him from Germany. Having the wherewithal to create and file a patent suggests that the family was doing fairly well.

Schwendner wrench in use, 2021.[30]

Reading had a solid manufacturing sector, anchored by the Philadelphia and Reading Railroad and, beginning in 1902, by the relocation of Duryea Motor Company from Massachusetts and arrival of other "Brass Era" automobile companies. Working for a hardware company supplying this emerging industry gave Max the inspiration and means for his patent.

Max married Reading stocking-maker Amelia Kirmse – born in 1868 – in Philadelphia in 1892 and he was naturalized in 1893. Amelia died in 1899 at age 31, and the same year Max married Margaret Pfeiffer.[31] The Schwendner children were: Irwin born 1893; Frederick born 1894; Evelyn born 1902; Edwin born 1903; and Allah – who would become the infamous "Slim" of this story – born 1906.[32] The older two brothers worked for Ford Motor Company according to the 1920 census. Given their father's death back in Reading, as well as Edwin's occupation as a press operator in Reading, it is most likely that Max never left Reading, and that his sons ventured west on their own. Apart from his eldest son's marriage record (Frederick to Helen Chadwick in 1936), Max does not appear in any Michigan records.

By the time Allah reached 5, the family resided on quiet North Front Street in Reading. Houses had front yards. The streets were not chaotic business locales. While today the house is gone, and only a parking lot remains, the houses in the area were built around the time of Allah's birth. Judging from the area today, the neighborhood was far cry from the squalid city tenements into which many immigrants landed in New York City. The family may have lived in a larger detached home as Max had his garage in the rear. Over time, the Schwendner family accumulated four homes at the corner of Windsor and North Front Street, with a 1930s assessment totaling $28,200.[33]

Row houses built in 1905 across the street from the Schwendner home in Reading, Pennsylvania. Google maps.

The family lived and breathed mechanics. Max had a garage in the backyard for 8 years and worked for Reading Hardware Co. for 15 years as a designer. He was one of the founders and later President of the Temple Malleable Iron and Steel Company of Temple, Pennsylvania. The Company, founded in 1911, was still in business in 2022, 111 years later.[34]

The family was also involved with St. Paul's Church[35], and Max was a member of the Bavarians. The church and its school were 1.4 miles from 824 North Front Street, certainly walking distance for the athletic family (Evelyn placed 2nd in a shoe race, a skating race and 4-legged race in a 1920 contest[36]). Given the family's membership in the church as well as the school's German teaching staff – The Sisters of Christian Charity had come from Germany to America, many due to German sanctions against the Catholic Church, and were centered at Wilkes-Barre, Pennsylvania[37] – it is highly likely that the relatively well-off Schwendner children were educated there.

St. Paul's School.

The teaching would have been very religious and likely strict. Allah would have spent eight years under that regime. As any young boy would attest, a key goal would have been to evade punishment while sidestepping edicts. Deference and a stone face would avoid the wrath of the nuns. While Allah may have been an ideal student and very religious, the subsequent historical record argues otherwise. He was joyriding by age 13.

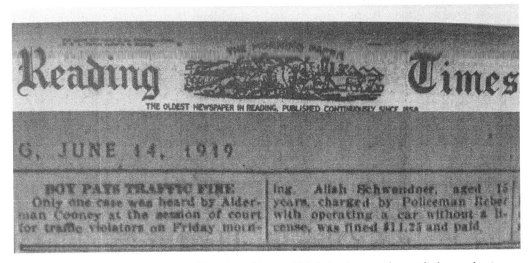

Allah Schwendner joyrides in 1919 and lies about his age. This behavior together with the pandemic may have encouraged his parents to ship him off to Detroit to join his brothers. Clipping provided to Judith Landis by Richard Wiles.

From Reading to Detroit

The allure of Detroit at the time of the father's patent in 1907, as his oldest two sons were about to exit school, must have been irresistible. Detroit was rapidly becoming the epicenter of an immensely popular new technology, and most of the new competitors were concentrated in that single urban area. Irwin, the oldest son, was out of Reading and in Detroit by 1910; Frederick by 1920 though likely shortly after Irwin's arrival. Allah was likely reminded time and again of his brothers' successes at Ford.

In 1918, the Spanish Flu pandemic arrived in America. It is difficult to know what Allah's parents were thinking when the deadly virus swept the east coast. From September 4, 1918, to January 11, 1919, deaths per 1,000 were 7.9 in Philadelphia but only 2.7 in Grand Rapids, Michigan.[38] Perhaps the Midwest appeared safe and, with two older sons there, they may have been eager to send their youngest westward. For the next three years, many parents longed for a safe haven for their children.

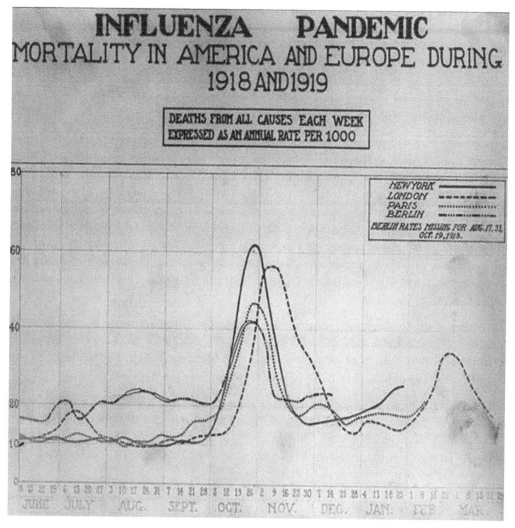

New York death rate skyrockets starting end of September, 1918.[39]

School was not a social or political priority at the time. Immigrant families arrived and only hard work would put food on the table. In 1895, a compulsory school attendance law was passed in Pennsylvania, requiring children between the ages of 8-13 years to attend school for 16 consecutive weeks.[40] The typical age limit for compulsory education was no more than 14 by the time Allah was 14.[41] Half of Chicago children, for example, were leaving school before the 8th grade, while the "majority [left] on the fourteenth birthday or as soon as the law allow[ed]."[42]

It may well be that Allah was enticed to Detroit by one of the innumerable garages popping up in the wake of Ford's massive growth in the period following World War I. The Roaring Twenties were emerging, and the auto was propelling that economic miracle. With high school education optional and child labor laws non-existent, children were sent into the workplace at an early age. Allah left for Detroit in his early teen years. Opportunities were abundant, even for the young. Children were cheap labor and, at Ford especially, not inclined to agitate for unionization. And they were sober. The U.S. Fair Labor Standards Act which protected children did not arrive until 1938.

Automobiles were still relatively new, breaking down on a regular basis, particularly given the condition of roads at the time.[43] And there were lots of them. The demands of World War I had juiced the Ford assembly lines. Over 800,000 cars rolled off the Ford lines in 1919, about half of the industry total for the year. Cars and trucks on the road totaled about 6,000,000[44]. In 1918, only 1 in 13 families owned a car. By 1929, 4 out of 5 families had one. In the same time period, the number of cars on the road increased from 8 million to 23 million. In fact, the industry grew so fast, by 1925 over 10% of all people in the workforce had something to do with production, sales, service, or fueling of automobiles[45]. By 1927, Henry Ford watched the 15 millionth Model T Ford roll off the assembly line at his factory in Highland Park, Michigan.[46]

The business of bootlegging required armies of these new vehicles to transport the recently-declared contraband, and a broken car in the middle of nowhere might lead to a lost shipment. It is likely that local Detroit garages in cahoots with the Purple Gang were hiring talent at top dollar. They had to in order to compete against Ford.

Railroads, on the other hand, had reached their peak route miles in 1916.[47] Despite the over 200,000 miles of track, the route from Reading to Detroit was convoluted, requiring several connections. Using the New York Central Lines, four connections were required in 1919. Getting to Detroit was made easier on May 29, 1920 when the Pennsylvania Railroad began passenger rail service from Detroit to eastern cities.[48]

Allah would have taken the train to Philadelphia and from there caught the line to Detroit, ending at the Romanesque style Union Depot on Fort Street. The PRR had operated its Broadway Limited from New York to Chicago since 1912, and this route would have been available but would have necessitated disembarking in Crestline, Ohio, and finding an alternate route north to Detroit. As well, the Broadway Limited at that time was all sleeper cars, a pricey proposition.

Above: Broadway Limited in the 1920s. Postcard. Below: Fort Street Union Depot in Detroit. Postcard.

Also in 1920, the Baltimore and Ohio Railroad reached Detroit from Philadelphia. The B&O had been acquired out of bankruptcy by PRR in 1901 but operated as an independent entity. Thus, getting to Detroit from Reading was not difficult in 1919 or 1920. Once there, Allah had his brothers who could help him navigate the new world of Detroit. As with many immigrants working for Ford and other auto-related businesses, Allah boarded with a local family. His older brother Irwin (13 years older) was boarding on Woodward Avenue near Ford's new sales office – down on the Detroit River – when the 1920 census was taken. The oldest brother, Frederick, lived in Ford's backyard, Highland Park. Both brothers were a couple miles apart, and either was likely amenable to helping his little brother.

Campus Martius (looking up Woodward Ave.) in 1917, as Ford boomed. Photo courtesy Detroit News.

Whatever the impetus, Allah likely landed in Detroit during the summer of 1919, though not likely in the comfort of a sleeping berth on the Broadway Limited. When he stepped off the train, he might have been shocked by the sight of his oldest brother. Irwin had scars to show Allah and might have lost a limb, having been severely wounded on January 11, 1919 – between two of the many Armistices attempting to end the War – in a fight on the Meuse River in France.[49] A description of action seen by Company G of Michigan's famous 126th Infantry, 32nd Division leading up to that time is unnerving.[50] The Meuse-Argonne Offensive of the previous winter was the deadliest in American history, resulting in 350,000 casualties on both sides, including 54,000 dead over the battle's 47 days. The shock of Irwin's condition must have reached deep into the youngest brother. Violence flowed through the times.

U.S. soldiers firing at a German position in the Argonne Forest during the Meuse-Argonne offensive. Photo credit U.S. Signal Corps / Wikibooks

Frederick had also returned from France in July of 1919, having served with an ammunition train company.[51] The combined battlefield experiences of Irwin and Frederick were very likely transferred to Allah in vivid detail when he arrived in Detroit. The new arrival in Detroit heard their combined political views as well. Anti-German sentiment was likely deep on the Ford assembly lines as well. If the older Schwendner brothers harbored any resentment of capitalists, they likely kept those opinions away from the factories. The post-war depression which hit Ford hard meant that holding onto a job was a top priority for returning soldiers.

It may well be that the parents were as eager to have Allah in Detroit to help his older brothers as they were for the brothers to help Allah. As the three brothers met in Detroit, the older two provided a very realistic, very dark view of life to the young Allah.

When a younger brother shows up at the doorstep of two older brothers – 11 and 12 years older – in a new place, strange things can happen, usually revolving around poor parenting, but standard brothering. One of the first things the older brothers may have done is to take their kid brother to the ballpark.

Slim Love the year before arriving in Detroit.

In January, 1919, the Detroit Tigers signed lefty pitcher Edward Haughton "Slim" Love – at 6'7" – who had just sat out a season with the Boston Red Sox but had been a star with the New York Yankees. Despite an injury in March, Love and compiled a 6–4 record in 22 games with a 3.01 ERA. On August 24, 1919 – Allah having passed his 14th birthday – Love allowed Babe Ruth's 42nd career home run in Detroit, in the sixth inning. That game would likely have drawn massive crowds to watch The Sultan of Swat.

It is likely the eldest Schwendner brothers actively weaned their little brother from eastern baseball teams and accustomed him to the local baseball team and its fortunes. To be conversant in Detroit Tigers baseball would have been a business asset, if not just good assembly-line conversation. With the nickname "Slim" circulating widely at the time, probably many lanky kids were given the pitcher's nickname. No doubt the older brothers teased the younger Allah with the title, with the younger relishing the new-found fame. Families with multiple brothers can appreciate this likely chain of events.

One can only imagine the torment and active neglect the younger brother received at the hands of the elder two. Any self-respecting parent in the 21st century would recognize this as a recipe for disaster. Today, Child Protective Services might have stepped in. At the start of the Roaring Twenties, it was every brother for himself – the more traditional view of sibling interaction. Allah was thrown to the wolves. And, thus, Allah became Slim.

Whether this new Slim landed in Detroit with a job already in hand, or needed to look around, he likely found a position rapidly. He was a slender, good-looking young man that could fix a car. That was all the resume that was needed. His adolescent years are a mystery, and only conjectures can be made. Whatever his career path, the Purple Gang was well known to all in the Detroit world, and they were hiring.

The Purple Gang was unique in that most were teenagers and, being Russian Jewish, faced incessant exclusion and segregation. The gang's original core group was sent to the Old Bishop School, a separate school for unruly children in the Detroit districts who were evicted from other schools for truancy, fighting, delinquent behavior, or learning disabilities. There they encountered isolation by being placed in the school's Ungraded Section. Students in the other section of the school were referred to as the "normal students," while their peers placed in the Ungraded Section were treated differently and not expected to improve.[52] Abe Bernstein had walked through its doors 10 years earlier.

But this was not the world of Slim. He would have easily slid into the world of mechanics, guided by his brothers. Education was not a priority for someone with hard skills. Those skills were sorely needed by the Purple Gang, the other large business in Detroit.

Allah likely took on the alias "William Al Gerhart" both to hide from his family should he be caught and to protect them. Kidnapping was one of the revenue models of the Purple Gang as well as other gangs, and so distancing himself from his brothers meant Allah would be protecting them. Another possibility for the name change was a notorious murder by suicidal 17-year-old Margaret Schwendner in 1911: she had bashed the skull of her month-old child.[53] Certainly, from an employment standpoint, the last name was an albatross, though fast fading from memories.

It may well be that no one in the Purple Gang knew his true identity. He might simply have been that lanky[54] – "Slim" – guy who could drive a car well and fix it when it broke down. He explained to a judge in a 1925 case that he was a chauffeur for gangsters, nothing more.[55]

Abe Bernstein, de facto leader of the Purple Gang.[56]

For the next decade, Slim was likely working for the Purple Gang and, more precisely, for Abe Bernstein. He probably started fixing cars, but may have moved quickly up the ladder with either wits or violence, or a combination of the two. Regardless, by the end of his teenage years, Slim was under the good graces of the Purple Gang and, more importantly, its financial muscle.

Having absorbed Slim, the Purple Gang and its experiences are all that are available to us to understand this young man's adolescence. Michigan had gone dry in 1918, so the profits from bootlegging were flowing. The Purple Gang had ascended to leadership of the Detroit underworld, led by its alignment with the older Oakland Sugar House Gang. Those elders surrounded themselves with the strong-arm Purple Gang members. At the same time, the gang become prodigious builders of brewing plants.[57]

The activities of the Purple Gang during the 1920s covered the full gamut of the underworld: control over the Detroit vice, gambling, liquor, and drug markets; hijacking liquor shipments; terror; murder; kidnapping; murder-for-hire; bombing; arson; theft; hijacking; insurance fraud; and extortion, such as during the Cleaners and Dyers War. Within gangland, there were vicious turf wars. Retaliations were commonplace, the police unconcerned with gang-on-gang violence. In 1927 the submachine gun was first used in a Detroit mob killing. The violence escalated and political pressure to end it rose in tandem.

In the summers, the Purple Gang's cars would be moving on all the roads between the Midwest's booming cities, carrying the bosses to their summer playgrounds. In the winter, the lightweight "Whiskey Six" Model T's would slowly cross the river to avoid breaking through. The autos were replaceable but landing in the river was certain death for the driver, though that fate was preferable to that meted out by an angry Al Capone if his Canadian Club shipment went missing. Skilled drivers and mechanics were needed year-round. Someone with both skills was invaluable.

The auto mechanic career path led to the top of the Purple Gang. In that promising path – very handy on long auto trips – Slim would have had ample opportunity to impress his bosses. As a young, educated, and certainly rising star in the Purple Gang, Slim received a further hands-on education in construction, accounting, and violent persuasion. As a younger member of the Purple Gang, he may be seen as the heir apparent – life was short for gangsters and a succession plan may have not been overlooked by the senior members of the gang. Perhaps, at the same time, those bosses were imaging some future retirement up North, removed from the action and danger of Detroit.

In 1924, Slim's father died. Slim was 18 years old at the time and definitely in Detroit,[58] proving his worth in the context of the automobile: moving or stealing booze, possibly moving liquor across the frozen Detroit River from Ontario during the winter, ensuring that the vehicles were in good shape and that they kept moving across the ice.

A view of bootlegging operation along the Detroit River near Riopelle Street. Courtesy of the Burton Historical Collection/Detroit Public Library

Detroit supplied about 75% of the nation's alcohol during Prohibition.[59] Obtaining the supply was not trivial:

> Ingenuity carried the day: cargo was dragged beneath boats, old underground tunnels from boathouse to house were reopened, sunken houseboats hid underwater cable delivery systems, and even a pipeline was built. Between Peche Island and the foot of Alter Road, an electronically controlled cable hauled metal cylinders filled with up to 50 gallons of booze. A pipeline was constructed between a distillery in Windsor and a Detroit bottler. In winter, with the ice frozen, anyone from a single skater towing a sled to a loaded caravan of 75 cars could be seen.[60]

Less visibly, tunnels were in the bootlegger's toolset, a defensive as well as offensive weapon. One of the notable tunnels in Detroit was at Tommy's on 3rd Street. The secret passageway led to Fort Street Presbyterian Church (across the street) and was also likely part of the Underground Railroad. It was repurposed during Prohibition as the Purple Gang kept the neighborhood stocked with bathtub gin.[61]

A tunnel used to transport alcohol between buildings is discovered during a Prohibition raid in Detroit. These tunnels likely inspired the later tunneling at Club Manitou. Photo courtesy Walter P. Reuther Library, Wayne State University[62]

By 1925, at age 19, Slim fit the gangster image well. He was charged, as "Allah Schwendner", of bastardy and jailed until he paid a $700 bond to support the new child.[63] Allah may have adopted the alias "Al Gerhart" – a foreman at Ford – to avoid paying this child support.[64] However, as suggested earlier, the name change was likely to protect his older siblings.

From Detroit to Harbor Springs

From the riverfront, the liquor needed to be shipped out to places as far away as Chicago, St. Louis, and Mackinac Island, far north in Michigan. The gang was well-acquainted with the Harbor Springs area and its financial potential. By 1927, the Purple Gang was considering its options for opening in the North, and looked for a building site and management. Slim was on the short list, having possibly secured by then the coveted job as Abe Bernstein's personal chauffer.[65]

Perhaps a more immediate concern to the Purple Gang leadership was its supply chain issues. Distribution was severely impacted by the murder of their key distribution partner for Missouri, Illinois, and Detroit, Johnny Reid, in December of 1926.[66] Most likely, however, the gang was simply trying to re-invest its money. The bootlegging trade generated $215 million in 1929 alone[67] ($6 billion in 2020 dollars), second only to the auto industry. On top of that were all the other rackets of the gang, including murder-for-hire.

An alternate source of funds may have been Sam "Fatty" Bernstein, Abe's cousin and classmate at Bishop School.[68] Sam worked alongside Slim at Club Manitou. At 5'5" and 225 lbs.,[69] he would have been a more formidable bouncer, or rather blocker, than Slim. Sam's purpose at the club may have been one of oversight, ensuring that his uncle's money was fully accounted for. How else could a thief trust a thief?

Sam "Fatty" Bernstein mug shot by the Detroit police. Photo courtesy Walter P. Reuther Library, Wayne State University.

More likely, though, Sam was part of the investor group. He had become rich over the first 10 years of Prohibition, itching for investments by 1928-29 when the investment into Club Manitou was required. His daughter-in-law described Sam as "very wealthy, had lost a lot of money in the stock market crash and was involved in selling illegal alcohol."[70] Sam was a central figure in the Purple Gang, making several appearances in their many police line-ups.

Early photo of Sam counting cash at Club Manitou. Photo courtesy Wendy Morris.

Sam Bernstein (aka Sam Burnstein, Sam Stein) in 1935 Detroit Police Department mug shot. Photo Courtesy Walter P. Reuther Library, Wayne State University.[71]

A few years older[72] than Slim, Sam may have developed a close and influential relationship with Slim when Slim first engaged with the Purple Gang. And, with a close relationship to the gang's leader, Abe Bernstein, Sam was likely at the table for many gang decisions. However, not quick to escape tight situations with the police, Sam had a rap sheet that was a gangland resume in full.

```
28205.....SAM BURNSTEIN alias BURNSTEIN alias SAM STEIN.
Age 23---1926. Height 5-5 5/8. Weight 225. Eyes Blue. Hair
Brown. Complexion Florid. Build Stout. This man has been
arrested in Detroit on charges of Prohibition Law, Attempt
Breaking and Intering, Grand Larceny, Robbery Armed and also
Extortion. He has been convicted several times. He is also
WANTED for questioning by the U.S. Immigration Authorities.
He is not known to be in jail at this time....10-12-32.
```

Sam Bernstein (aka Burnstein) FBI summary.[73]

Not being a member of the Bernstein family, Slim may have been more of an operative than decision-maker. He likely took directions and followed them as required by his superiors. The Purple Gang boat was not one to be rocked.

Slim may have been privately re-evaluating his relationship with the gang when, in January 1928, the gang gunned down a policeman, Vivian Welch.[74] While Welch was clearly on the take, the murder crossed a boundary line that had been tacitly sacred. If law enforcement was not safe, the game had changed. Later that year, the 22-year-old Slim – possibly together with the 25-year-old Sam – traveled to Harbor Springs to build and operate Club Manitou. Assuming that discussions for the project were mature, he was likely involved in its planning no later than 1927, the year of the Purple Gang's notorious Milaflores Massacre, another gang turf war.

Perhaps Slim had had enough. Or, perhaps the Purple Gang was simply eager to continue its expansion, diversify its portfolio, and increase its distribution channels, and Slim was the more educated of the gang. Likely both played a part. Public sentiment was starting to turn against Prohibition – eventually repealed throughout the U.S. in 1933 – and alternate revenue streams were being developed by the gang. The needs of Slim and the Purple Gang were aligned.

As well, the gang may have been finding ways to get its counterfeit money into circulation. If, at the close of the Civil War, one-third of all currency in circulation was counterfeit[75] and the funding of the Secret Service minimal and inconsistent, then likely the world of Slim swirled with fake notes. In early 1920, the Secret Service head told the House Appropriations Committee that counterfeiting had doubled in six months.[76] The large-scale counterfeiting scheme of "Count" Victor Lustig – who had earlier swindled Al Capone – lasted from 1930 until 1935 and injected vast amounts of money into the U.S. economy.[77]

The Purple Gang was involved in getting these or other counterfeit notes into the system, and Slim played a part. In 1935, Slim was ensnared in a wide-ranging sting by the Secret Service – throwing $2,000 in bundled fake bills out his hotel room window when surrounded – and pled not guilty though ultimately was freed.[78] That sting was part of an effort to stop a Toledo counterfeiting operation with connections to New York. Surely, the gang's involvement in counterfeiting came long before that. Trunks-full of the bills must have been traveling the roads of the U.S., and the paper money was much easier to move, particularly from Detroit to Harbor Springs.

Questions arise about Slim and Sam's aptitude for building Club Manitou. However, they likely engaged local talent, including a general contractor, to handle all aspects of the build. Their roles, then, would have been to approve plans and pay the workers. Many folks with lots of money handle construction in this fashion. The workers' pay, however, may have been counterfeit, though they would have been unconcerned as long as others accepted the notes.

Whatever the underlying motivations, Slim was sent north, far from Detroit but at the behest of its most powerful gang, to open an exclusive speakeasy and capture the lucrative summer market there. The mechanical training wrought by his father would be apparent in the construction of that venture. The techniques for hiding and moving liquor would also be incorporated into its design.

Detroit Slim (Al Gerhart) reconciles receipts at the Club Manitou in the 1930s, the first known photograph of Slim. Photo courtesy Wendy Morris.[79]

To understand Slim is to understand Club Manitou.

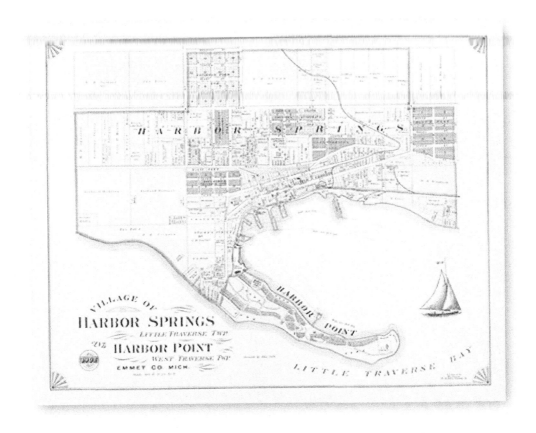

Plat of Harbor Springs, 1902. Courtesy Harbor Springs Area Historical Society

3   Harbor Springs, Petoskey, and vicinity

"Where?" is a third planning hurdle. Slim and the Purple Gang sought to tap the greatest concentration of wealth they knew: they would take their product to the most lucrative market within private shipping distance of Detroit but not in direct competition with the Chicago gang under Al Capone, one of their best clients.

Long a magnet for the wealthy of Chicago, Detroit, St. Louis, Cleveland, and other cities with rail connections there, Harbor Springs and Petoskey were destinations of choice for broiling millionaires and other well-offs during the Heartland's miserable summers, their annual journeys starting in the late 19th century. The Midwest in summertime was and continues to be oppressively hot and humid. The lake breezes and northern cool of Little Traverse Bay, together with its warm sunny beaches during the day, made it an enticing destination. Nearby lakes, such as Crooked Lake and Burt Lake, were equally attractive. Small cottages dotted those lakes, all connected by a series of small rivers. Major League Baseball Commissioner Kenesaw Mountain Landis – Reed Landis' father – made Burt Lake his summer destination. The area's natural beauty and enticing weather combined with the lumber industry to kick the area's development into high gear.

In 1878 resorts had been formed at Harbor Point and Wequetonsing. By 1881, the small town called Little Traverse had been organized as the Village of Harbor Springs with its citizens electing their first village president. Ten years later,

> Harbor Springs had reached a population of more than 1000 and it had since about doubled. It is an up-to-date village, with good water, electric light, clean well paved streets, and a thorough system of public schools. A community of noticeably intelligent people it has naturally given much attention to its educational institutions, and its schools are of the best.[80]

The town was situated on an eastward-facing harbor, giving safe anchorage to ferries. In 1912, "the steamship 'Northland,' the finest passenger steamer on the Great Lakes, owned by the Great Northern Railroad company, made Harbor Springs the only port of call on the east side of Lake Michigan, while many others steamers, including the 'Manitou,' plied between Chicago and Harbor Springs."[81] The Grand Rapids and Indiana Railroad connected the town with Petoskey, 8 miles to the east along the Little Traverse Bay coast.

Harbor Springs, ca 1920. Photo courtesy Harbor Springs Library.

Sited between Harbor Springs and Petoskey, the Ramona Park Hotel was built in 1910. Its large east wing added in 1929 with the financing Cheboygan gambling racketeer Mert Wertheimer,[82] possibly a member of the Purple Gang.[83]

Ramona Park Hotel. Image courtesy of Little Traverse Historical Society.

Slim became keenly interested in the hotel and eventual bought it to stifle competition.

Slim and Sam strategically sited their Club Manitou across the road from the Harbor Springs Airport. Flights brought in lobster every Friday from New York to the club[84], and flights likely also brought in the well-heeled from Chicago and Detroit for the weekends. As reported by the Aeronautics Department of the Smithsonian:[85]

> aeronautical smuggling, but it picked up in the United States immediately after the war as a response to the rising tide of local, state, and ultimately, federal prohibition of the import and transportation of alcoholic beverages.

Harbor Springs Airport, July 11, 1930. Club Manitou's front lawn (facing south) is circled on the right along what is now M-119. Photo courtesy Walter P. Reuther Library, Wayne State University

Simultaneously there was an almost overnight availability of war surplus airplanes like the JN-4 and DH-4, as well as a pool of trained pilots who were deeply frustrated that they saw little to no opportunity to engage in combat before the Armistice. As a result, smuggling arguably became the most profitable and expansive commercial enterprise in American aviation for much of the 1920s. Aerial bootlegging occurred over both the northern and southern borders and was highest near urban markets and distribution centers like Chicago, Detroit, Seattle, San Diego, and Miami.

While there are no shipment manifests or passenger logs – both being inconvenient records in a raid – the proximity of Club Manitou to the airport was likely no accident. There would be far fewer police in the air than on land, and the route was likely less turbulent that the rutted roads below.

Alcohol being unloaded during a Prohibition raid.

Because radar was not available for either smugglers or law enforcement, a modest cloud cover could provide enough coverage to go undetected. Once at the Harbor Springs airport, greased police relations would guarantee successful transfer of the goods to their destination.

Emmet County

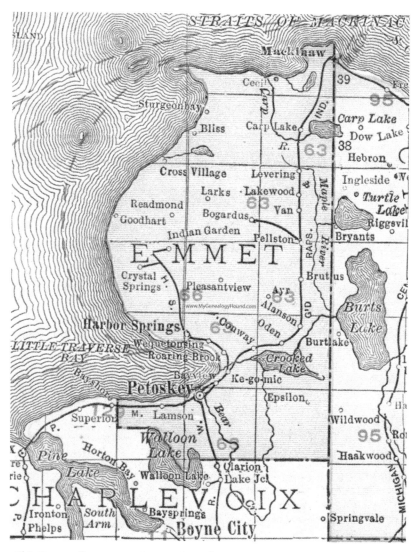

This Emmet County map is a portion of a 1911 Michigan map by Rand McNally.

The most important jurisdiction in our story is Emmet County, encompassing both Harbor Springs and Petoskey, as well as Alanson, Crooked Lake, and Crooked River, all of which are interesting to this story. Club Manitou was sited outside of (but adjacent to) Harbor Springs in an unincorporated area. Thus, the Sheriff of Emmet County is a silent but very important character in this narrative.

As historian Robert Knapp observes, ""I never ran across any law enforcement people who gave a hoot for the fact some of these guys were underworld characters. Not in Roscommon County, not in Cheboygan County, not in Emmet County."[86] If one needed a one-stop-shop for avoiding prosecution, it was the Emmet County Sheriff. The FBI recognized the collusion between the Purple Gang and Emmet County as will be explored below.

Waterways

The inland waterways of Northern Michigan are crucial to understanding the movement of contraband during Prohibition.[87]

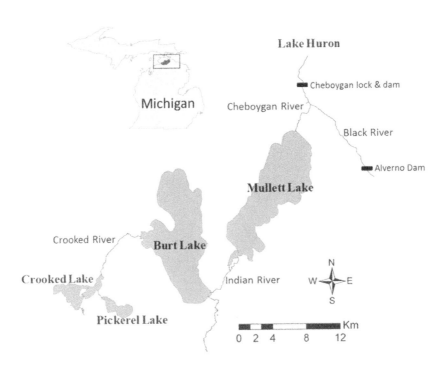

Waterways leading from Emmet County in the lower left up toward Cheboygan on Lake Huron.

The Feds were already active in clamping down on the flow of booze along this route in 1922, as reported by the Cheboygan Democrat: "Prohibition enforcement officers swooped down upon the city Monday morning unheralded and at once commenced serving warrants on thirteen parties who they complained of as having been soiling or dealing in liquors in violation of the federal prohibition laws."

CHEBOYGAN, MICHIGAN, THURSDAY, MARCH 30, 1922.

PROHIBITION OFFICERS LIFT NETS SET IN CHEBOYGAN

Prohibition enforcement officers swooped down upon the city Monday morning unheralded and at once commenced serving warrants on thirteen parties who they complained of as having been selling or dealing in liquors in violation of the federal prohibition laws. Before it was time for the noon train to go south on the M. C. Ry, the thirteen parties complained of were taken to the depot and left on the noon train in charge of the officers for Bay City for arraignment before United States Commissioner Frank S. Pratt. They all appeared before the U. S. commissioner on the following day where they were arraigned for hearing on April 6th or 7th, and gave bonds in the sum of one thousand dollars each for their appearance on those days. Attorney H. H. Quay was retained by several of the men detained and went down with them. The men arrested are Chas. Sias, who has been running the Michigan Central place near the M. C. Depot, James P. Clune and clerk R. A. Massey, Tom Lewis, Lawrence Neelis, John Mushlock, Jack Elliott, Peter Asselin, Eugene Lafrinere and Eugene H. Lafrinere, A. Morris and Joseph Wezell.

Cheboygan Democrat, March 30, 1922, first page.

It is no wonder, then, that Club Manitou was located at the junction of Lake Michigan, the Inland Waterways, and the Harbor Springs airport, all touching Emmet County. It is also not surprising that the Purple Gang owner of Club Manitou eventually retired in Alanson, on Crooked Lake and in the heart of Emmet County. Slim eventually donated a park to Alanson after his retirement there.

Alanson Hillside Garden, gift from Slim for years of protection.

The siting of Club Manitou was no accident; rather, it was very intentional. The location was ideally suited to serve the motives and markets of the business that was soon to open there.

Club Manitou, 2nd Edition

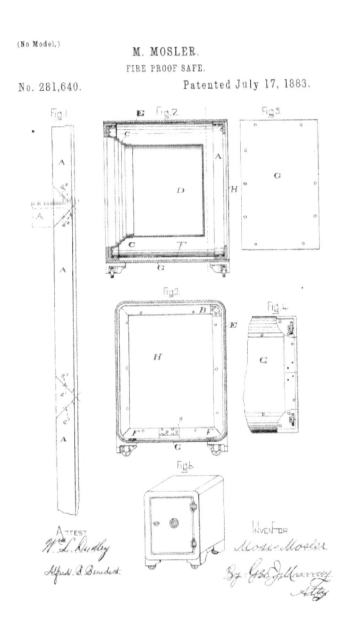

Patent No. 281,640, July 17, 1883, by Moses Mosler, of Cincinnati, Ohio, for "certain new and useful Improvements in Safes." https://patents.google.com/patent/US281640A/en

4 Motive

"Why?" is at the heart of any business plan. Why invest here, now, and for this purpose? Is the purpose because no other options are available? Or, is it because there are many options, but the chosen course is the most compelling among several choices?

As the Purple Gang suddenly raked in millions of dollars in Detroit each week, its leaders must have felt the growing pressure from a citizenry fearful of the brazen killings in the cities. Prohibition was coming undone, and that revenue stream would dry up soon. What to do with the money?

Diversification was an attractive option. While the savvy 1928 gangster might realize that alcohol would soon revert to a legal product, gambling was not headed in that direction. Packaging the vices would keep the profits flowing once the country reversed its dry course. Patrons would pay a premium for the contraband, ensuring good use of the money. Even the alcohol might continue to be a cash cow, as long as taxes were evaded.

More importantly, perhaps, the club could launder other Gang cash through established banking channels. Gangsters could not simply walk into banks with wheelbarrows of cash. But the cash needed to find a safe haven. It needed to be laundered. Given this objective, it may have been that the books of the club were rosier than its actual results. The club would operate only from the weekend before July 4 until the weekend after Labor Day. However, phantom "private parties" and other "events" throughout the year might justify cash flowing into the bank no matter the month.

Thus, such a club could serve several purposes, all important to the Purple Gang enterprises. Likely, the idea for the club was circulating in 1927, the year before construction began. Somewhere, someone was drawing up plans and scoping out sites.

Even after Prohibition, the Club could capture the Sunday cocktails crowd: Harbor Springs prohibited alcohol sales to encourage church attendance:[88]

> Gerhart hired a bartender from Saginaw who was unfamiliar with both the observance and enforcement of liquor laws in the Michigan wilderness …

"What do you do on Sundays?" the bartender asked.

"The same as you do on Saturday," Gerhart replied.

"But you can't serve on Sundays," the bartender protested.

Gerhart paused: "Well, don't sell to anyone with a badge."

The key for the Club Manitou business was to provide goods and services that were in high demand but with a government-stifled supply. No competition was good competition.

Markets and profits

If revenues were actually important to Club Manitou, dining would provide one source of income. But booze was the key. As the well-tested restaurant adage goes, "the profit is in the drinks." The profit margins in restaurants are low, generally below 10%. Bars, in fact, prefer not to sell food because doing so lowers the profit margin. This explains why many states require that bars sell food.

Focusing on the bar, at peak season a club such as Club Manitou with 300 people going 6 hours might require 2,000 pours. While the cost of drinks is not known (low-end speakeasies were charging about $0.35[89]), we can assume a price of about $1. Given inflation – a dollar in 1928 had the buying power of $15 in 2020[90] – that translates to $15 in 2020 dollars. The cost of the booze was nearly free – much simply stolen – so this may have all dropped to the bottom line. Raking in $30,000 each evening – before gambling – would result in monthly gross revenue of about $1,000,000. This would be fine for the months the dining room was open. Gambling and the larger community, however, provided a boost to this income.

Gambling revenue can only be inferred from currently reported numbers. In 2017, monthly revenue per slot machine in Las Vegas was about $7,000.[91] If the crowd in a Harbor Springs club might support a half dozen slots and a few roulette tables mixed in, this revenue would be incidental to the profit from alcohol sales. Gambling may have simply been part of the entertainment mix, its revenue incidental to the enterprise.

The community helped the alcohol sales. While it lasted, Prohibition gave Slim a quick $85 per case of high-quality gin, regardless of dining and entertaining revenues. Slim explained, "I think I sold to 99% of the resort people – I might have missed one or two, but I'll go 99 – if they had their $85."[92] This would be $1,275 or more in 2020 dollars: not small change.

If we assume some community distribution of perhaps 10 times that within the club itself – the club being as much as storehouse as an entertainment venue – then the summer season starts looking rosier. It may well be that the club paid for its initial investment in its first summer of operation. That would have made the Purple Gang happy – and allowed Slim a freer hand in its operation.

Finding and capturing these markets was certainly at the top of any list of goals the gang may have kept. The profit margin was enormous, at 1,000% to 2,000% (10-fold to 20-fold). "Commercial stills in New York could put out 50 to 100 gallons a day at a cost of 50 cents per gallon and sell each one for $3 to $12. By 1930, the U.S. government estimated that smuggling foreign-made liquor into the country was a $3 billion industry ($41 billion in 2016)."[93] Stolen liquor was even cheaper to procure, though created some bad blood.

Regardless, capturing market share and enforcing dominance there were certainly primary objectives of the gang and its new venture.

The winter season may have shut down the dining and entertainment at the club, but the winter festival in Petoskey may have pulled in crowds large enough to justify keeping the bootlegging going even when the roads were nearly impassable.

1933 Petoskey Winter Sports Carnival Ice Throne Sculpture by Stanley Kellogg ~ Submitted by Geoff Guillaume from the collection of his grandfather Harold Guillaume[94]

A follow-on problem was where to keep all that money overnight, or indefinitely, until it could be deposited or moved elsewhere. For this, a safe would be required.

Mosler Safe Company from Cincinnati, Ohio, provided the large, wheeled safe having at least 7 layers of plate – perhaps some fireproof – to discourage blow torches and other attempts to break in. The wheels on the safe would be handy should the safe need to be moved rapidly toward a tunnel for hiding or further extraction.

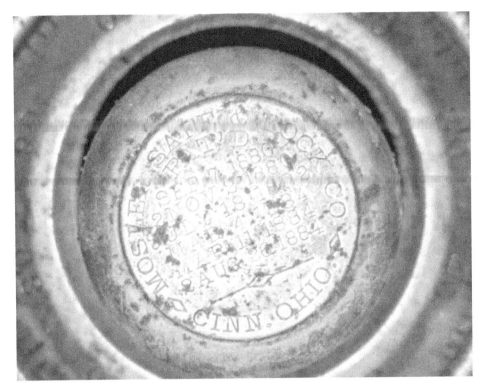

Dial on the Mosler safe. Author's photo.

Because the safe's dial places the Mosler Company in Cincinnati, the safe was bought used: Mosler had moved the company to Hamilton, Ohio, in 1891. That the safe was second-hand suggests that the managers of Club Manitou were not spendthrifts: they were beholden to someone else's bottom line.

Mosler safe. Located in kitchen outside Slim's office. Author's photo.

Investment

What that initial investment looked like is well hidden. What is certain, however, are the dimensions of the resulting edifice named Club Manitou. The basement – location of the kitchen and illegal activities – dominated, with over half the square footage of the entire building on that level.

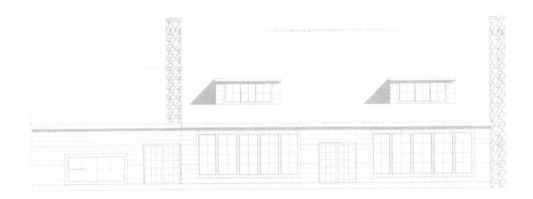

Club Manitou rendering, south elevation.

Floor	Length (E-W)	Width (N-S)	Area
Basement (lounge)*	65'	65'	4,225 sf
Main (dining)	60'	35'	2,100 sf
Top (bedrooms)	40'	25'	1,000 sf
All			7,325 sf

*includes tunnel areas adjacent to main rooms but not the tunnel extensions into the yards; all dimensions are approximate

It is difficult to know today exactly how much such a structure would cost to build in 1928 in Northern Michigan. However, if average construction cost of a typical single-family home in a 2019 survey was $114 per square foot, and we factor higher for high-end finishes demanded by a high-end club, then the construction cost was around $1,000,000 in 2020 dollars. The land may have been relatively inexpensive due to its location on the eastern fringe of Harbor Springs, but nonetheless added to the required investment.

There would be other start-up costs as well, both fixed and recurring: furnishings, salaries, printing, foodstuffs, etc. Perhaps only the booze was free. It may well be that contractors were paid in-kind, and the deal was largely one that could not be resisted. The client, after all, was a gangster and this was no secret.

This is not the sort of money a 22-year-old saves, even in the best of times. While one might imagine a a large cache of counterfeit money "lost" during the disintegration of the Purple Gang, this hypothesis has trouble with the presence of Sam Bernstein, likely around to protect Abe's interests. Some complicity between Sam and Slim to Abe's disadvantage would have been highly risky if not downright stupid. Most likely, the club was simply financed with a very large infusion from the Purple Gang at the direction of either Abe or Sam.

It may be that the entire purpose of the operation was to launder money through a legitimate business. If this is so, then the investors may have been satisfied with a break-even operation: profits would be secondary to getting money into the banking system. If profit was a requirement, the task would be difficult – but not impossible – given the short operating season. Many restaurants have operated with this limitation in resort areas.

BUILD

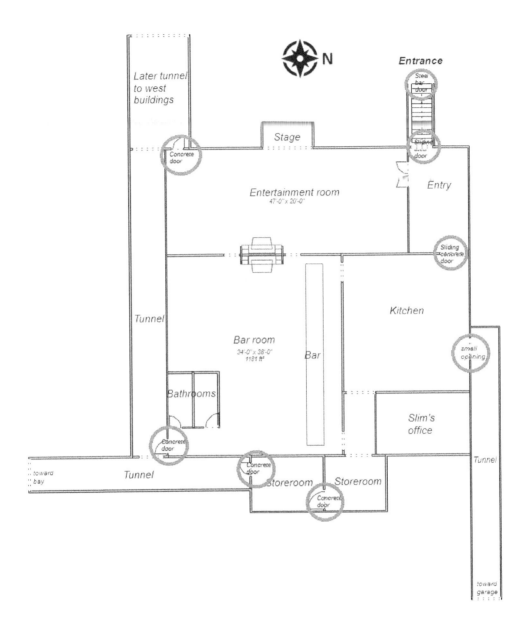

Slim's Lounge floorplan highlighting barrier doors.

5 Risk Management

Building the club meant solving unique business issues. The plan to bundle vices meant increased risks of police raids.

To repel these likely raids, Slim and Sam relied on four defenses. The first was to keep the police in their pockets. With the arrival of the stock market crash and Great Depression in 1929, the local police and politicians were reluctant to bust revenue-generating activities.[95] Well-timed payments and bottles-to-go kept the police amply satisfied. According to a 1935 FBI report, agents determined the local sheriff was protecting the gangsters and "no doubt is receiving some remuneration in that connection."[96]

The second defense was to ensure patrons were not only fully vetted but intimidated. As Slim recounted:

> We weren't interested in anyone unless they were introduced by a friend. ... And during the speakeasy days it was strictly a locked door proposition. [T]he head waiter, Paul Pepper, decided who got in.[97]

The reputation of the Purple Gang, and their unspoken presence at the club, was likely sufficient to keep lips sealed. Besides, why risk losing a follow-on invitation to the club?

Third, locals were employed to warn of impending raids: protection was a community affair. Switchboard operators were well-rewarded, purportedly sending light signals toward the club when a raid was imminent.

Finally, all else failing, there were the doors, locks, and tunnels: doors and locks for delay, and tunnels for hiding or escape.

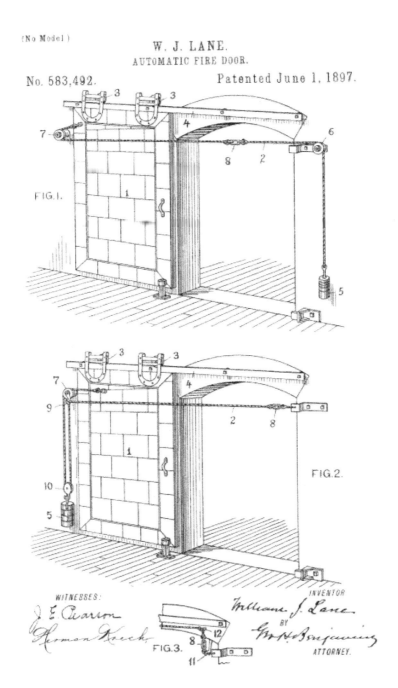

Patent 583,492 for a sliding fire door, easily adapted to preventing entry to any person possessing a blow-torch.

Steel and concrete barriers

The final defenses against a raid were delay and escape. The underground area needed to be designed to allow for time to move or destroy evidence. Raiders would need to get through four locked doors – two steel and two concrete – in order to get to the north tunnel to the garage. To get to the east tunnel leading toward the airport, five steel and concrete doors would have to be breached. Both tasks would be nearly impossible without blow torches and jackhammers. The social defenses – bribes and threats – may have been sufficient: there is no evidence the doors were ever forced open.

The composition of the doors was their most intriguing feature. The first door was made of steel bars; the second of ¾" steel plate; the remaining doors of steel-reinforced concrete. These doors were not for privacy; they were for protection from some likely armed force on their far side.

Steel had been invented in 1868 by British metallurgist Forester Mushet. Two centuries earlier, the Great Fire of London suggested an important application of that invention. The inferno of 1666 had destroyed most of the city's buildings and rendered 100,000 citizens homeless. Fire had made short work of wooden doors, which had no built-in fire protection. This got the wheels turning inside the minds of engineers and creators like Charles Dahlstrom. Mr. Dahlstrom invented and held all original patents on the first fire-rated steel door. In 1904, The Dahlstrom Metallic Door Co. was born. The idea of sliding doors on top tracks was not new: such doors have been unearthed in Pompeii, dating to the first century AD.

A second distinctive feature of the barrier doors – beyond their heft – is that they close and lock on the side farthest from the staircase, the only entry into the lower level. These were not doors that were shut as one was leaving the basement by a normal route. For the tunnel doors, in fact, it would be very difficult to close the door from the side closer to the staircase. Now why would that be? If the tunnels were simply for storage, their doors would open from the other direction.

The first barrier door was the steel-bar door atop the steps leading down to Slim's Lounge[98]. That jail-style door was likely kept locked at all times – except to let a guest pass through – to avoid surprise visits by law enforcement.

Steel door lock. Photo by author, 2022.

At the bottom of the stairs was a solid steel door hanging from an overhead track.[99] Once closed, a bar would be jammed into the trailing edge to prevent the door from being opened from the side facing the outsider. The narrowness of the staircase would also prevent raiders from bringing a large object to ram against the door.

Staircase to the basement lounge with the rolling steel door (second barrier door) in the foreground. The steel-bar door (first barrier door) toward the top of the stairs has been removed and is now stored at the Harbor Springs Area Historical Society. Photo by author, 2021.

A raiding party, if it successfully breeched the first two barriers, arrived at the cashier's room, with doors to the right leading to the entertainment area and a large concrete door hiding the kitchen – and behind that Slim's office, another concrete door hidden behind shelving, a storeroom, and finally a concrete door to the tunnel.

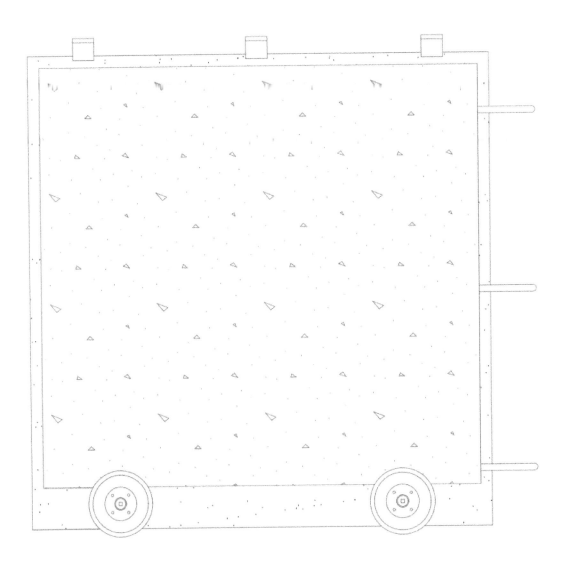

Elegantly impenetrable design of the sliding steel-reinforced door leading to the kitchen. The pins on the leading edge would fit into holes drilled into the concrete foundation wall.

Barrier 3: Door between cashier's area and kitchen, from the kitchen side. Photo by author, 2021.

The steel-reinforced concrete door to the kitchen rolled using a set of double-flanged wheels on a track laid into concrete. The track was on the side furthest from a raiding party: there would be no levering the door off the rail in a raid.

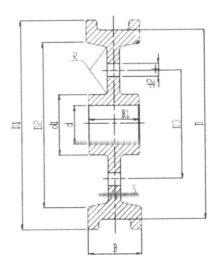

Double-flanged wheel.

Track and wheel of door leading to kitchen. Photo by author, 2022.

On the kitchen side, a large incinerator would have been busy at work sending evidence up the chimney. Booze and slot machines would be carted back toward a storeroom hidden by bookshelves.

On the far (eastern) side of the kitchen from the sliding door was Slim's office and, just past the office, a storeroom. The concrete door to the storeroom was half the width of the wall. Once closed, the door was flush with the other half and simply looked to be part of the wall. Shelves in front of the wall and door would further suggest to the raider that there was nothing more to be found.

Barrier 4: Door outside Slim's office to the storeroom. Brackets for shelves are on the left of the door. Once closed, the door appeared the same as the wall to the right. Photo by author, 2022.

A raiding party at this point may have quickly become disoriented if they did not bring a compass. Lights may have been shot out. Once inside the storeroom, the fleeing gangster would see the might of the steel encased steel-reinforced concrete door. As the door was pushed shut, a locking mechanism at ground level would snap up and lock the door shut.

The storeroom door from the inside. The ceiling of the storeroom is about 6' high. At the base of the door opening is the roller of the locking mechanism. The bracket for the securing timber is at the bottom of the door. Photo by author, 2022.

In addition to the quick lock from below, the gangster could use large timbers to secure the roller in a locked position while bolting the door shut.

At the far side of the storeroom was another steel-reinforced concrete door – the fifth bunker-quality barrier – closing again from the inside. This fifth barrier led into the tunnel which headed south into the sloping yard and toward the airport. Again, a locking roller would snap into place as the door was shut, quickly preventing the door from being pushed open from the raiding side.

Barrier 5: Door to east tunnel. The passage was filled with concrete in the 2020s due to a collapsing sidewalk above. However, the likely terminus near M-119 exists. Photo by author, 2021.

Roller locks

An ingenious system of rolling locks secured the doors on either side of the second storeroom against the raiders. These were not doors meant to welcome uninvited guests. The doors were likely open during operating hours as stored liquor was transported to the bar and beyond. To prepare against the raid, however, the locks on the inside were easily triggered, operating in one of five ways:

1. **Normal, doors open**: As the fleeing gangster pushed a door shut, the closing door would push a long rod down and, as the door finally shut, snap the rod and its roller up and into place.
2. **Normal, doors closed**: If the doors were already closed but unlocked and no one was inside to lock them, a rotary control cable from outside the door could be used to push the roller locks for both doors into place.
3. **Recovery 1**: If the doors were already closed, or if the fleeing gangsters were not available to re-open the door, a rotary control cable from outside the door could be used to release the lock by lowering the rod.
4. **Failsafe**: If the second door was open as the fleeing gangster passed through it and the rod was in a lowered position (i.e., not able to return up to lock the door), the gangster could lock the door by stepping down on the far end of the rod and a fulcrum would lift the roller into a locked position.
5. **Recovery 2**: If the second door was closed and a fleeing gangster wanted to return through it, a manual override was available by lifting the rod manually.

1] Normal, doors open

If either of the two storeroom doors (barrier doors 4 and 5) was open, anyone on the inside of the tunnel would be able to shut the doors. As a door shut it would press down on the top of a bar with a roller and, as the door reached a closed position, the bar would snap a roller up, locking the door.

Looking into the tunnel from the second door southward toward the road and airport. The lock is seen along the floor. The roller is at the bottom of the picture and the spring at the far end of the bar. Photo by author, 2022.

2] Normal, doors closed

If the doors were closed, the interior roller lock could be lifted (into a locked position) or lowered (into an unlocked position) by means of a rotary control cable which attached to a jack at each pole and which was operated from outside the doors.

Rotary cable and housing at the wall next to the first door. Photo by author, 2023.

At the first door the rotary cable was attached to a mechanical apparatus operating a scissor jack under the rod.

At the first door, the control cable on left attaches to the scissor jack under the pole. The pole's roller can be seen at the top of the photo at the end of the pole. Author's photo, 2023.

A sub-floor allows a control cable to continue back to the second door.

Looking down below the tunnel's concrete floor at the second door. The control rod can be seen pressing against the brickwork which appears to be at least 5 layers deep. Photo by author, 2023.

Under the second rod which lifts the roller to secure the second door, a different jack is used to lift and lower the rod.

Jack mechanism at the second door. The control cable can be seen coming up from the subfloor chamber and attaching to the gears which lower and lift the rod. Author's photo, 2023.

3] Recovery 1

The rotary cable could also be operated to lower the bar and unlock the door should no one be available to unlock it; for example, if the gangster had exited the tunnel near the airport and flown far, far away. But what would prevent law enforcement from doing the same? Perhaps there was a recessed key on the outside of the door that would hinder a quick pursuit by the law. What is interesting is that, from the outside, the exit of the cable is not visible. Perhaps it has been cemented over.

4] Failsafe: Fleeing but the second door did not lock

The mechanism was ingenious if a bit over-engineered. At the door end was a roller attached to a 10' metal pole which had an attached fulcrum about 2' from the roller. At the other end, the pole was attached to a spring hanging from the ceiling thereby keeping the roller in an unlocked position.

Tunnel door locking mechanism: the fugitive steps on the pole, causing the roller to rise and block the door from opening.

To lock the door, the gangster would push down on the pole at its far end, the fulcrum thrusting the wheel up the door and locking it. The gangster could then uncouple the bar from the spring and the lock would stay in place.

5] Recovery 2

If the gangster was in the tunnel and wished to return to the Club but the second door was locked, he could use the process above but instead would lift the pole in order to lower the roller. A similar recovery appears available for the first door but without the spring keeping the pole in an unlocked position.

Exits

Original and eventual purposes

While the basement location minimized the risk that law enforcement would break in through a door or window, there nonetheless needed to be entry and exit, for people, booze, and air. There are four types of openings from Club Manitou's basement to the outside: fireplace flue, entry staircase, ventilation openings, and tunnels.

The fireplace flue would suck air from the room into the fire and send heated air and smoke up and out. No human could ascend or descend this opening, so the Feds would not enter this way. Given the cool dampness of the basement, the fire likely was going year-round, even in the heat of the summer.

In fact, the fire would be important to set up the convection current to ventilate the basement. The air forced up the chimney by the heat would create a vacuum, sucking in cool air through other openings. The most efficient source of this outside air would be down the staircase to the basement, the second opening into the basement. The steel-bar door at the staircase top would allow for a locked entrance, but also the movement of fresh air down the staircase and into the basement.

Convection in Gases

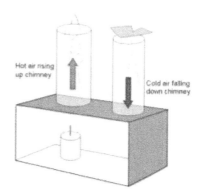

- When the air above the candle is heated, it **expands**.
- The expanded air is **less dense** than the surrounding air and **rises out of** chimney B.
- Since the surrounding air is cooler, it is **denser** and therefore **sinks into** chimney A.
- The difference in the densities of the air at the different chimneys sets up a **convection current**.

The basement fireplace would draw in air from the outside to replace that sent up the flue. The volume of the entering air would only be as great as that exiting.

While the staircase would provide ample air intake – at least as much air as that being pushed out the fireplace flue – the tunnels might have also assisted this air intake. Air shafts in the tunnels suggest that air movement was a priority. Those shafts perhaps were intended as the inflow for the kitchen blower sending hot kitchen air out the tunnel headed toward the garage.

The third opening into the basement, a kitchen ventilation system, shows an intake for small packages such as cases of liquor and a fan which would push air out of the kitchen. The unit is at ceiling height. This opening was also the western end of the north tunnel, a tunnel designed for moving cases of booze using carts, ropes, and pulleys.

Finally, there are the tunnels leading into and out of the basement. Simply delaying the raid was useful but would not thwart the raiders forever. The very existence of delaying tactics was near admission that illegal activity was underway. However, without witnesses or evidence, the police would have nothing to show the courts. Therefore, if it couldn't be incinerated, evidence needed to be concealed; better yet, removed to a safe place. To accomplish this, Slim designed three tunnels under walkways around the eventual restaurant. The Feds would not be after the guests; they were keen to bust the owners and their deputies.

The tunnels have several design aspects that suggest their original purpose was more sinister than air movement:

1. As noted earlier, the staircase already provided sufficient air to replace the air leaving through the fireplace flue.
2. The tunnels are long and have no apparent mechanism for moving air in any direction. Without blowers, the air would stagnate.
3. The concrete doorway entrances, at about 4' high, are placed at ground level, their tops at least a foot below the tunnel ceilings, impeding if not preventing efficient air flow.
4. The doors themselves are 6"-thick concrete. What purpose would that choice of door serve for airflow (or storage)?
5. The tunnel from Slim's office would logically be for escape. If he needed fresh air in his office, he could easily have run another air shaft to the exterior as is found in the east tunnel. Air did not need to laze in from hundreds of feet away to keep Slim breathing.
6. While the height and width of the tunnels reduced the friction loss of the air flow, the quality of the air – assuming it flowed – might nonetheless be an issue. The tunnel air would be dank, the fresh air blowing above the tunnels in the sunlight. Even if air flowed in from the tunnels, would it be smart to get it from the garage? That's where the north tunnel terminated. More likely, it terminated there because there was something of interest to be moved between the garage and the club. Air

may have been vented out from the kitchen to the garage but, again, why not simply run a vent directly skyward as shown above?

Air shaft in the east tunnel. Photo by author, 2022.

7. The locks for the doors are on a side convenient for fleeing people but not for anything else. The locks presuppose that the person locking the door is *inside the tunnel already*.
8. If large enough for law enforcement to breech, they would certainly have a steel-bar grating to prevent entry, else the barriers just discussed would be useless.

Regardless, the tunnel doors may have been kept open during normal – i.e., non-raid – operations to assist the flow of air in whichever direction that air could flow, though doing so would have defeated the purpose of the many doors designed to prevent entry. More likely, the doors were open to allow for ready escape as well as access to stocks of liquor stored behind them. The safest approach for air movement was what the owners designed: a locked steel-bar door at the entrance, allowing air through but not uninvited guests.

Would cross-ventilation have been one of the tunnels' purposes? This is unlikely due to the requirement for different air pressure – produced by wind – at opposite ends of the building. Underground ducts would not give rise to this pressure difference. The pressure difference would need to come from either convection, as described earlier, or fans. No such fans have been found, and no electrical system allowing their operation is installed. Finally, the tunnels are at the far ends of the basement, with several doors and obstacles in between. Air, even if entering through the tunnels, would be caught by these barriers.

The smoking guns, perhaps unassailable evidence, suggesting that the primary role of the tunnels was far from ventilation are a wheel and flange found in the eastern tunnel. Stuff was being moved along the tunnels, below the gaze of prying eyes.

Wheel and flange in the east tunnel. Photos by author, 2022.

Lastly, the heights of the east and south tunnels are human-friendly. An occupant of the tunnel need only hunch over – or crawl in the north tunnel[100] – to move through the tunnel or to hide until any threat passed. While this movement would not have been comfortable, it would be far preferable to beds at the Michigan State Penitentiary.

While there was never a confession by anyone regarding the tunnels' purposes, neither was there denial.[101] Slim was coy: they were for kitchen purposes, though it's difficult to justify a long tunnel for storage when a room with shelves would be better suited to that purpose. As well, one of the tunnel exits is on the far side of the basement from the kitchen.

The tunnels' real purpose is easily inferred and ties in with the purpose for the doors. It all fits perfectly into a strategy for saving one's skin in a raid. If the raid came from the only direction it could – down the staircase at the northwest corner of the basement – the massive iron door would be shut there, then the massive concrete door would slide shut allowing time to incinerate evidence, and finally important people would be whisked into the tunnels, the concrete tunnel doors shut and locked, with their escape routes being to the east and the south, far from the Feds. No leap of faith is needed to conclude that such was the intent of the tunnels. The FBI thought so.

A more practical and comfortable view is that the tunnels only functioned to hide and transport cases of liquor into the club and, in the case of a raid, to provide a sealable, hidden storage location. If the tunnels were for liquor movement, did the eastern tunnel stretch downhill, under the road, and to the airport? The tunnels were probably built in straight lines, the one toward the airport along the shortest route. The tunnels did have exterior exits; the question is: where?

Description

There were three original tunnels – north, east, and south – with a later tunnel added to the west likely in the late 1940s.

North tunnel

Entrance to the north tunnel from inside the garage. At the base of the visible opening is a smaller tunnel about 3' high leading to the kitchen. Photo by author, 2022.

The north tunnel led to the garage or, more appropriately, came from the garage. Starting in the garage where shipments could be loaded onto carts in the tunnel, it led under a sidewalk that also ran between the garage and kitchen. In fact, the tunnel may have also been used for any shipment needing to reach the kitchen, avoiding the only other entrance to the basement: the staircase on the west side of the club. This would have been handy if the club was open for business and the chefs needed some supplies.

There is no doubt that the north tunnel connects to the garage. The only question is what moved in that tunnel. It was not meant to be for escape due to its low height. The garage exit is interesting in that it is convenient for getting down to, but not up from, the garage floor. A raid would not start here due to the slow crawl needed to get through the tunnel.

North tunnel looking west from the bottom of the shaft in the garage. There is a possible rail in the lower part of the photo. Photo courtesy of the Harbor Springs Area Historical Society.

What also might suggest this north tunnel was used for moving supplies? An empty champagne case from a New York importer was found at the bottom of the garage tunnel entrance. It is likely that workers in the garage used this discard to help them in and out of the tunnel entrance.

An unfortunately empty champagne case from New York found in north tunnel. Photo by author, 2022.

The north tunnel ended at the kitchen. Here, cases of contraband could be moved either to storage or directly to the bar. The tunnel also functioned to move heat and air out of the kitchen, though Kelvinators were also used to condition the kitchen. A mostly intact Kelvinator, likely a part of the refrigerator, still rests where the refrigerator had been.

Air conditioning compressor for the Kelvinator refrigerator. Photo by author, 2022.

These "kitchen-related" purposes of the north tunnel were not the same as those for the east and south tunnels, those being meant for human passage.

East tunnel

The east tunnel led from the storeroom outside Slim's office toward the airport. The far southern terminus has not been definitively located, and may settle some interesting questions once discovered[102]: was the tunnel for escape to the road, or the airport? Was it for the most important guests who might arrive by plane? Was it ever used? It may have been an unfinished project, intended to transport booze to and from the club but discarded in favor of simple payoffs to law enforcement policing the airport.

There is also what appears to be evidence of a staircase leading down from ground level just after moving through the 5th door. Coloration of the wall leads to this observation, as well as the remains of concrete stairs overhead.

Vanishing stairs into the tunnel from ground level. The outline of the staircase is visible on the wall to the right of the photo. At the top are still existing concrete steps leading nowhere. Photo by author, 2023.

We have three hypotheses about the now-gone staircase:

1) *Alternate escape exit*: if all the commotion during a raid was at the northwest corner of the building (entrance to Slim's Lounge), why not exit at the southeast corner, brush off some dust, and walk away into the darkness? This theory would allow for the tunnel to be used on opening day even if the entire tunnel length had not been completed to its eventual terminus.
2) *Escape entrance*: if one was near the dining entrance as raiders headed to the northwest corner of the building, one could slip into the tunnel from surface level. This, however, would require another entrance into the lower area and a much larger security risk. If there was an entrance, it could be found.
3) *Construction entrance*: the stairs were only used during construction and then decommissioned.

South tunnel

In the southeast corner of the basement was a door to the tunnels that, when turning to the left, joined to the east tunnel or, when turning right, ran along the south edge of the basement. This tunnel entrance is interesting in that there is a second door inside that, if shut, would funnel the escapees away from east tunnel leaving that tunnel for the exclusive use of the gangsters.

It seems likely that this would have been one of two for guests if they so desired. However, if all the contraband was gone when the raiders arrived, perhaps the patrons would simply continue listening to the band, feigning ignorance while partaking of legal dancing.

The south tunnel led from the southeast corner westward along the south wall of the basement, linking to a tunnel entrance at the southwest corner of the basement. That tunnel has collapsed and filled-in, but somewhere along its length another tunnel joined it and led southward into the sloping yard. The outside entrance of this exit tunnel is approximately 20 yards from the house, beyond the gaze of law enforcement in the driveways or at the entrances to the club.

It is unlikely the south tunnel served any other purpose than to link to the east tunnel in order to get escapees out in the direction of the main road and airport. Of course, a yard full of the more than 100 guests would be a nightmare for law enforcement with all manpower needed for handcuffing and transporting the decoys. The gangsters would be long gone before the police made their way into the south tunnel which would only lead back to the dance floor and bar area.

Door to south tunnel. Inside the door, a tunnel leads to the right and along the southern edge of the house or to the left, connecting with a tunnel headed south toward the bay. Photo by author, 2021.

Escape exits

There are two candidates for the east and south tunnel exits. The first is south of the house approximately 20 yards. An underground cavity collapsed there and was subsequently filled in. As well, this is the location a neighbor[103] claims he exited prior to the collapse. This location would conveniently hook into the south tunnel which was accessed on the east from the door at the southeast corner of the bar room and on the west from the door at the southwest corner of the dance room.

Stakes showing the location of the exit from the south tunnel into the yard. Stakes placed in the yard by members of the Lake Superior State University Geology Department. Photo by author, 2023

Guests filing out the southwest door to the south tunnel would draw the attention of raiders, diverting law enforcement activity to that route which led, eventually, to the middle of the lawn. It was a feint. While the police, in theory, would round up the 100 or more guests exiting onto the south lawn, the gangsters would escape on the far side of a retaining wall below the yard, crossing the main road there under cover of dark, and possibly board planes to whisk them into the night.

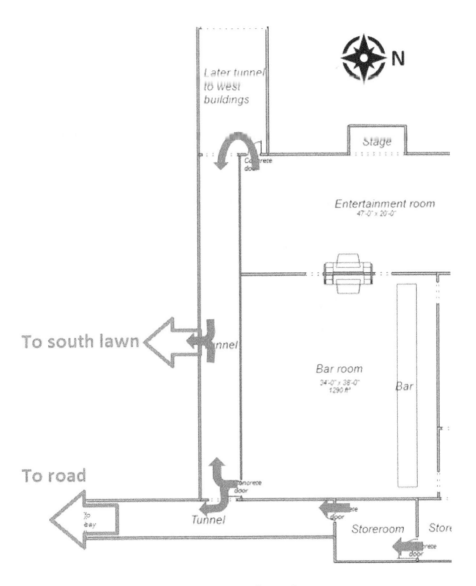

The escapes to the south.

Thus, the second escape exit is more intriguing: close to the road directly south and in-line with the east tunnel. A local merchant[104] noted that this was the "traditional" entry into the basement for the local teenagers bent on adventure while a band member who played in the basement venue corroborated the existence and likely purpose of the east tunnel's southern terminus.[105]

Likely east tunnel exit near M-119, directly in-line with the east tunnel at the main house. Photo by author, 2022.

A top-level gangster boss, flush with cash, might have envisioned as a retirement plan an arrival at the airport. While this might be followed by a private car to Club Manitou or nearby accommodations, the return trip might be complicated by a raid. If things got hot, the boss would slip into the tunnel, get a bit dirty, but arrive somewhere close to an airplane that could magically disappear into the night sky. Radar was a thing of the future. Unfortunately, bottlenecks at the entries into the tunnels from within the basement meant that the police stopped most escapees before they even entered the tunnels. However, this would provide the diversion needed. By also closing the southeast tunnel entry from the basement, even more confusion would ensue and the gangsters leaving by way of the storerooms would disappear. The guests would simply be bait.

The interior of the east tunnel exit at M-119. Photo by author, 2022.

The southeast tunnel may also have had a series of steps as it descended the south lawn slope.[106] The concrete exit chamber, with an opening on top and another possible opening collapsed to the north, is clearly large enough for several people to stand. It measures approximately 6'x6'x6'. A heavy beam supported something above ground, but that something is now gone. The pit of the chamber is filled with debris caving in from the north where the tunnel to the house would be expected.

Excavation of east tunnel exit, south of the retaining wall and near M-119. Photo by author, 2023

Excavations in 2023 to the north of the exit shaft unearthed many broken and intact whiskey bottles – some branded and some likely home-brewed – at depths from a foot above the top of the shaft to a couple feet below that level. These appear to be bottles discarded by either workers during the construction of the shaft and tunnels, or guards in place later. An empty .44 shell casing was recovered by the author during these digs.

Whiskey cap and shard from dig near shaft. Author photo, 2023.

West tunnel

The larger west tunnel – added nearly 20 years after the club opened – was to shuttle more traffic between a building constructed in the 1950s and the original building. The west tunnel was taller and wider than the other tunnels, allowing easy passage of staff and guests between the buildings. At the building of Club Manitou, this tunnel may have been smaller and connected to the south tunnel just as the east tunnel did.

Club Manitou, 2nd Edition

Club Manitou rendering, north elevation. Lookout is on the left. The chimney is from the incinerator in the kitchen of the lower level.

6   Construction

While we do not have details of the construction plan, we have some idea of how quickly the club was constructed. These were the days before planning departments and construction permits. The Grand Hotel on Mackinac Island was built in 93 days: the land purchased in 1886 and the hotel opening on July 10, 1887.

Grand Hotel on Mackinac Island.

The construction timeline for Club Manitou was similarly aggressive, starting in 1928 and opening on the July 4 weekend the following year. A critical path would have been obtaining the 12 steel girders required to span the length of the basement and, directly above, the dining room.

Excavation of the ground may have started immediately, with the goal of having an enclosed structure by the time winter arrived, allowing for interior finishing work to continue while snow piled up outside. Alternately, following the timeline of the Grand Hotel, the design and planning were accomplished in 1928 – and critical materials stockpiled – and ground-breaking as soon as possible in the following spring.

Either way, the construction site would have been extremely hectic. One imagines, however, that Slim would reward milestones with some of the Purple Gang product.

The site was also likely well-guarded, keeping prying eyes away as the tunnel system was put in place. Outside knowledge of the exits for the tunnels would have defeated their purpose.

Supporting the upper floors were large steel beams, six supporting the main floor and six supporting the top floor. The edifice was built to last.

Steel girder supporting the top floor. Photo is taken in the room to the west of the main dining room. The stonework is the backside of the fireplace in the dining room.

The basement had the most remarkable superstructure, with concrete and steel used all around. The building was clearly designed to outlast explosives if not all time.

Basement superstructure: steel poles supporting steel girders supporting steel girders atop them. This photo is taken of the southeast corner of the kitchen. Photo by author, 2023.

Club Manitou, 2nd Edition

OPERATE

Michigan roads and rail, 1928, from the Complete Atlas of the World.

7 Operations

Follow the booze.

A probable sequence for getting Canadian Club from Windsor, Canada to the mouths of Club Manitou patrons in July was perhaps as follows:

A Cincinnati Brewery Company truck is seen at the loading dock of a Canadian warehouse across the river from Detroit in 1925. Photo courtesy The Detroit News Archive.

First, the liquor was loaded onto a waiting truck at the (legal) distribution point on the Canadian side. As Slim described it: "There were as many export docks in Windsor, Ontario, as there are clothing stores in Petoskey. The liquor would be dropped off on the U.S. side of the river and we would arrange to truck it to the Harbor Springs area."[107]

Coast Guardsmen dump cases of beer into the Detroit River during Prohibition. Photo courtesy The Detroit News Archive.

On the Detroit side, the cases were loaded into cars, and delivered to, often, barns and other buildings housing plants that watered-down the booze such that only a quarter of the bottle was the original liquor. At any point, the liquor was likely to be stolen by the Purple Gang.

The Purple Gang may have preferred to steal the liquor on the U.S. side, rather than attempt the riskier river crossing: U.S. Customs agents plied the waters of the river continually. Likely, the gang used several channels to maximize the probability of success. The gang ensured the agreed deliveries made their way to Al Capone in Chicago and other contracted recipients. Some loads, however, were destined for the north of lower Michigan where summer vacationing and winter skiing entertained the wealthy of the Midwest.

The northbound drivers would take the cache, likely by random routes, north and west over 270 miles to Harbor Springs. At a speedy 40 miles per hour – paved roads were still to come – this was a 7 hour journey. At Club Manitou, the car would be driven into the garage on the eastern edge of the property where, in the far southeast corner, boxes hiding a tunnel were moved, and the load lowered down onto a wheeled cart.

This cart would be rolled along the north tunnel from the eastern entrance under the garage toward the kitchen, where staff might inventory it then whisked it into the storeroom protected by barrier doors 4 and 5. The first storeroom was accessible to both the bar room operations and a smaller storeroom which led to the east tunnel and away from raiders.

Path to the garage at the left in this aerial photo. The tunnel led west to the main house. Photo courtesy of Wendy Morris.

During a raid, the liquor from the bar would be moved into this second room where, time permitting, it would be moved into the more secure smaller room to the east. In the event the transfer was incomplete, law enforcement could pat itself on the back with the haul from the larger room. The entrance to the smaller storeroom would likely be well hidden. From the smaller storeroom, the liquor could be further hidden in the tunnel itself. From there, if law enforcement was aggressive, the booze could be diverted into the east tunnel and down toward the bay.

Or, it might be that the liquor was simply written off: abandoned to the raiders. If law enforcement found any booze, in the tunnel or not, the entire gig was up. More important for the gangster would be to be far away from the actual raid. Once law enforcement left with the booze and perhaps some unfortunate staff, the club owners could return and resume operations post haste.

Patrons, on the other hand, would be crowded into the south tunnel where they could make their way south toward the main road and away from the raiders. It is unlikely that they would need to do this if the alcohol and gaming equipment had been removed from their presence. The guests were there simply to listen to good music and kick-up their heels, both allowed in Prohibition.

No doubt the staff had the raid operation plan well-rehearsed. Should it fail, it meant years in jail for many and a likely end to the club. The risks were high; the risk mitigation therefore necessarily great. On a good day, however, the booze simply filled the bar in Slim's Lounge.

That plan would have been useful until December 5, 1933, when the 21st Amendment repealed the 18th. Michigan was the first State to ratify it. But illegal distilling and gambling continued. After the repeal of Prohibition, the procedure for thwarting a raid was likely similar to protect the ever more expensive slot machines. While wooden roulette tables and cards could be incinerated, the more expensive machines would likely have followed the route of the retreating booze: first into the small storeroom, then the large, finally the tunnels if need be.

One might wonder why a patron might not be pressured into testifying against Slim and his club. No doubt, stories of the Purple Gang were well known. These stories chilled to the bone. As well, the social ostracism of such a move would be great. Slim vetted the patrons; his lounge was not open to the general public.

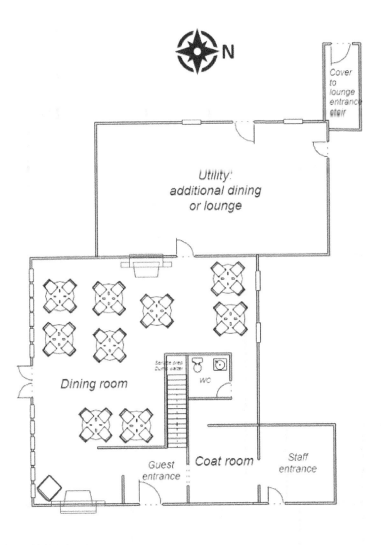

Main (dining) level of Club Manitou superimposed over Slim's Lounge. Placement of tables representative only. The coat room may have had kitchen functions. The staff entrance is also called the "Lookout".

8 Guests at Club Manitou

From downtown Harbor Springs the club was a short 10-minute drive east toward Petoskey or 15 minutes from Petoskey headed west. Approaching Pleasantview Road, the guests would notice the club up the hill, then turn north on the road and take the next left into the driveway, seeing the new club with its car valet waiting.

The exterior of the club evoked North Woods. Despite this informality, both staff and guests donned jackets and ties. Semi-formal was *de rigueur*.

Club Manitou, ca. 1930. Photo courtesy of Wendy Morris.

But you were watched. As your car rambled up the driveway, eyeballs were watching from the northeast corner "Lookout." This location afforded a view of both the garage – where incoming shipments headed – and other vehicle traffic headed toward the main entrance.

Northeast "Lookout" of Club Manitou. The door was not for guests. The windows conveniently spied on the garage operations and incoming vehicles. Photo not taken in high season.

Had your vehicle been flagged as suspect, staff would scurry to secure the joint. You would be politely greeted and, if no proof of Slim's approval available, promptly sent back to Pleasantview Road. The Michigan State Police were no exception: no warrant, no entry.

Given proper clearance, valets would open your car doors, with the parking valet whisking your car down the driveway to the parking area. You and your guests would be escorted – always warily – toward the front entrance. If a shipment was arriving at the garage, no doubt you'd raise an eyebrow, but stay quiet for your health's sake.

The front entrance on the east side of the building led into an entrance hall where you were greeted by diminutive, stone-faced Paul Pepper. When liquor became legal, the small lounge off to the left might have served you cocktails as you awaited you table, or Paul might have offered you beverages on the deck.

As you passed through a small reception area, a large fireplace foretold the massive fireplaces you would be seeing throughout the club, particularly the lower level. You would immediately see Little Traverse Bay through the large windows to the right of the fireplace. As you turned the corner into the main dining area, you would see the windows stretching across the entire south wall of the club.

Above: Maître d'hôtel and gatekeeper, Paul Pepper, stands by the main entrance. Below: east fireplace in the reception area. Photo by author, 2022.

Perhaps you then relaxed on the south-facing porch overlooking Little Traverse Bay as the long days encouraged the outdoors. Other guests might have strolled the grounds as they waited for their table, tea-cups in hand. The yard sloped gently downward toward the road. Picnic-style dining might have been an option if the demand exceeded the available indoor seating.

Club Manitou front lawn, ca 2021. Building siding is not original, nor is player. The back of the player's t-shirt reads "Camp Judy"

Or, the large windows overlooking the Bay would be flung open and the summer day brought indoors. During Prohibition, small drinks might arrive in teapots and teacups, quickly whisked away if needed.

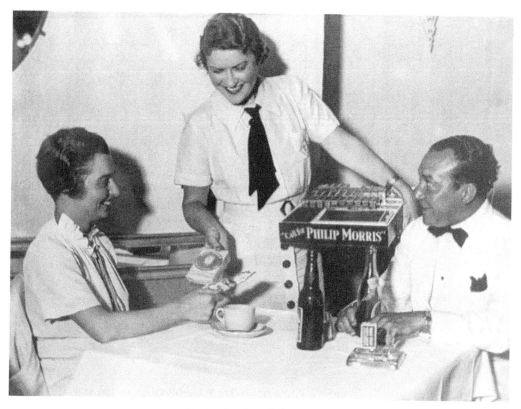

Having "tea" at Club Manitou.

The view to the south from the dining room was and remains spectacular. Through a dozen large window and the young maples growing in the sloping south yard, the vast expanse of Little Traverse Bay would greet the diners. The far shore would be visible, and a tiny cement plant there would later grow but then be sold off to the developers of Bay Harbor.

View from the dining room – in front of the east fireplace – toward Little Traverse Bay. Author's photo, 2020.

Small bi-planes, eventually single-winged aircraft, from far-off cities might start arriving on Friday as corporate executives in those cities came north to join their families who were spending a summer in Harbor Springs and surrounding communities. This pattern persists to the present.

After some conversation and "tea" on the porch, you would be shown to your table in the main dining area in front of the fireplace that sat above the larger basement fireplace. Clamor from below would be faintly audible, the band's drums vibrating the floor under your feet.

The south face of Club Manitou, taken ca. 1970. A porch was off the large set of windows and double doors.

The male waiters in their white uniforms would take orders, then return with meals they had retrieved from the dumb-waiter coming up from the basement kitchen.

According to Slim's wife, Jean Gerhart:

> We catered to society clientele. And we had a reputation as one of the finest eating places in the country. Nothing but French chefs, and dinners that consisted of course after course. ... Our guests remained seated and were served by male waiters.[108]

The main dining room was intimate. Perhaps 9 tables with 36 guests were seated at one time in the main room. It is possible that the large room behind the fireplace was also utilized for seating guests, perhaps doubling the capacity for dinner, though more likely this area was used for laundry and other dining room operations.

Dining room fireplace, 2021. Blue floor paint and rail surround are later additions. Photo by author, 2021.

Perhaps you had lobster flown in from the East coast or a steak from Chicago. Either way, you enjoyed the dinner on fine dinnerware from Shenango China. That dinnerware had reached the Club from Albert Pick-Barth Company in New York, a short-lived enterprise having been incorporated in 1929, cancelled by the tax department in 1933,[109] and dissolved shortly thereafter.

Coffee cup from Club Manitou. From the collection of Ed and Judy Meyer at the Harbor Springs Area Historical Society.

Shenango China was located in New Castle, Pennsylvania, and area rich in the soft coal needed to fire up the beehive kilns, but also rich in investment money from the steel barons of the area jealous of the thriving pottery industry of East Liverpool, Ohio.[110] The company fared better than its New York distributor, staying in business until 1989 after several changes in ownership.

The pattern on the dinnerware echoed the Art Deco interior of the restaurant. The ambience was all New York, where the Chrysler Building and Empire State Building arrived shortly after Club Manitou opened.

Club Manitou dinner plates. From the collection of Ed and Judy Meyer at the Harbor Springs Area Historical Society.

Pattern detail.

The Art Deco feel was reflected in the columns supporting the massive steel beams. The columns had clean, simple, rectangular capitals. But the ceilings were beadboard, a favorite of the Craftsman Cottage style popular in the early part of the 20th century.

Capital of a dining room column. Photo by author, 2021.

Given perhaps four seatings throughout the evening (each 90 minutes duration), about 280 guests eventually headed toward the west side of the dining room and toward a small door. While dinner was the legitimate part of the business, it was likely not the most interesting part of the evening for most guests.

Exiting a door on the west side of the building, you would be led to what appeared to be a shack, but which was the entrance door for the downstairs. Your host would unlock a steel-bar door, and you would carefully descend a long set of stairs, a hint of smoke wafting up the stairs from below.

Entrance to Slim's Lounge on the right at the northwest corner of the Club. The main house is behind. View is toward the east. Photo by author, 2021.

The jail door at the top of the stairs leading down was likely always locked to avoid surprise visits from law enforcement. The noise and smoke would quickly escalate as you descended, laughter and music dominating. At the bottom of the stairs, you would look right and into Slim's Lounge. But first you paid the dinner bill and bought chips.

What were you, fine guest, thinking at this point? The risks were escalating with each step. But you were a gambler, so the greater the odds, the greater the pay-off. The thrill must have been immense for those who enjoyed the uncertainly, but unnerving for any conservative companion. That companion might have tossed a coin in the wishing well for good luck at the start of the evening.

Wishing well with new addition behind.

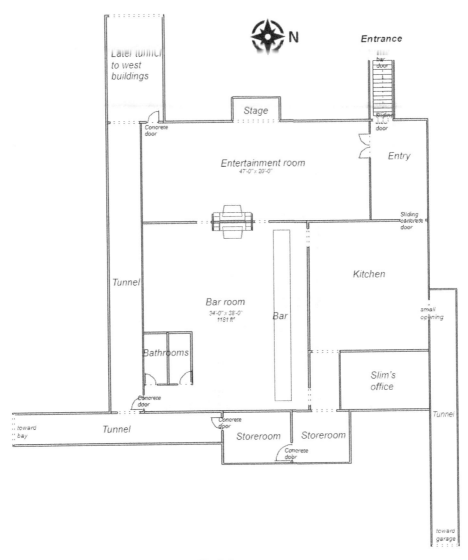

Slim's Lounge.

9   Slim's Lounge

The lower level was where the action was at. The space was divided into three principal areas (excluding the tunnels and Slim's office): dance (west) room, bar (east) room, and kitchen. A monstrous fireplace heated both the east and west rooms.

Room	Length (E-W)	Width (N-S)	Area
Dance (west) room	20'	47'	940 sf
Bar (east) room	38'	34'	1,290 sf
Kitchen	26'	25'	650 sf
Entry and other areas*			1,345 sf
All			4,225 sf

*includes tunnel areas adjacent to main rooms but not the tunnel extensions into the yards; all dimensions are approximate

But first, business needed to be transacted. Whoever gave access to the guests at the top of the stairs likely led that group down and to the cash wrap at the bottom. While bar bills would be settled here at the conclusion of the evening, guests needed to get their gambling chips for the roulette tables. The concierge would slide behind the cash wrap, insert his key into the cash register, lift open its top, and politely ask how many chips would like to be purchased, cash only.

National Cash Register out of Dayton, Ohio, was the cash register of choice. Born out of the many James Ritty patents for "Ritty's incorruptible Cashier Machine,"[111] the company was both successful and forward-thinking, introducing in 1893 such novel business practices as daylight factories and hot lunches. While Slim and Sam likely had a lower-end model, in 1928 the company acquired "the Ellis Adding Typewriter Company that produce[d] the only machine available that combined a typewriter with an adding machine in one unit [making] detailed accounting reports possible for the first time [leading to] the most flexible accounting machine to exist in pre-electronic era."[112] If the gangsters were not aware of it, they were set up with the best financial apparatus of the time.

1920s Advertising Blotter from the National Cash Register Company.

And, with that, Club Manitou extracted ever greater amounts of cash – some likely of their own counterfeiting – from the guests. But, with the drinks flowing freely, the guests were likely considering this no more than the price of admission to some of the best entertainment in the Midwest. The guests' cash disappeared into Model 736, a technological wonder.

National Cash Register Model 736, top opened.[113]

National Cash Register Model 736, top closed.[114]

The guests may have even resolved their dining room bills here as well, keeping the risks lower for Slim, Sam, and their investors. The convenience of keeping all the cash on the lower level, and near the safe, was probably a top concern of management.

Alcohol was lubricating the process. Neither guests nor Slim likely gave a moment's notice to where their money had originated, counterfeit or not. The point was that it was an agreed-upon medium of exchange, and so the party rolled on. If the U.S. government had not confiscated the bills, they must be legal tender, or so all agreed.

Here, at the cash wrap, Slim may have even emerged from his office at the far end of the kitchen. He was known as a "superb raconteur"[115] and likely mingled with his guests, particularly if Norwegian figure skating champion and movie star Sonje Henie was among them. She owned a mink ranch on Mink Road a half mile east of the club.[116] Sonje was three-time Olympic champion in 1928, 1932, and 1936 during the heyday of Club Manitou.

Sonje Henie in 1932. Photo courtesy IOC Olympic Museum, Switzerland.

The presence of high-profile figures only magnified the allure of Club Manitou. The higher, the better.

Dance (west) room

The first room the guest entered after squaring accounts was the dance room. A dancing floor fronted a small stage sufficient for a four-piece combo.

The more energetic guests would be seated here, though a greater number continued under one of the arches on either side of the great fireplace and into the east room where the bar stretched the full length of the room's northern side.

House band poses on stage in the Dance Room. Photo courtesy Wendy Morris.

Vacationers had flocked to Harbor Springs for its perfect summer weather and the watersports that went with it. They crammed into Club Manitou for the night life. Swing music was emerging out of a combination of jazz and dance orchestra popular in the 1920s. Trumpet-playing Louis Armstrong – the Great Satchmo – modified traditional New Orleans Jazz, "accenting the second and fourth beats and anticipating the main beats with lead-in notes in his solos to create a sense of rhythmic pulse that happened between the beats as well as on them, i.e. swing."[117]

In 1927 Armstrong worked with pianist Earl Hines, who had a similar impact on his instrument as Armstrong had on trumpet.

The house band on stage in the dance (west) room. Photo courtesy Wendy Morris.

Hines' melodic, horn-like conception of playing deviated from the contemporary conventions in jazz piano centered on building rhythmic patterns around "pivot notes". His approaches to rhythm and phrasing were also free and daring, exploring ideas that would define swing playing."[118]

Detroit area bands were influential in the development of Swing prior to the arrival of Benny Goodman's band in the mid-1930s.

At the same time Swing dancing began to replace the heel-kicking Charleston in the late 1920s as hemlines fell and long skirts demanded different steps. Hot swing music also fit well with jitterbug dancing – a faster and jumpier version of swing – that became a national craze alongside the swing craze.

Jitterbug dancers in 1938. Photo courtesy Library of Congress Prints and Photographs Division. New York World-Telegram and the Sun Newspaper Photograph Collection.
http://hdl.loc.gov/loc.pnp/cph.3c34893

But by 1939, Duke Ellington and others were dissatisfied with the creative state of swing music. Shortly, he and other bandleaders moved into more ambitious but less danceable orchestral jazz, while soloists gravitated toward small ensembles and bebop, which gave way to rhythm and blues by the early 1950s, shortly before the demise of Club Manitou.

Nonetheless, jitterbugging continued its popularity through the war years and beyond; the "frenetic leftover of the swing era ballroom days that was only slightly less acrobatic than Lindy"[119] lasted into the rock and roll era.

All this was squeezed into Club Manitou's dance room, and all the while waiters would be scurrying back and forth from tables to bar to ensure the patrons' wallets and purses were fully emptied.

As time passed into the 1940s, the demand for space to allow for larger bands and dance-floors increased. Slim added his west buildings in 1945-6 to accommodate these needs. By that time, only the gaming needed to be hidden from the authorities.

Bar tenders and waiters in front of the fireplace.

Fireplace

Across from the stage in the dance room was the grand fireplace. The centerpiece of the downstairs, the fireplace separated west and east rooms, with guests and staff passing through the stone arches on either side. The subterranean basement would naturally be cool but not cold year-round, so the fireplace kept the rooms warm if not toasty. Its heat also created the convection that sucked fresh air into the rooms.

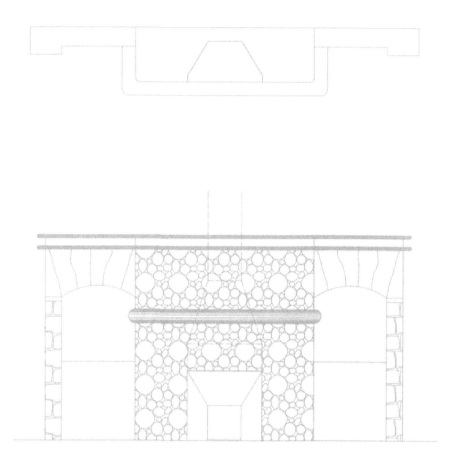

Fireplace elevation, approximate

The fireplace was likely not needed for warmth, the bodies crammed into the lounge – and dancing to the band – being sufficient for that, but it would provide a convenient convection for air to leave the room.

The fireplace also lent grandeur to the underground space. Its scale would have been impressive to the guests, particularly given they were all seated nearly in its belly.

Left archway of the fireplace leading from the entertainment (west) room back to the bar (east) room.

Gaming

Spread throughout the lounge were slot machines and roulette tables. Guests would rest from their jitterbugging by ordering some cocktails and playing the 5-cent slots.

Slim, second from right, poses in front of the lounge's fireplace with slot machine to the far left.

While the roulette wheels and other wooden gambling devices could be incinerated in a raid, the slot machines would need to be wheeled to safety – likely through the tunnel entrances at the southeast and southwest corners of the lounge. In front of the fireplace stood a Rol-A-Top Slot Machine from the Watling Manufacturing Company.

"Thomas W.B. Watling who was a founder of Watling Manufacturing and his older brother John, both Scottish immigrants, had begun their enterprising careers selling carnival games and equipment. Through this work they came into contact with Daniel Schall, who in 1895 introduced a version of the Schultze automatic payout counter wheel to Chicago." Imitations arose. "Watling stayed in the competition with imitations and lower prices, though they did come up with a few innovations of their own designed for the operator. Watling was the third largest maker of slot machine before World War I."[120]

"The Rol-A-Top slot machine model was the most popular model of the Watling Manufacturing Co. The brilliant idea of adding around coin escalator on top of the slot machine was first implemented by Thomas Watling in the early 1930s, and soon it became one of the most popular slot machine models of the century.

"This amazing slot machine design consists of a very attractive front board with a coin front theme and two front vendors. Moreover, it comes with twin jackpot slots, increasing the chance of winning jackpot. Apart from that, it has a nicely positioned three reel-spinning slot, a list of winning combinations, and a Rol-A-Top coin escalator. The coin escalator also has a button on the back, which can be used to unjam the coin if it gets stuck.

"When it comes to playing this slot machine, the gameplay is just as any other slot machine from that time. All you have to do is enter a 5 cent coin into the coin slot at the top of the coin escalator and pull the slot machine handle attached on the side. Once the handle is pulled, the slots start spinning and when they stop, they reveal the lucky combination you have scored.

"If you score a jackpot combination or any other winning combination from the given list of combinations, the machine automatically dispenses the accurate amount. However, if you score anything other than a winning combination, you win absolutely nothing, also losing the coin you have entered.

"It is an extremely fun way to gamble your money and the excitement keeps on increasing with every turn. Due to the machine's addictive gambling nature and its one handle design, this slot machine, along with other slot machines with a similar one handle design, was given the nickname as 'one-armed bandit' "[121]

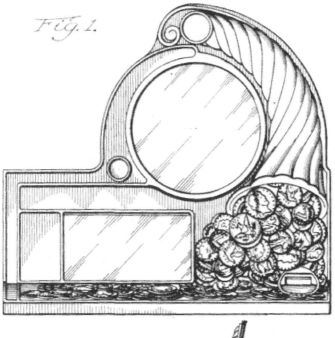
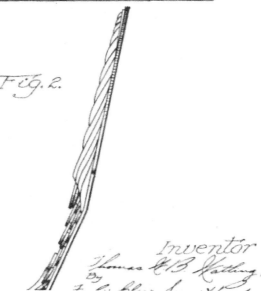

Design patent 94,718 to T.W.B. Watling, design incorporated into the infamous "one-armed bandit." Courtesy patents.google.com.

Watling Manufacturing's Rol-A-Top Slot Machine, manufactured from 1935-38, similar to that shown in the preceding photo in Slim's Lounge.

Slots were not the only gaming device to separate the guest from his or her dollar. Roulette tables assisted this effort. Their added advantage was that they could be stuffed into an incinerator in the case of a raid. No evidence: no crime.

The romantic and exciting image of the roulette table further enticed the summer vacationer to Harbor Springs. In Las Vegas, a new pinpoint on the map, the game was very popular, evoking the great European casinos in Monte Carlo.

Roulette in a nascent Las Vegas, 1932. Photo courtesy UNLV Libraries digital collection.

Bar (east) room

The bar room, unsurprisingly, was furthest from the entrance and closest to the tunnel entrances, both at the far eastern end of the room. Law enforcement needed to enter through the northwestern staircase, after battering down an iron jail-door and the top of the stairs and then a sliding iron door at the base of the stairs. That effort, if even possible, allowed for ample time to evacuate or burn evidence.

Bar (east) room with fireplace and arches leading to entertainment (west) room.

The bar was the main focus of the room. Spanning 37' across the north side of the room, it likely was not fully stocked – or perhaps even did not exist – until after 1933, to allow for quick clean-up operations during a raid.

Guests lounged at small, intimate tables with white tablecloths. The noise level would have been more sociable with the band in the adjacent room. However, the flow of alcohol probably incited more laughter and louder voices.

Bar in the east room after 1933. The liquor license is prominently displayed.

Bar, west end. Representation approximate.

Bar, east end. Representation approximate.

Bartenders at the bar, 1936. Photo courtesy Wendy Morris.

The bar was possibly inspired by the bar at The Stork Club in New York, founded in 1929. That bar featured the colonnaded bar-top, mirrored backing, and window-paned, mahogany cabinetry. The Stork Club's first iteration was a speakeasy that Sherman Billingsley, a former bootlegger from rural Oklahoma, operated with mobsters before it was smashed up and shut down by federal agents enforcing Prohibition laws.

> From Table 50, the journalist Walter Winchell gathered materials for his nationally syndicated gossip column and radio show, ensuring that the Stork Club's legend loomed large.[122]

Its second location had the beginnings of Billingsley's opulent vision, drawing fans like Winchell and the underworld boss Frank Costello. This iteration survived past Prohibition's end in 1933.[123]

The Gerhart's prided themselves on the reputation of Club Manitou as The Stork Club of the West. Everything that could be imported from New York was, including champagne, lobster, and chefs.

The proprietor of Jim Brady's, a Manhattan pub that went out of business at the start of the pandemic, said that a bar once part of the fabled Stork Club was brought piece by piece to his tavern in the 1970s. Credit Lila Barth for The New York Times.[124]

The whiskey of choice at Club Manitou was Canadian Club:

> Hiram Walker founded his distillery in 1858 in Detroit. He first learned how to distill cider vinegar in his grocery store in the 1830s before moving on to whisky and producing his first barrels in 1854. However, with the Prohibition movement gathering momentum and Michigan already becoming "dry," Walker decided to move his distillery across the Detroit River to Windsor, Ontario. From here, he was able to export his whisky and start to develop Walkerville, a model community that Walker financed to provide housing and services for his employees.
>
> Walker's whisky was particularly popular in the late 19th century gentlemen's clubs of the United States and Canada; hence it became known as "Club Whisky." Walker originally positioned the whisky as a premium liquor, pitching it not only on its smoothness and purity but also its five-year oak barrel aging.[125]

More likely than its long history and established reputation, Canadian Club's ready availability from Windsor and other Canadian trans-shipment points was probably its most appealing trait. Its local competition – home-brewed whiskey – could not begin to compete. The great whiskies from the Appalachian region were not to be available until after Prohibition's repeal. Finally, Al Capone had a fondness for Canadian Club, and the importance of that distribution channel was not lost on Slim and Fatty.

And so the Ford trucks rumbling across the roads of Michigan, Ohio, Indiana, and Illinois – originating from Purple Gang bootlegging and theft, were laden with Hiram Walker's product.

Canadian Club Whiskey, bottled 1930 (replica).[126]

Archeological digs near the east tunnel terminus near M-119 also turned up numerous fragments and a tell-tale bottlecap from Consolidated Distillers of Montreal which was later folded into Seagram.

Consolidated Distillers whiskey bottle similar to cap and shards found at east tunnel terminus.

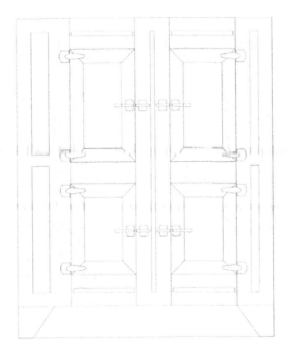

Kitchen refrigerator, front view above, side view below.

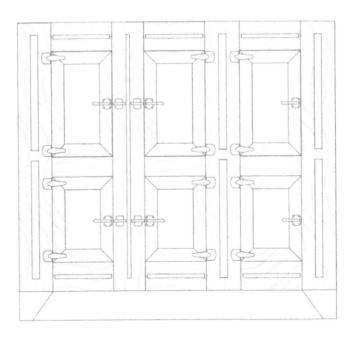

Kitchen

While guests turned right at the bottom of the stairs and proceeded into the noisy west dance room, the kitchen staff would head straight back and into the kitchen. It was tight quarters for the chefs and cooks.

The kitchen served the upstairs dining room, the front for the lounge operations below. A dumb-waiter hoisted the meals upstairs, and returned dirty dishes down.

Kitchen staff in front of refrigerator. The double doors in the rear led to Slim's office. The safe was nearby. The photo was taken from the approximate location of the 3rd barrier door. Photo courtesy Wendy Morris.

Dominating the kitchen was a Kelvinator refrigerator. The whole idea of refrigeration had been radically altered by William Carrier in 1902.

> Using what he already knew about heating objects with steam by sending air over hot coils, Carrier altered the process by filling the coils with cold water to produce cool air.

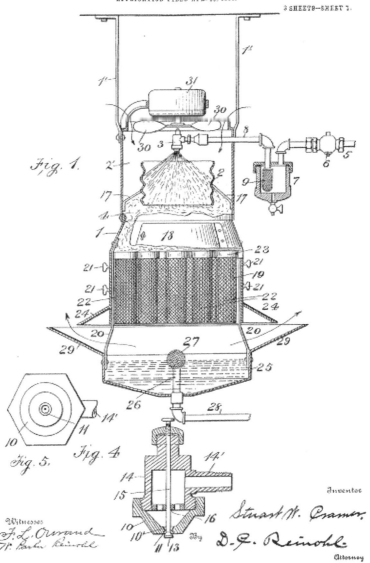

This was an electrical method of evaporation that reinvented the strategies of the ancient Egyptians and Chinese. It also circulated and cleansed the air. He revealed the innovation in 1902. The patent for the Apparatus for Treating Air was granted in 1906.

Around the same time, textile manufacturing executive Stewart W. Cramer was looking for ways to control the temperature and humidity of the air in North Carolina's cotton mills. In a speech at the American Cotton Manufacturers Association's 1906 annual conference, he "used the term 'Air Conditioning' to include humidifying and air cleansing, and heating and ventilation." His technology for doing so, the Humidifying and Air-Conditioning Apparatus, was granted a patent in 1907.[127]

The refrigeration ideas were then applied to cold storage as well as living spaces, both utilized in the kitchen area of Slim's Lounge.

Kelvinator icebox. Photo by Daderot - Own work, Public Domain, https://commons.wikimedia.org/w/index.php?curid=66555781

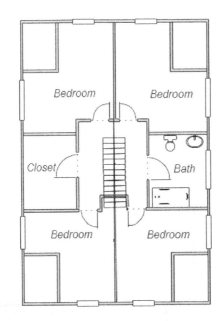

Upper floor of Club Manitou, with four bedrooms for staff, superimposed over lower floors

10 Personnel

About 30 staff were involved in the operation of Club Manitou. The size of the payroll meant that Club Manitou was an important employer in the area and that many families were dependent on those checks, particularly as the Great Depression hit. It is no wonder that the local police were more interested in the Club's survival than in enforcing unpopular laws.

Club Manitou staff with the band in the lower right, chefs in the upper right, and waiters in the upper left. Slim and Sam are noticeably absent.

Slim picked the best to prepare and serve dinners for his guests, reaching to New York's Vatel Club for great chefs.[128] The Vatel Club -- an organization of French chefs that conducted all of its business in the mother tongue[129] – was a founding member of the American Culinary Federation (ACF) in 1929. On May 20, 1929, New York's leading European chefs, each representing their respective culinary associations — Louis Jousse, John Massironi, Charles Schillig, Rene Anjard, Joseph Donon, Louis Paquet, Charles Bournez, Charles Lepeltier and Charles Scotto — came together to form The ACF.[130]

Slim was serious about his menu. Likely his chefs were lured by a lucrative short-term contract – July and August – and a chance to get out of New York's stifling summer heat. It would make sense, given their demanding schedule, that they were lodged on the second floor of the club. The croupiers were imported from Ballard's Resort in French Lick, Indiana.[131]

Chefs in the kitchen. This photo is difficult to reconcile with the basement lounge layout. Was part of the kitchen upstairs in or next to the lookout? Photo courtesy Wendy Morris.

Club Manitou, 2nd Edition

11 Competition

Slim and Sam opened their operation in a region well acquainted with their business plan. The Colonial Club in Charlevoix opened around 1916 as a "high-class gambling club and gourmet restaurant."[132] This was followed by Cook's in Charlevoix in 1925, then the Beach Hotel Casino in Charlevoix, the Ramona Park casino in Harbor Springs, and the Grand Hotel Casino on Mackinac Island.[133]

The best way to beat the competition is to have none. The Ramona Park Hotel a couple miles from Club Manitou was a problem. Both competed in the same illicit markets.

The Ramona was owned by Jimmy Hayes, "an extremely powerful gambler who ran all the gambling operations in northwestern Ohio during the early 1930s."[134] After a run-in with the mafia who had wrested control of Detroit-based mob activities from the Purple Gang, Hayes was found murdered in a Detroit alleyway, shot in the head with a shotgun.

Hayes' wife and business partner continued to run the Ramona for two more years, but finally sold the hotel to Slim, who promptly tore it down. The competition was not just beaten, it was beaten in traditional mob style.

With the boards from the Ramona, Slim built a new restaurant in downtown Harbor Springs on the waterfront, Al's Pier Bar. Slim now had a monopoly on gambling and associated activities around Little Traverse Bay, though his original investors had disappeared into various jails or assorted cemeteries.

The competition Slim could not snuff out was up at the Grand Hotel on Mackinac Island between lower and upper Michigan. "Al Capone and the Purple Gang came north to keep Canadian whiskey passing through Sault Ste. Marie to Chicago and Detroit. Federal enforcement agent John Fillion double-crossed both his office and the bootleggers. The Grand Hotel on Mackinac Island survived due to gambling and fine Canadian whiskey brought in by rumrunners, sometimes assisted by the Coast Guard."[135]

> During the early 1900s, the Grand Hotel on Mackinac Island hired fake nannies to smuggle spirits in from Canada. Women pushing baby carriages full of alcohol strolled up the storied Mackinac streets, pausing periodically on their routes to enjoy the sunshine and avoid suspicion from law enforcement or church officials. The nannies unloaded their goods at the Grand Kitchen's door and went on with their days.
>
> The Grand Hotel staff unloaded the goods and doled them out to notable guests. Perhaps iconic hotel visitors like the Armours and Swifts (the meat packing families), Marshall Field (the department store founder), Cornelius Vanderbilt, and Mrs. Potter Palmer (whose husband founded the Chicago's

Palmer House Hotel) imbibed, or perhaps that was all before their time, but who can say for sure?[136]

But as much as the Hotel was competition for Slim, it was also an effective and busy conduit for his gang's contraband:[137]

> To the north was Canada where liquor literally poured into the United States. Again private individuals with fast speedboats picked up the liquor, many times aided by young Coast Guardsmen, brought it through the labyrinth waterways of the St. Mary's River. Mackinac Island, across the Straits from Mackinaw City, was the staging area. Liquor reached the Grand Hotel much to the delight of guests who also enjoyed gambling. Liquor landed at the island was then shipped south to Capone in Chicago and to the Purple Gang in Detroit. However Mackinaw City was the terminus of the notorious Purple Gang's rum running highway north.

> Across the Straits at St. Ignace, a fellow known as Black Jack was an outlet for Canadian rye whiskey. He operated quietly using his home as a front selling maple syrup. When raided at one point by Treasury agents they wanted to know who would buy 36 bottles of maple syrup? Black Jack naturally had no idea except that they were eating piles of pancakes.

> On the Straits boats plied their illegal cargoes. Sometimes coal-carrying boats had liquor stored in sacks beneath the coal. At one point in May 1928 the Coast Guard chased the Geronimo loaded with 4,000 cases of liquor worth $250,000 on its way to Chicago. It was in the wee hours of the morning and the captain thought either he could outrun the cutter or he would be lost in the mist. The captain refused to stop; the Coast Guard fired a warning shot, and then disabled the vessel west of the straits. Two years later it was seized again, this time loaded with $600,000 worth of booze. The placid and magnificent Straits was busy during the era of Prohibition.[138]

Club Manitou's success may have also attracted copycats. After the 1931 Collingwood Manor Massacre in Detroit – which put three Purple Gang members behind bars for life – "One-Armed" Mike Gelfand – a member of the gang – came up with the "novel" idea for a "restaurant and dancing pavilion to cater to local residents while providing a safe house for gangster fugitives."[139] Located about half-way between Detroit and Harbor Springs, Graceland Ballroom in Lupton, Michigan quickly became the retreat of first-resort.

Mike purchased the property for one dollar from his sister who had inherited it from an uncle's estate. No one knows where the money to build the ballroom came from – but little doubt it was the Purple Gang.

The original inhabitants of Lupton would not have been amused by the activities of the denizens of the Graceland Ballroom since those early settlers were Quakers. The town was named for Emmor Lupton, who came to the area in the 1880s and in 1889 built a sawmill and shingle mill. Lupton became a railroad stop and grew to have a blacksmith, grocery store, hotel, livery stables, a meat market, a milliner, a shoemaker, hotel, drug store, and more. However, as the lumber depleted, people moved on and the Purple Gang moved in.

"Some customers spoke of bullets in the ballroom's ceiling and gangsters standing guard at the upstairs windows, watching for the police to come down the gravel road from Rose City. If the law ever did come, the gangsters knew they had just minutes to get out through one of the many tunnels that led from the basement into a ravine 100 feet north, where a creek ran across the property. Others told of safes, presumably stolen from Detroit merchants, that were opened with explosives as a highlight of an evening's entertainment. It's not known how many of these stories were true, but they added to the building's mystique."[140]

Graceland Ball Room in Lupton

Above: Ironton Ferry, opened 1926. Photo courtesy Charlevoix Historical Society. Below: Michigan State Prison

12 Business interruption

Shortly after their first summer of business, Slim and Sam faced a nation plunging into the Great Depression. The stock market crash of October 1929 no doubt affected their high-wealth clientele. Yet, the attraction of whiskey and gambling appeared to overcome the troubled economy. The wealthy were buying lottery tickets by heading to Club Manitou: just one good ticket and all problems would disappear.

State and local officials were reluctant to shut down the tourist trade during the Depression. Jobs were needed. But Slim's next hurdle was himself. He engaged in other gang activities from his Harbor Springs base, likely taking direction from his counterparts in Detroit. In early 1935 he was arrested for counterfeiting by the Treasury Department's Secret Service in a ring that extended from New York City through Toledo and into Michigan.[141] He beat that rap: gangsters were adept at navigating the justice system.

Slim was not shy with a gun. Desiring more greenery for his club at the lowest price, he went to the Charlevoix County nursery in Ironton and stole some small cedar trees. When the owner started to chase them, Slim pulled out a pistol and shot at the owner. Or, that was the story Slim gave the court. He was charged with intent to murder.[142]

More likely: a bootlegging operation had gone awry and Slim was going to set it aright.[143] Ironton had a small landing, and may have been a trans-shipment point for one of the gangs that had spread tentacles throughout Michigan.

This landed him in the Michigan State Penitentiary in 1935, but he returned to the club in 1936 for its 8th season.[144]

In that interval, the Purple Gang had self-destructed. Sam seems to have disappeared as well. When Slim returned to the club, his benefactors and their expectations had disappeared. The Detroit gangsters had their own legal reckonings to contend with. Moreover, the time in the pen may have shaken Slim. He started to settle down, perhaps confident that the club would provide sufficient income going forward.

As Allah Joseph Schwendner, Slim married Jeannette Violet Kenick on March 27, 1937, in Richmond, Indiana.[145] Jeannette had grown up in Detroit with her parents, Vincent and Jennie. However, according to the marriage certificate, she was living in Richmond at the time of the wedding.

A graduate of the nursing program at the University of Michigan, Jeannette might have been a profoundly down-to-earth influence on Slim.

JEANNETTE KENICK

"The mildest manners and the gentlest heart."

House of Alice Freeman Palmer; Greenfield Park School; Nurses Training, Highland Park Hospital; University of Michigan.

HELEN KENYON

"Unspotted faith and comely womanhood."

House of Alice Freeman Palmer; Hutchins Intermediate School;

Jeannette's Northern High School yearbook entry, 1926.[146]

What was the "House of Alice Freeman Parker" mentioned in Jennette's high school yearbook? It may provide a clue into Jeannette herself[147]:

Alice Freeman was born in 1855 to a farmer in New York State. She was the eldest of four children. Her father had greater aspirations than farming and left his family in order to gain further education and went on to become a doctor. Alice and her mother ran the farm and raised the other children in his absence. Alice wanted desperately to go to college but at that time 0.7% of all young women 18-21 were attending college, and a poor family like hers would not waste money on educating a girl when they had boys to raise and educate. Alice promised her parents that if she were allowed to attend school she would help to pay for her younger siblings educations as well. Her parents agreed and in 1872 Alice Freemen began attending the University of Michigan. Only two years earlier U of M had begun allowing women to attend classes. While going to school she fulfilled her promise to her family and took teaching jobs to support them.

After she graduated Alice Freeman became a principal at a boarding school in Wisconsin. Due to her outstanding reputation, the founder of Wellesley College, Mr. Henry Fowle Durant, offered her a position to teach mathematics, then Greek and finally a professorship in History. She accepted the third offer. When Durant died in 1881, the trustees of Wellesley College elected the then 26-year-old Alice Freeman, president. She was the 1st female to head a nationally known college. Prior to her leadership, the school was considered a religiously based college. Freeman is credited with creating a well rounded and intellectually stimulating Liberal Arts College.

During that time she met George Palmer, a forward-minded Philosophy professor at Harvard. In July of 1887 Alice Freeman announced her engagement to George Palmer and her resignation as President of Wellesley College. For the next two years Alice Freeman Palmer was an active public speaker focusing on Women's higher education. She was appointed to the Massachusetts Board of education and was one of the founders of the American Association of University Women.

How Jeannette came to meet Slim and wind up in Richmond may remain a mystery. Perhaps the town was usefully distant from Michigan law enforcement eyes. Whatever the story of their meeting and courtship, together they expanded Club Manitou.

Aerial view of Club Manitou ca. 1948 showing new addition to the west (left) of the original structure.

13   Expansion and threats

Michigan eventually legalized 3.2 percent beer, marking the beginning of the end for Prohibition. At 6pm on May 11, 1933, beer could be legally served. The newspaper kept a close eye on the city's legal beer supply as the date approached. In 1935, the Purple Gang ceded control of Detroit wire services and essentially all mob activity to the Mafia.[148] With that power change, it behooved Slim to keep a low profile and distance himself from the Purple Gang. Many of the Purple Gang leaders not already incarcerated were murdered by rival gangs with scores to settle. Slim avoided that fate.

The Manitou Club continued to prosper in the later 1930s but new competitive pressures were emerging. A tectonic shift in U.S. entertainment was underway and, given his tentacles into the mob world, Slim was likely well aware of it.

The Hoover Dam project in Nevada kicked off in 1931, and swelled Las Vegas' population from 10,000 to 25,000, mostly young men. To capture the paychecks of these new workers, the State of Nevada legalized gambling at the local level the same year. By 1941, the first resort opened on what would become known as the Las Vegas Strip. The mob arrived shortly thereafter.

Flamingo Hotel, ca. 1949. Photo courtesy Las Vegas Museum.

Intrigued by legal gambling and the profits pouring though the existing casinos, mobster Bugby Seigel designed in 1945 then opened "The Flamingo" in December of 1946, the year of the Club Manitou expansion. Gambling had gone Hollywood: size mattered.

At the same time, bands were demanding larger venues to accommodate not only their larger size but also the burgeoning crowds enticed by radio.

With mobility in the U.S. unleashed by rail, then the automobile, and now aircraft, competitive pressures mounted for Club Manitou. Music, convention, and gambling venues were rapidly becoming available wherever they could be financed and built.

Prior to World War 2, the writing was on the wall. In 1934, the time to travel from New York to Los Angeles by plane was 25 hours. In 1938, it was cut by 50%[149]:

> On an early evening in late 1938, a gleaming American Airlines DC-3 departed Newark Airport, bound for Glendale, California. The takeoff, wrote a Fortune magazine reporter aboard to record the still-novel experience of cross-country air travel, was effortless. "Halfway along the runway," he recounted, "she left the ground so smoothly that none of the first fliers in the cabin realized what had happened until they saw the whole field rushing away behind them and the factory lights winking through the Jersey murk ahead."
>
> By the time the flight crossed over Virginia, passengers had already polished off a dinner of soup, lamb chops, vegetables, salad, ice cream and coffee. After a refueling stop in Nashville, the DC-3 continued west. Beyond Dallas, the journalist added, "visibility was limited only by the far horizons of the curving earth." Despite head winds, the plane arrived on schedule at 8:50 a.m. Total time was 18 hours 40 minutes, including several ground stops.

A year earlier, Howard Hughes had dropped the transcontinental time to 7 hours 28 minutes. Technology was pushing forward.

Post-war air travel added to the wealthy American's mobility. Commercial aviation, in particular, grew rapidly and at first used war surplus to transport both people and cargo. Heavy and super-heavy bombers like the B-29 and Avro Lancaster were easily converted into commercial aircraft, and the DC-3 was ideal for longer commercial flights. The British de Havilland Comet was the first commercial jetliner to fly, although it had some major issues. In 1946, United DC-4s and TWA Constellations managed one-stop transcontinental flights[150]. Yet, it was the imminent arrival of commercial jet transportation that was to drop the transcontinental time to Howard's liking.

1945 advertisement for the American Airlines System, Douglas DC-4 Flagship

While airlines focused on international flights to available airports, the major U.S. cities were racing to attract trans-American flights. Situated across from the Harbor Springs Airport, Slim and Jeannette were well-aware of the aviation changes of the post-war years, and the allure of Las Vegas. Time to expand.

Above, 1948 addition viewed from the northeast. The original building is on the left.

Slim was drafted into World War 2 on October 28, 1940[151] but did not serve.

In 1945, Slim and Jeanne decided to triple the club's size. The new addition opened on July 4 the next year. "The dining and dancing portions of the nightclub had been moved into the new addition while the illegal gambling activities (such as roulette, poker, baccarat and chuck-a-luck) remained in the steel-door-protected basement portion of the old building."[152]

It was an immediate success. That success carried the club forward, years past its initial plan.

INTERIOR OF the Club Pony Tail as it was in the early 1960's. (NEWS-Review file photo.)

Interior of the pavilion in later days. A tunnel connected it to the original building. Photo courtesy Petoskey News-Review.

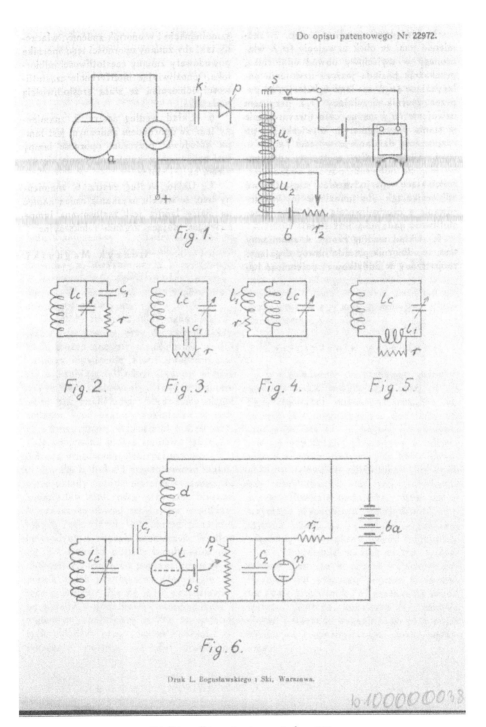

Walkie-talkie patent, granted 1936[153].

14   Disruptive technology

Radio, patented in 1904, had been perfected on the battlefields of Europe during World War I. At the same time, the National Guards from across the U.S. were called into service, leaving the states short on law enforcement. Fearing that German agents and militant labor groups would disrupt the vast war production in Michigan, the Michigan governor organized state police in 1917 and promptly sent them to the Upper Peninsula to quell strikes at mines in Gogebic County, Ironwood, and Palmer.[154] While fiscally prudent legislators and "jealous militia companies" sought to disband the 300-strong force, Governor Sleeper kept the troops to respond to the escalating violence of the bootleggers.[155]

The Department of the Michigan State Police was established on March 27, 1919. With liquor moving along the rapidly growing road systems, the purpose of most state police systems centered on highway enforcement.[156] Notably, none of the original posts of the Michigan State Police were near Harbor Springs.[157] By 1929, spurred by the success of the Detroit Police Department with radio, the state police set up a state-wide radio system.[158] No longer could the gangsters simply bust through police lines: those lines could radio ahead and more substantial obstacles – such as logs – placed across the roads. Modern communications were playing havoc with the free-for-all of the earlier world where disappearing into the dark was easier.

Next, the first patent for the walkie-talkie idea (patent filled on 20 May 1935, granted on 19 March 1936) was granted to a Polish engineer, Henryk Magnuski, who worked after 1939 on Motorola's first walkie-talkie. The boon to law enforcement was immense. Now, coordinated assaults on unseen forces could be mounted by the military or local law enforcement. The first usable walkie-talkie appeared in 1942. Its impact on the outcome of World War II is unknown but likely significant, as was its impact on law enforcement in the U.S..

As well, night-vision devices were introduced in the German Army as early as 1939 and were used in World War II. After World War II Vladimir K. Zworykin developed the first practical commercial night-vision device at Radio Corporation of America (RCA), intended for civilian use. Zworykin's idea came from a former radio-guided missile but was not a commercial success. Nonetheless, technology to thwart the enemy – whoever that might be – was proceeding at a furious pace, led by the military.

The tunnel and other labyrinthine, subterranean hideouts had suddenly become less secure. Technologies of defense were giving way to technologies of offense. Law enforcement could be deployed widely, to cover multiple opponent moves, and yet stay coordinated, in even the darkest environment. The confusion of the rat den was no longer a defense; the tunnel was no longer safe.

At least as important as the arrival of these technologies was the expanding role of the Federal Reserve in clearing checks.[159] While the stated goal of the central clearing was to provide a bulwark against the regular business cycle recessions, a less appreciated result was that monetary transactions could be both regulated and recorded. Suddenly, any customer presenting a check that was subsequently cashed created a transaction that could be presented in court. The anonymity of cash disappeared; legal hazard arose.

Volume of checks processed by Federal Reserve Banks

	Millions of checks	Dollar value of checks ($ billions)	Value of checks processed by Reserve Banks as a percentage of checks cleared through clearinghouses (%)
1915	8.8	4.7	2.9
1920	452.1	156.5	35.6
1925	716.5	247.2	49.4
1929	852.1	351.7	49.1
1934	754.7	171.9	65.1

Source: Gilbert (2000, 131)

Check clearing becomes the norm.[160]

After a series of raids by the Michigan State Police in the 1950s, the Michigan Liquor Control Board revoked the club's liquor license in 1953. The Gerhart's did not open the club for the 1954 summer. Club Manitou had ended its 25-year existence.

But the building was still there, and Slim still alive. Club Manitou followed both in spirit. Slim was not finished.

Charleston, West Virginia News-Gazette, August 28, 1960.[161]

Colonial Club near the Greenbrier

Slim moved to White Sulphur Springs, West Virginia, where he operated the Colonial Club adjacent to the prestigious Greenbrier Resort. As expected, the club ran with law an afterthought. Now, however, without the threat of the Purple Gang silencing witnesses, Slim's venture ran upon the rocks.

Colonial Club in White Sulphur Springs.[162]

Federal agents investigated the Colonial Club in 1962 and then Federal officers raided on September 18, 1963. The investigating agent was sent a poker chip by Slim, a less than smart move. Slim was found guilty, and his appeal failed.

The operation of the Colonial Club reflected the importance of money laundering to the criminal enterprise, and how that use of the banking system ultimately became the undoing of many of those illicit businesses. In United States v. Gerhart, 275 F. Supp. 443 (S.D.W. Va. 1967), District Judge Michie wrote on October 1, 1967[163]:

> Convicted by a jury on three counts of violating 18 U.S.C. §§ 1952 and 2, William Al Gerhart moves this court in arrest of judgment and for a new trial. None of the multitudinous grounds urged in support of each of these motions, I conclude, is sufficient to warrant overturning the conviction. ...
>
> Advantageously located adjacent to the Greenbrier in White Sulphur Springs, West Virginia, the Colonial Club, a gaming establishment owned and operated by the defendant Gerhart, flourished for several years prior to a raid by Federal officers on September 18, 1963. The club, testified Gladys Brown, a former employee, had a seasonal operation running from April to November of each year. She had worked there beginning in September, 1961 and except for the off-season continued to be employed until July, 1963. Gambling equipment at the club, she also related, consisted of a roulette wheel, two blackjack tables, a

dice table and five slot machines. Corroborating her testimony concerning the activities conducted at the club is the description of the club and the gaming operation there carried on related by Special F.B.I. Agent William B. Anderson, Jr. who had visited the club in an undercover capacity in September, 1962 and again in August, 1963. Another F.B.I. Agent, George Patterson, related at trial the substance of two conversations he had had with the defendant, one in March of 1962 and the other in May of 1963 which would lead one to believe that the defendant was engaged in conducting at the Colonial Club a gaming operation of a substantial nature which he planned to continue indefinitely. Several patrons of the club also testified for the Government and described the games of chance in which they had engaged while there. All the testimony adduced from these sources demonstrated that both for some time prior to, and also for some time after the dates on which the proscribed use of the mails occurred, the defendant, except for seasonal variations, continuously operated the Colonial Club as a gaming establishment.

It was customary for the defendant to cash at the Colonial Club checks drawn on out-of-state banks. Not only did he take such checks in exchange for cash, but also according to the testimony at trial he accepted checks drawn on foreign banks directly in satisfaction of gambling debts and as payment for chips. Mr. Paul Slattery, a patron of the club over Labor Day week-end, 1962, cashed with the defendant two checks totaling $200.00 drawn on the Union Trust Company, Washington, D. C. Defendant's endorsement and the stamp of the Bank of White Sulphur Springs established that these checks were negotiated there. Government witness John Crawford who had visited the club in May, 1963 issued to the defendant checks drawn on a New York bank totaling $19,000 directly to cover gambling losses. ... The United States mail, testified the bank president, is the means used by the Bank of White Sulphur Springs to transmit checks to the Federal Reserve Bank of Richmond, Virginia. The gravamen of the offense alleged in the two counts of Indictment No. 513 is that the defendant Gerhart used or caused to be used a facility of interstate commerce, in this case the United States mail, by causing checks to be sent by mail through the normal clearing channels.

On December 18, 1962 Special Agent William B. Anderson, Jr. received at his home in Pennsylvania what amounted to a Christmas card enclosed in an envelope. The envelope containing the card was postmarked White Sulphur Springs, West Virginia and bore the return address of the Colonial Club. The card inside which contained a facsimile of a poker chip carried the endorsement "Greetings of the Season * * * Redeemable on presentation at the Club for full value by customer only" and additional notations indicating that it came from the Colonial Club. The card bore the signature of the defendant

Gerhart, affixed apparently by mechanical means. The single count of Indictment No. 522 charged defendant with the use of the mail for the purpose of sending this card which was designed to promote and facilitate the operation of the Colonial Club.

Of course, it was also necessary for the Government to show that the defendant's operation was carried on in violation of the laws of West Virginia. Games of unequal chance favoring the proprietor of the house are proscribed by West Virginia law. Special Agent Anderson described the odds at roulette. The odds at roulette, he explained, are 38 to 1. The Colonial Club paid 35 to 1; the disparity favored the house. Witness John Crawford, an expert on many gambling games, described the odds present in the game of craps as it was conducted at the Colonial Club. He said that a cautious, knowledgeable player could keep the odds as low as 1.4% in favor of the house; the average player, he said, generally plays in such a manner that the odds favor the house by as much as 5%. Two of the slot machines seized by the Government during the raid of September 18, 1963 were examined in the F.B.I. laboratories. F.B.I. employee Bruce Fisher, who had tested the machines thoroughly, derived statistics showing that the 25-cent machine retained approximately 27% of all monies played and that the 50-cent machine retained approximately 33% of all money inserted for playing purposes.

Apparently, Slim's use of the U.S. Mail to send the poker chip to the FBI agent was unwise.

Slim sold the Club Manitou buildings to Stan and Jean Douglas of Petoskey in 1962, likely needing cash for his problems in West Virginia. As well, Jean's father had died at The Greenbrier in 1957, having possibly been in costly assisted living at the exclusive resort. The West Virginia exile, then, was very unpleasant for the Gerharts. At least time in a West Virginia jail was avoided. Slim and Jeannette returned to a modest, quiet retirement in Alanson, a small town a few miles from Harbor Springs. There, on the banks of Crooked Lake, they could peer out at the waters that had once teemed with their shallow-draft boats laden with contraband.

Crime scene photo that shows the bodies of Isadore Sutker, left, near bed; Hymie Paul, right, foreground; Joe Lebovitz, center, background after they were gunned down by members of the Purple Gang. Caption reads: "Scene in the bedroom, hall and living room of apartment 211 - 1740 Collingwood Ave (City of Detroit). Taken September 16 1931 at 4:00pm by Detective Edward Crimmins." Walter P. Reuther Library, Wayne State University.

15 The road not taken

Slim was born in 1906. Three Fleisher brothers were born a few years earlier – Harry in 1903, Lou in 1905, and Sam – and came to the U.S. with the other Russian Jewish immigrants soon after their birth. They were members of the juvenile Purple Gang and attended the Old Bishop School.[164] Like most members of the younger branch of the gang, but unlike Slim,

> [they] graduated into the world of organized crime with the advent of Prohibition. Both Harry and Lou served their apprenticeships as members of the Oakland Sugar House Gang .... Both Fleishers gained reputations as strong arm men and hijackers. ... Harry Fleisher became known as a killer. ... The Fleishers' father was known for his skill at building hidden gun compartments into the side panels of touring cars. This was a sideline business at the family junkyard.[165]

In 1936, Harry and Sam were convicted of violating the Internal Revenue Act by manufacturing liquor illegally, and were sent to Alcatraz for a 8-year sentence, though only served 4½ years, released early for good behavior.[166]

Louis, on the other hand, was arrested in Detroit in 1926 for the murder of William Glanzrock, a partner in Lou's bootlegging operation but, for insufficient evidence, he was released. However, he quickly ran afoul of the law again, and was sentenced to 10 years at Leavenworth Penitentiary in 1928, but was released in 1934.

On his release, Lou joined his brothers at the junkyard. Within two years, Sam and Lou were questioned about 50 burglaries in the Jackson area. In 1938, Lou and his wife were found guilty of 14 counts of federal firearms violations. Lou was sentenced to 30 years.

In 1940 Harry and Sam Fleisher were released from Alcatraz. Soon, Michigan State Senator Warren G. Hooper was dead. Hooper had been one of the State's chief witnesses in the Grand Jury's ongoing investigation into graft by government officials. Harry Fleisher was eventually convicted of conspiracy to murder Hooper.

Was Slim of this ilk? The question is difficult to answer. His rap sheet might suggest he had all the makings if not the opportunity. In 1926, before making his way north, he was charged with bastardy, but he skipped on a $700 bail – nearly $20,000 in 2021 dollars – intended to protect the new child. Then, just prior to opening Club Manitou, he was arrested south of Detroit and admitted to picking up a load of liquor. While the driver of his car had a bullet in his head, Slim was not charged with the May 25, 1929, murder. He was also picked up in a counterfeiting scheme in 1935, though not convicted. Finally, as mentioned earlier, Slim did serve 9 months in 1935-36 for felonious assault.

Purple Gang roundup by Detroit police in March of 1928: Sam Axler, Eddie Fletcher, Sam Goldfarb, Phil Keywell, Abe Zussman, Willie Lake, Harry Fleisher, Jack Stein, and Abe Axler (seated)

Slim was active, therefore, in all the enterprises, violent and not, that define a gangster, even as Club Manitou was open and operating. Assuming the arrests only account for a small fraction of his actual activities, he was a very busy man. Yet, the differences between Slim and the Fleisher brothers are pronounced if not glaring. The escalating violence of the Detroit gang likely encouraged him to stay away and manage Club Manitou to accomplish other gang objectives in a less violent environment.

Was Slim an actual member of the Purple Gang? If we are to accept the simplest explanation for all his activities based on Occam's Razor, then clearly 'yes'. As well, who is the slim guy with the slick, dishwater blond hair in the right of the police line-up in the following photo? One wonders.

Purple Gang line-up. Photo courtesy Detroit Free Press.

DEPUTIES RAID GAMBLING DEN; POLICE QUIZZED

Grand Jury Will Hear Charges Against Local Police.

COMPLAINTS NOT ANSWERED, REPORT

Turrets, A Steel-Lined Office, Guns Found By Raiders.

Following a complaint that Dearborn police refused to raid an alleged gambling establishment, members of the Wayne County sheriff's staff, led by Deputies Rockard and Freckelton, wrecked a resort known as the Atlantic Athletic Club, 2809 Salina avenue, at 1:10 a. m. Thursday.

Fifteen men were found grouped around two large dice tables in the center of the room. Dice cups, dice and money were found on the tables, according to the deputies. Three revolvers and a large sum of money was confiscated. The raiders reported that they found a steel-lined office and turrets commanding the "club" and its entrance.

Charges that the Dearborn police had, on several occasions, refused to raid the gambling house, caused Harry S. Toy, Wayne County prosecutor, late yesterday to order grand jury subpenas served on all prisoners arrested in the raid. The subpenas are returnable Monday.

The charges against the Dearborn police department and the alleged threats on the life of John Kowalski, 2779 Amazon avenue, will be placed before the grand jury for investigation, it was stated at the prosecutor's office Thursday.

The raid, according to Toy, had been conducted by the deputies in a legal manner following the complaint placed before them by Kowalski that his two sons had lost their entire earnings of two weeks at the "club." The investigation will also include the report that Dearborn patrolmen are forbidden from entering establishments while on duty in the "south end" section of the city.

According to Kowalski, a com-
(Continued on Page Six)

DEPUTIES RAID GAMBLING DEN: POLICE QUIZZED
(Continued from Page One)

plaint was made to the Dearborn police three weeks ago when he went to Detective Arthur Linske with the information that gambling was in progress at the place. Linske, according to the statement, told Kowalski that he would investigate the report. Several phone calls were later made by Kowalski, and Linske repeatedly promised to accompany Kowalski to the establishment.

When the detective failed to accompany Kowalski to the "club," the complainant placed a complaint in the office of Chief William Linsday, who promised to do something. Nothing was done, according to the report. Another call to the Dearborn police, it is charged, resulted in information being given that the Dearborn police were doing nothing in the case.

Kowalski also informed the county authorities that he had been threatened with death by two gunmen after he had made an effort to recover the money lost by his son.

The men taken by the county police were brought before Common Pleas Judge Leonard L. Scheiman in Detroit, Tuesday afternoon. Three of the men, Michael Youngdov, John Harniby and

Dearborn Independent, January 30, 1931, accusing Dearborn Police of failure to raid.[167]

16 Law un-enforcement

Where were the forces of the law during those 25 years of Club Manitou's existence? They seemed to rush in only after a quarter century of having known full-well what was going on at the club.

Stepping back 10 years before Club Manitou arrived, the acquiescence was noticeable at the Grand Hotel on Mackinac Island, an hour north by car (4 hours by bicycle if inclined). From 1919 to 1921 there were three successive raids by the Michigan State Police toward the end of each season in late August. In the first raid, the equipment was confiscated. In the second, equipment was lost, and three $100 fines levied. In the last raid, again the equipment was sent to Lansing for supposed destruction, and the manager fined $250. There was no jail time for anyone, and no arrests of guests.

In 1927 the Michigan Governor hosted the National Governors' Convention at the Grand Hotel. Later it was found that "a significant portion of the $25,000 appropriated by the legislature to pay for the national conference had gone to buy liquor."[168]

Down in Detroit, the Purple Gang wiggled out of several Imperial Entanglements – until 1931. Acquittals were handed down in the 1927 charge of extortion from the Detroit Wholesale Cleaners and Dyers. That same year, no charges were brought after the Milaflores Massacre and the later murder of rogue cop Vivian Welch. In 1930, no charges were brought in the murder of radio reporter Jerry Buckley. However, finally, in 1931, four members of the gang were found guilty in the Collingswood Manor Massacre, the start of the gang's self-destruction.

Club Manitou had similar brushes with the Michigan State Police in 1938 and 1947. There were perhaps other raids, none of which netted anything.

What was going on? Several things, including:

- Copious pay-offs to local officials kept local enforcement feeble.
- Local officials had no motivation to curb the economic boom fueled by gambling and alcohol.
- The threat, real or not, of reprisals by gangsters likely outweighed the risk of small fines for both law enforcement and possible witnesses.
- The illegal and essentially victimless sins were commonplace in private residences; that those same foibles occurred in more public places would be expected, and be simply an extension of habits already well-formed in the public.
- Without evidence and witnesses, the courts were reluctant to convict, such convictions likely to be overturned on appeal. Good gangster lawyers likely

used the words "hearsay" and "circumstantial" quite often. Good gangsters surrounded themselves with good lawyers. It was a cost of doing business.

And so the public, law enforcement, and the courts were equally reluctant to chase down the more benign of gangster activities. When enforcement and justice prevailed, it was likely more the result of gangster sloppiness than bona fide detective work.

Al and Jeannette Gerhart, on left, with their lawyer. Photo courtesy Wendy Morris.

Club Manitou, 2nd Edition

Homicides increased 67% during Prohibition. Meanwhile, arrests for drunk driving increased 81%.[169]

17 Unintended consequences

What are the lessons from planning, building, and operating a speakeasy? The first is that it is a highly profitable business while its tools stay ahead of the law and its tools. Whether the constant danger was troubling to Slim is unknown; it may be that those threats added to the excitement of the day. Certainly, the money and other benefits must have compensated for the risks.

But the second and far more important lesson relates to the public policy and sin: prohibitions of private, victimless behavior simply drive that behavior underground, encouraging black markets and crime. A far more effective and less dangerous policy, as was learned through prohibition, is the "sin tax", which discourages the activity by squeezing profitability out of the black market. Would the Mafia have gotten a foothold in the U.S. without the 18th Amendment?

> Bootlegging opened up a glittering world of rum-running, roustabouts and riches for the ordinary people of Ecorse [an island in the Detroit River] and allowed gangs like the Purple Gang from Detroit to provide a foundation for the Mafia and entrench themselves in American society.[170]

Slim and his cohorts thrived in the U.S. for several decades, and the Mob – the successor to the Purple Gang in Detroit and elsewhere – still rears its ugly head. Slim was in business – with either the gang's or his own illegal ventures – for nearly half a century, somewhere around 1919 until 1962. That's a long time to evade the law and enjoy doing so.

To what degree did grinding poverty and ethnic ostracism contribute to the rise of gangs? No doubt, it played a part and, in the case of many gangsters, the biggest part. Certainly, the normalization of violence as the stories of World War I returned home with its veterans did not help to staunch the rise of violence within the gangs. But that must be considered a secondary consideration; poverty and teen-age hormones were more likely complicit.

Families in which the parents participated in criminal activities generally but not always had problem children: the beer smells of the barrel as with the Fleisher family. Three of the four children were violently criminal. On the other hand, Slim's older brothers worked for Ford and his father was a successful businessman. Slim, while a part of the mob world, appeared to be far less violent than the Fleisher kids. His family background may help explain the difference.

The disaster known as Prohibition ended almost as quickly as it had arrived. But it managed to concentrate wealth into the hands of gangsters who then channeled it into quasi-legitimate businesses for decades afterwards.

But the lesson was unlearned.

The Marijuana Tax Stamp Act of 1937 required anyone who hoped to sell cannabis to pay a tax and get a license. However, the law was designed so it was practically impossible to do so (with the exception of during World War II, when the feds actually encouraged hemp production). Selling pot without a license was treated as tax evasion and could draw a substantial prison sentence.

States banned marijuana under their own laws in a process that started well before 1937; Massachusetts was the first to do so, in 1911. By the time the 1937 law took effect, the drug was illegal everywhere in America under both federal and state statutes.

In 1969, the Supreme Court tossed out the Tax Stamp Act, saying it violated the constitution by forcing people to incriminate themselves when asking for the stamp. However, the next year Congress and President Richard Nixon enacted the Controlled Substances Act, a harsh statute that declared marijuana to be among the most dangerous substances in the world.

The Controlled Substances Act organized various legally controlled substances into "schedules" according to how dangerous, addictive, and medically useless Congress considers them to be. Marijuana has always been in schedule 1, the most highly restricted category, along with ecstasy and heroin. And that's where things stood for nearly 30 years, giving rise to a whole new generation of gangsters. Gradually, starting in 1996, medical marijuana was accepted, followed by recreational use. But by then, the criminal organizations were entrenched, in the U.S. and elsewhere.

The opportunity to focus resources on the more destructive drugs was lost as resources were piled into corrections facilities to house casual users. For example, in late 2021 a fentanyl operation was finally broken up in Seattle after operating three years. Two men a backyard pill-pressing operation with fentanyl powder they ordered from China beginning in 2015 — just as the synthetic opioid was taking hold as a cheaper, more powerful and more deadly alternative to heroin. They obtained stamps that could mark their product "M30" — making the small, blue pills appear to be pharmacy-grade oxycodone, not fentanyl.

Between May and September of 2022, U.S. Drug Enforcement seized enough fentanyl in Michigan and Ohio to kill 4 million people:[171]

> In Michigan, the DEA seized 2,586 pills, representing 1,137 deadly doses of fentanyl. In Ohio, it seized enough 87,000 pills and 65 kg of fentanyl powder or enough to kill 4,700,022 people.
>
> Fentanyl routinely travels between Michigan and Ohio along the I-75 corridor. It's likely that fentanyl seized was heading to or coming from Michigan, the DEA said. The ultra-deadly synthetic opioid is mixed with heroin and pressed into counterfeit pills that resemble Percocet or oxycodone or Xanax.

It is also pressed into rainbow fentanyl, colorful pills that look like candy, which the DEA says represents a deliberate attempt to get young people hooked on the drug. The DEA has found rainbow fentanyl in Michigan and Ohio, [Orville Green, special agent in charge of the DEA's Detroit Field Division] said. ...

A record-breaking 107,000 people in the U.S., including 3,040 in Michigan, died of drug overdoses [in 2021] and the majority of those deaths were caused by fentanyl. The synthetic opioid is up to 50 times more powerful than heroin and up to 100 times more powerful than morphine. According to the DEA, 2 milligrams of fentanyl — enough to fit on the tip of a pencil — is enough to be lethal.

The Seattle and Michigan busts came on the heels of the Oxycontin epidemic raging in the early 21st century. Almost half a million people died from opioid overdoses, including prescription and illicit opioids, from 1999 to 2019, according to the Centers for Disease Control and Prevention.

It was these deadly drugs – starting with cocaine – that the legislatures and law enforcement needed to interdict, but resources were spread thinly chasing red herrings.

TRANSMOGRIFY

Cotton being picked on the Billups farm in Lowndes County, Mississippi, ca. 1898. Photo courtesy The Dispatch (Columbus, MS)

18 Songs of Freedom

When spoken words are impossible or inadequate vessels, singing is a superpower, resonating through the body, shifting the atmosphere, and communicating beyond the words. This superpower was critical to Africans enslaved in the United States. They found solace and strength in African song as well as songs birthed from the trauma of chattel slavery. Through forceful removal from Africa, the dangerous middle passage, to inhumane treatment on the plantation, song served important purposes including recreation, prayer and worship, and work songs or field hollers. Beyond the musical aspects, singing provided religious and social commentary. All were cultural repositories connecting people from various African tribes. As Folklorist, Ralph Metcalfe observed, music is and was one of the most stable aspects of West African culture because of a reasonably cohesive musical system and the function of music at the core of African society. For Frederick Douglass, the deep, soul-stirring singing he grew up hearing "was a testimony against slavery and a prayer to God for deliverance from chains..... To those songs I trace my first glimmering conceptions of the dehumanizing character of slavery."[172]

Wilson

In 1860, Thomas and Joseph Billups owned 315 slaves in Lowndes County, Mississippi,[173] on land developed by speculators earlier in the century who had "purchased" it from the Chickasaw tribe.[174] Life for the slaves was brutal.[175] Out of the depths of this suffering and the desire to gather and read came hymns reflecting the folk tunes of the slaves' original homes in far-off Africa.

According to the 1890 census, the county had "Whites: 5,940; colored: 21,105."[176] Among the non-whites was Tom Ransom, born in 1858 to unknown slaves. In his 42nd year on the plantation, his wife, Becky Sanders, gave birth to Eliza Mae. Over the years, Eliza attended Billups Chapel with her mother and she became an excellent choir singer.[177] The music of freedom flowed in the family.

After the death of her father in 1915, Eliza married Jack Wilson and lived in Columbus, Mississippi, then joined the Great Migration and the two made their way north to Detroit, fleeing Jim Crow laws and the Ku Klux Klan – and drawn by the booming auto industry in Motortown.[178] Over 1,5 million Africa-Americans migrated north between 1916 and 1930. The music of Billups Chapel followed with Eliza.

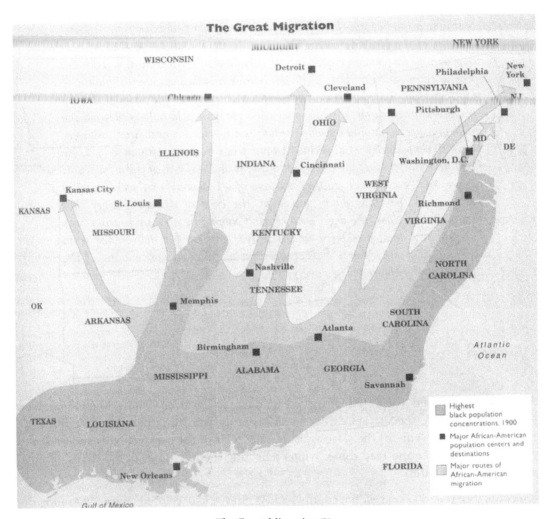

The Great Migration.[179]

Gordy

Berry Gordy I – grandfather of the Motown founder – was the son of James T. Gordy, a white plantation owner in Georgia, and one of his slaves, Esther Johnson, who was 14 at the time of Berry's birth.[180]

Berry Gordy II (also Berry Gordy, Sr.) was the son of these freed Georgia slaves who had become sharecroppers of a 168-acre patch of barren farmland that had yielded barely enough to keep the family going. Twenty-three children were born there, but fourteen died at or shortly after birth. Those who survived were tough.

Berry Gordy II. and Bertha Gordy in 1923[181]

Berry Gordy II was a short, wiry man who did not get to high school until he was 22 because his family could not spare him from its backbreaking farming. He was 30 – mature by local standards – when he married Bertha, a 19-year-old schoolteacher of African and Indian descent [born in 1899 in Milledgeville, Baldwin County, Georgia[182]]. In 1922, three years into their marriage, Gordy made a deal that changed their lives: he sold a load of the farm's timber stumps for $2,600, a small fortune in rural Georgia. As word of the sale spread, the family worried that local whites might rob Gordy, so he traveled to Detroit, where his brother had recently moved, to cash the check. Once there, he never returned. Bertha and their three children joined him a month later.

The promise of assembly-line jobs in auto plants had lured many southerners to Detroit since the mid-1800s. The Motor City's population boomed 1,200 percent during a fifty-year period that ended with the Great War. Ford was the first to break the racial barrier when it began hiring black workers in 1914. During the Roaring Twenties, Detroit had become America's fifth-largest city and its second-fastest-growing. And although Jim Crow laws were still widely entrenched and the city largely segregated, to many southern blacks Detroit offered genuine possibilities for progress.

Berry Gordy II's start was not auspicious. Shortly after arriving, he used his share of the $2,600 windfall as a deposit on a cramped two-story home. It looked like a decent buy – at $8,500 – until the Gordy's moved in and discovered it was falling apart. Rotting plasterboard was hidden by fresh wallpaper, and bursting pipes had been concealed under duct tape. In the small space, the Gordy's eventually had eight children who shared only three beds (soon after birth, Berry III slept with his sister Gwen). The house was rat-infested, and the children often piled into the kitchen and watched in horror and fascination as their father killed giant rats. Once, a rat jumped from the oven onto Berry II.'s face, leaving him blood-covered and the children screaming in terror.

For several years, Berry Gordy II hustled through a string of odd jobs and frequently rented an empty lot where he sold everything from ice to coal, wood, Christmas trees, watermelons, and old car parts. Finally, he landed a gig as an apprentice plasterer for black contractors and in a year earned a union card. He then found steady work and saved enough to launch his own businesses. He not only started a carpentry shop but also bought the neighboring Booker T. Washington Grocery Store, as well as a print shop.[183]

Bertha "managed the grocery store and meat market which the pair established. She co-founded a mutual insurance business and sold real estate, became an active figure in the religious community, earned university diplomas with honors, and raised, with Pop, a family of eight children, imparting life lessons to all of them."[184]

By July of 1929, it was apparent that Bertha was again pregnant with now her seventh child. The parents would name the child, if a boy, Berry Gordy III.

In the Winter of 1930, Seattle musician Paul Tutmarc met with a fellow musician and tinkerer, Art Stimson from Spokane. They ended up going down to his workshop in the basement and they started messing around trying to electrify things.

Stimson took off for Los Angeles, and the brief partnership was ended, although we don't know what, if any, verbal arrangements were made concerning what the two of them had come up with in Tutmarc's basement. It must have come as a surprise in 1932 when a company called Dobro began marketing an electrified guitar. One imagines Paul Tutmarc wondering, "How can that be? How did THEY get a patent?"

He looked into it and found that someone had, indeed, patented the pickup and the guitar as a package. That somebody, according to the patent, was Art Stimson. To make matters worse, according to Peter Blecha, Stimson had sold their pickup design to Dobro for just $600.

The first electrically amplified stringed instrument to be marketed commercially was designed in 1931 by George Beauchamp, the general manager of the National Guitar Corporation, with Paul Barth, who was vice president. The maple body prototype for the one-piece cast aluminium "frying pan" was built by Harry Watson, factory superintendent of the National Guitar Corporation. Commercial production began in late summer of 1932 by Electro-Patent-Instrument Company, in Los Angeles. In 1934, the company was renamed the Rickenbacker Electro Stringed Instrument Company. In that year Beauchamp applied for a United States patent for an Electrical Stringed Musical Instrument and the patent was later issued in 1937.[185] By 1935, Electro String Instrument Corporation had achieved mainstream success with the A-22 "Frying Pan" steel guitar.

The electric guitar changed the music industry by making music louder and heavier, giving artists more ways to alter their sounds and allowing genres like blues and rock to flourish. The evolution of rock began with the addition of a louder, faster, and more aggressive beat to the blues and boogie-woogie patterns.

More importantly, small bands could now play to large audiences. The entire outfit could be crammed into a station-wagon along with the equipment, traveling between venues easily if not luxuriously. During their travels in the North, musicians performed to larger and louder audiences on electric guitars, and their performance was heard above the crowd. Going electric was more than just a pragmatic decision in the early 1950s, it was an idea that reflected the spirit of the time.[186]

19 Baby Boom

They were the Greatest Generation. The GIs returning from Europe and the Pacific between 1943 and 1945 had fought horrendous battles, seen buddies die next to them, and won victory for the Allied armies. The world had been saved from fascism for the time, and these men and women wanted to celebrate. More than that, they wanted to enjoy life and living. They started families. Lots of families.

Almost exactly nine months after World War II ended, the cry of the baby was heard across America. More babies were born in 1946 than ever before. It was estimated about 3.4 million, 20 percent more than in 1945. In 1947, another 3.8 million babies were born; 3.9 million were born in 1952; and more than 4 million were born every year from 1954 until 1964, when the boom finally tapered off. By then, there were 76.4 million Baby Boomers in the United States. They made up almost 40 percent of the nation's population.

Despite the optimism of family-building, the returning soldiers understood that nothing was certain. They had fought and won a brutal war – but had also lived their childhoods in the Great Depression. For many, the army provided regular meals for the first time. But there was sacrifice in the military: many did not return from the two fronts.

The G.I. Bill gave many of these soldiers the ability to secure a college education. Armed with those degrees, they marched America into a post-war economic boom that rivaled any previous boom in history. These children of the war-tested would start to reach their teen-age years in the late 1950s as their parents pressed them to snap-to and secure their future as well.

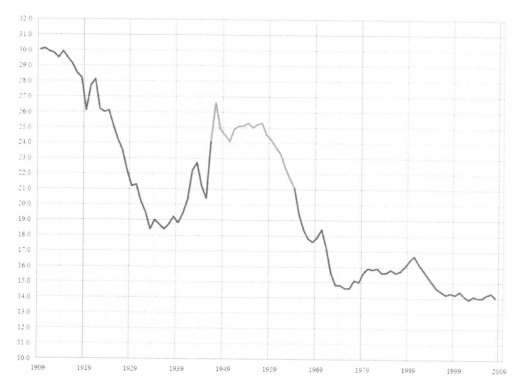

United States birth rate (births per 1,000 population per year): The segment for the years 1946 to 1964 is highlighted in red, with birth rates peaking in 1949, dropping steadily around 1958, and reaching prewar Depression-era levels in 1965.[187]

20 Vinyl

The first vinyl record arrived in 1948. Peter Carl Goldmark, a Hungarian physicist who immigrated to the US, created the first "Long Play" record. He presented his innovation in Atlantic City that year and was lauded almost immediately. Compared with the Edison and Berliner prototypes, Goldmark's record had many differences: a 23-minute play time, 30 cm diameter, and over 100 grooves per centimeter

Columbia Records innovated on Goldmark's design and marketed the Long Play record, while RCA marketed a new size and speed of record called the "45," because it rotated at 45 rotations per minute.

The record companies (Columbia and RCA Victor) had pursued their product research independently, but in the 1950s they did agree to standards on the needle size that would play their records as well as frequency standards, which stand even today. The music industry as we know it was born during this era.

At the same time, driven by the huge output of records, turntables became portable, less expensive, and ubiquitous. The Dutch company Philips imported a portable 45 rpm model that included a carrying strap. Music was now moving with its listeners. No part of the day, except the classroom, was devoid of music.

Advancing the vinyl boom, in 1957 the first commercially available stereo sound records were released to the public. In contrast to the earlier monophonic records, these recordings used spatial characteristics (namely a left and right channel) to create a more holistic listening experience.

21 Radio

According to producer Richard Fatherley, Todd Storz was the inventor of the "Top 40" format at his radio station KOWH in Omaha, Nebraska. Storz invented the format in the early 1950s, using the number of times a record was played on jukeboxes to compose a weekly list for broadcast.[188] The Top 40, whether surveyed by a radio station or a publication, was a list of songs that shared only the common characteristic of being newly released. Its introduction coincided with a transition from the old ten-inch 78 rpm record format for single "pop" recordings to the seven-inch vinyl 45 rpm format, introduced in 1949, which was outselling it by 1954 and soon replaced it completely in 1958. The Top 40 thereafter became a survey of the popularity of 45 rpm singles and their airplay on the radio. Some nationally syndicated radio shows, such as American Top 40, featured a countdown of the 40 highest ranked songs on a particular music or entertainment publication. Although such publications often listed more than 40 charted hits, such as the Billboard Hot 100, time constraints allowed for the airing of only 40 songs; hence, the term "top 40" gradually became part of the vernacular associated with popular music.[189]

With the mass production and popularity of records in the mid-1940s, as well as the birth of TV, a radio show could be produced simply by playing records and hiring a disc jockey to host the program. One of the first disc jockeys (later called DJs) was Dick Clark. Others followed.[190]

Music radio, particularly Top-40, has often acted as both a barometer and an arbiter of musical taste, and radio airplay is one of the defining measures of success in the mainstream musical world. In fact, the rise of rock music to popularity is intimately tied to the history of music radio. Early forms of rock had languished in poor areas of the South. It was enjoyed mostly by rural blacks, with notable exposure in Memphis, Tennessee due to the African American programming of WDIA.[191]

Rock music entered the mainstream during the 1950s because of controversial white DJs such as Dewey Phillips, Alan Freed, Dick Clark and Wolfman Jack with an appreciation for black music.[192] That music quickly dominated the Top 40.

22   Transistor Radio

Not only could the new generation tote around a turntable and record collection, fine for heading to a sleep-over, but the arrival of the transistor radio allowed the music to follow them to beaches, schools, and just about anywhere.

Following the invention of the transistor in 1947—which revolutionized the field of consumer electronics by introducing small but powerful, convenient hand-held devices—the Regency TR-1 was released in 1954 becoming the first commercial transistor radio.

Regency TR-1 Transistor Radio. Credit: Joe Haupt from USA, CC BY-SA 2.0 via Wikimedia Commons

The mass-market success of the smaller and cheaper Sony TR-63, released in 1957, led to the transistor radio becoming the most popular electronic communication device of the 1960s and 1970s.[193]

23   Television

Television was invented in the 19th century, gaining in popularity throughout the 1930s and 1940s, and sent into hyperdrive with the arrival of color TV in 1950.

TV did more than bring culture into the American home: it brought a conforming culture. The content needed to attract the largest audience, and so was mainstream in values and outlook. It became the mouthpiece of the business world and its interests. Its musical content, therefore, was not bleeding edge, not even leading edge. It, like the transistor radio, had saturated the American market and penetrated nearly every home by the end of the 1950s.

24 Motown

Wilson

Throughout the 1940s, Eliza Mae Wilson, who had lost two earlier children, doted on her only son, Jack Jr., and exerted a profound influence on him. He began singing early, accompanying his mother, an experienced church choir singer.[194] In his teens "Jackie formed a quartet, the Ever Ready Gospel Singers Group, which became a popular feature of churches in the area. Jackie wasn't religious, he just loved to sing and the cash came in handy for the cheap wine which he drank from the age of nine.[195]

Growing up in North End, a rough section of Detroit, Wilson was a habitual truant, belonged to a gang called the Shakers, and was continuously in and out of trouble. Twice he was sent to detention in the Lansing Correctional Institute. It was there that he learned how to box. Wilson dropped out of the school in the ninth grade, in 1950 at 16. He then competed in the Detroit amateur circuit, becoming a Golden Gloves welterweight boxing champion in Detroit. After his mother forced Jackie to quit boxing, he was forced to marry Freda Hood by her father after getting her pregnant, and he became a father at age 17.[196]

Jackie began working at Lee's Sensation Club as a solo singer, then formed a group called the Falcons that included cousin Levi Stubbs, who later led the Four Tops.[197]

Gordy

Meanwhile, Berry Gordon – Gordy – was frequenting Detroit's downtown nightclubs, and in the Flame Show Bar he met bar manager Al Green (not the famed singer), who owned a music publishing company called Pearl Music and represented Jackie Wilson.

The Flame Showbar in Detroit, opened 1949, closed 1963. Capacity: 250.

Gordy soon became part of a group of songwriters—with his sister Gwen Gordy and Billy Davis—who wrote songs for Jackie. "Reet Petite" was their first major hit which appeared in November 1957. During the next eighteen months, Gordy helped to write six more Wilson A-sides, including "Lonely Teardrops", a peak-popular hit of 1958. Between 1957 and 1958, Gordy wrote or produced over a hundred sides for various artists, with his siblings Anna, Gwen and Robert, and other collaborators in varying combinations.

Gordy reinvested the profits from his songwriting success into producing. In 1957, he discovered the Miracles (originally known as the Matadors) and began building a portfolio of successful artists. In 1959, with the encouragement of Miracles leader Smokey Robinson, Gordy borrowed $800 from his family to create an R&B record company. Originally, Gordy wanted to name the new label Tammy Records, after the song recorded by Debbie Reynolds. However, that name was taken, and he chose the name Tamla Records. The company began operating on January 12, 1959.[198]

25   The Club transmogrifies

After a series of raids by the Michigan State Police in the 1950s, the Michigan Liquor Control Board revoked Club Manitou's liquor license in 1953. The Gerhart's did not open the club for the 1954 summer. Club Manitou had ended its 25-year existence.

The Gerharts had a sizable indoor venue – the Pavilion -- and a complementary outdoor venue for summer concerts was not hard to imagine on the 4-acre property. The agents for the most popular music acts were demanding these larger venues to maximize ticket sales. The Gerharts could help with that, but they were planted in West Virginia. They lacked management. Moreover, they had just had their liquor license revoked, so the prospect of opening an adult club was not available to them, at least not directly.

The solution was two separate entities: a teen club at the former Club Manitou which would not sell alcohol, and an adult nightclub a few hundred yards north on Pleasantview Road. Given the Gerharts' familiarity with booking acts for Club Manitou during the early 50s, it is perhaps a safe bet that they were considering how to draw Detroit music to their Harbor Springs holdings as soon as Motown's[199] Miracles released their hit *Shop Around* in 1960. That song quickly sold its first million records. There was money to be had in helping to develop and promote these new acts. But who would own and manage these new enterprises?

How the Gerharts met the Douglases – eventual owners of Club Ponytail at the site of Club Manitou – is unknown. Stan and Jean Douglas operated a motel in neighboring Petoskey. It is very likely the Gerharts were aware of those accommodations and every other potential competitor in the area. Did the Douglases have the ready cash to simply buy the Club Manitou property? Perhaps, but the asking price was likely hefty. The Gerharts perhaps had some debt still to service from the construction on the Pavilion. And they had lawyers to pay in West Virginia.

Did the Gerharts approach the Douglases or vice versa? This may remain a mystery, but perhaps an unimportant one but might suggest what involvement the Gerharts continued to have in the newest incarnation of the entertainment venue.

It is very conceivable that the Gerharts were interested in keeping a stake in the venture and reaping some of its cash flow. They likely had very good connections still in Detroit. If the Douglases would assume this debt and share the proceeds, the cash needs would be far less. The Gerharts could help make the connections needed to get the bands to Harbor Springs. The deal was likely being negotiated throughout 1960 and into 1961.

Meanwhile, in Detroit Motown was created and prospered. The Tamla and Motown labels were merged into a new company, Motown Record Corporation, incorporated on April 14, 1960. In 1960, Gordy signed an unknown singer, Mary Wells, who became the fledgling label's second star, with Smokey Robinson penning her hits *You Beat Me to the Punch*, *Two Lovers*, and *My Guy*. The Miracles' hit *Shop Around* peaked at No. 1 on the national R&B charts in late 1960.[200] Motown's Marvelettes released the company's first U.S. number-one pop hit, *Please Mr. Postman*, in 1961. The company would have 110 top-10 hits over the next decade.

The Gerharts finally sold the Club Manitou property to the Douglases in 1961.[201] Soon after, Federal agents began their investigation of Slim's Colonial Club in West Virginia.

As 1962 neared, a huge chunk of the baby boom – those born prior to 1949 – entered its teen years. Those millions of teenagers were armed with transistor radios and were buying records with abandon. They and their older siblings were mesmerized by Elvis and other sounds coming across the AM radio waves.

But music is not all that is changing as 1962 arrives.

26 Late 1961

The cultural reputations of whole decades are particularly crude. No sooner do we enter a year whose final digit is nine than the great machinery of the media is flooding us with phrases to sum up the previous ten years. ...

There is a specific reason ... why "the Sixties" are still so heated a subject. To put it briefly, the genies that the Sixties loosed are still abroad in the land, inspiring and unsettling and offending, making trouble. For the civil rights and antiwar and counter-cultural and women's and the rest of that decade's movements forced upon us central issues for Western civilization – fundamental questions of value, fundamental divides of culture, fundamental debates about the nature of the good life. For better or worse, the ideas and impulses remain, transposed into other keys, threatening, agitating, destabilizing ...

- Todd Gitlin, "The Sixties: Years of Home, Days of Rage"[202]

The earliest boomers, now approaching 18, were driving culture and behaviors in the U.S. as the baby boom faded. While the age of majority in most states was 18, in Michigan it was 21. That was simply an inconvenience. No doubt, parental liquor cabinets were being raided.

The Cold War was escalating as the U.S. got entangled in Vietnam. In May 1961 President John F. Kennedy sent helicopters and 400 Green Berets to South Vietnam and authorized secret operations against the Viet Cong. At the same time, Cuba's leader, Fidel Castro, announced that Cuba was adopting socialism. By November, the U.S. had 18,000 military advisors in South Vietnam.

The Civil Rights Movement was gaining steam on the heels of the Supreme Court decision declaring the "separate but equal" doctrine inherently unequal. While many states began desegregating schools, many towns in the south simply closed the schools down. Rev.

Martin Luther King, Jr., had recently been released from four months hard labor in Georgia in early 1961 for having an Alabama driver's license while on probation in Georgia. The Freedom Fighters bus was fire-bombed in Alabama as it attempted to show the force of the Supreme Court's decision in Boynton v. Virginia forbidding segregation in interstate transportation facilities.

Man of the Year: President John F. Kennedy. Image courtesy eBay.

27   1962

Time Magazine named President John F. Kennedy "Man of the Year" on January 5 – his second time being chosen – despite the failed Bay of Pigs invasion of Cuba the year before. The Cold War now entered its most dangerous phase. By February, the U.S. broke off all trade with Cuba, and embargoed all cargo headed there. Time Magazine wrote of its nominee:[203]

> "Before my term has ended," he said in his State of the Union message last January, "we shall have to test anew whether a nation organized and governed such as ours can endure." In the years since Wilson, Americans and their Presidents have vanquished many threats from those who would abolish the "consent of the governed." But the test that faces the youngest elected and the most vigorous President of the 20th century — and all those who live under his leadership—is far greater: to meet and battle, in a time of great national peril, the marauding forces of Communism on every front in every part of the world. In his first year as President, John Fitzgerald Kennedy showed qualities that have made him a promising leader in that battle. Those same qualities, if developed further, may yet make him a great President.

On May 6, a test of a W47 warhead fired from a Polaris missile, the only time a nuclear missile has been test fired with its warhead detonated, occurred near Palmyra Atoll south of Hawaii. Nuclear tests start normalizing, with tests by the U.S. and U.S.S.R. occurring at regular intervals. Meanwhile, the space programs of the two superpowers mirror the Cold War,

On May 24, Project Mercury sent Scott Carpenter around the Earth 3 times in the Aurora 7 space capsule, narrowing the technology gap with the Soviet Union.

On June 4, plans to detonate an American nuclear weapon 40 miles above the Earth were halted one minute and 40 seconds before the scheduled explosion. Failure of the tracking system in the Thor missile led to the decision to blow the warhead apart without an atomic blast.[204]

On June 10, Operation Anadyr, to place Soviet nuclear missiles in Cuba, was approved unanimously by the Presidium of the Soviet Union on the recommendation of Defense Minister Rodion Malinovsky and Prime Minister Nikita Khrushchev. Under the plan, 24 medium-range nuclear missiles and 16 intermediate-range missiles were placed in Cuba, and a total of 50,874 Soviet military personnel were placed on the island to defend against an invasion.[205]

Race relations

An African American and a white girl study a sign in the integrated Long Island community of Lakeview, New York, on April 1962. It reads "Negroes! This community could become another ghetto. You owe it to your 'family' to buy in another community." The sign was an attempt to keep African Americans from exceeding the number of whites who want to live in an integrated town. AP photo.

Frustration seethed in cities nationwide as African Americans fought against ingrained poverty in their communities. For two decades middle-class white Americans had been fleeing cities for nearby suburbs. Businesses that had once provided jobs and tax funding in the cities were leaving as well. At the same time, more than three million job-seeking African Americans moved from the South to the cities of the North and West. Increasingly, the downtowns of large cities became home to lower-income minorities, many of them southern blacks. Unemployment among African Americans was well above the national average, and one-half of all black Americans lived below the poverty line (as opposed to one-fifth of whites). Not surprisingly, tensions ran high in black communities.[206]

Adolescent wave

Amid a rapidly deteriorating international scene and ingrained racial tensions, U.S. families were raising a wave of pre-teens and teenagers who now had unparalleled freedom to listen to dozens of news and music channels on their transistor radios.

Limited-channel TV had the effect of creating a single perspective of U.S. news to Americans. With families largely limited by budget to a single TV and single record player, life within families also tended to a single stream of influence from the outside. But the rapid uptake of the transistor radio was changing that homogeneity. New voices were appearing, and they did not follow the usual script.

28 Music

On January 1, 1962, the Beatles auditioned unsuccessfully for Decca Records with John Lennon, Paul McCartney, George Harrison and, at that time, drummer Pete Best. Two days later, Pope John XXIII excommunicated Castro for preaching communism. Another two days later, the first recording on which The Beatles played, the 45 rpm record My Bonnie, credited to "Tony Sheridan and the Beat Brothers" (recorded the previous June in Hamburg), was released by Polydor in the United Kingdom; "The Saints" was on the B-side.[207]

Motown

"Like the year before it, 1962 was a good year for Smokey Robinson. Already firmly entrenched as King of Motown, Smokey's biggest successes as both a singer and a songwriter were still yet to come. But 1962 was good; it was very, very good. With the

Miracles, he would rack up multiple hits and two songs on this list. As a songwriter, he would deliver a total number of three.

"But 1962 would see a lot more for Motown than just the simultaneous growth of Smokey's reputation and wallet. The year would produce a top 5 pop hit by way of the highly unlikely Contours. It would see Mary Wells rise from a promising R&B favorite to a pop chart sensation. Almost a full decade before the Prince of Motown would cement himself as soul music's most revered legend, he ditched lackluster jazz for R&B and found his first hit. Brought on board as a mini-Ray Charles gimmick by Miracle Ronnie White, Little Stevie Wonder would release his first, uneven recordings. And desperately waiting in the wings, Motown's two biggest groups, the Supremes and the Temptations, would keep on struggling (and keep on struggling some more) for a breakthrough hit.

"Not Motown's best year by a long shot, it was Motown's best year yet. And that was plenty enough. All that momentum had finally reached a breaking point, and Motown was at long last truly full steam ahead."[208]

The Beatles first entered EMI's Abbey Road Studios in London on June 6, 1962, and that fall produced recordings of *Love Me Do*, *Please Please Me* and *P.S. I Love You*. In mid-November, as Beatlemania intensified, police resorted to using high-pressure water hoses to control the crowd before a concert in Plymouth.

After the moderate success of *Love Me Do*, the single *Please Please Me* was released in January 1963, two months ahead of the album. It reached number one on every UK chart except Record Retailer, where it peaked at number two. In May 1963, the Beatles upstaged main act Roy Orbison.[209]

The music world was changed forever. The music appealed to a baby-boomer generation entering its teen years. A rock and roll revolution moved across the U.S. in 1962, fueled by the Beatles and numerous other bands. The afternoon broadcast of American Bandstand was a favorite of teenagers and united then glued their musical interest. In March of 1962, the first teenage nightclub in the U.S. opened in Las Vegas, Nevada.

A week after the Beatles entered the Abbey Road Studios – in the year the FBI began its investigation of Slim's Colonial Club in West Virginia – the new owners of the Club Manitou buildings opened Club Ponytail Teen & Collegiate Nite Club." No alcohol was officially served, once again, at the site.

Perhaps more important for Club Ponytail were events of two years earlier: the incorporation of Detroit's Motown Records in 1960 by Berry Gordy. In 1957, Gordy had met Smokey Robinson, a local 17-year-old leading a vocal harmony group. In 1958, Gordy released a single, *Got a Job*, by Robinson and his new group, the Miracles. The group would later play at Club Ponytail.

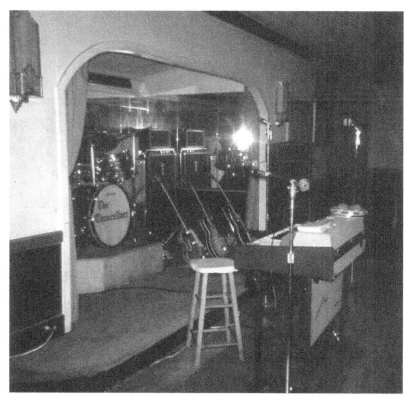

The Club Ponytail interior stage in the former Slim's Lounge. The club eventually had a stage in a new west pavilion and dueling stages in a sprawling outdoor patio.

Lower level in the old Club Manitou. The mirrored stage dates from that earlier club.

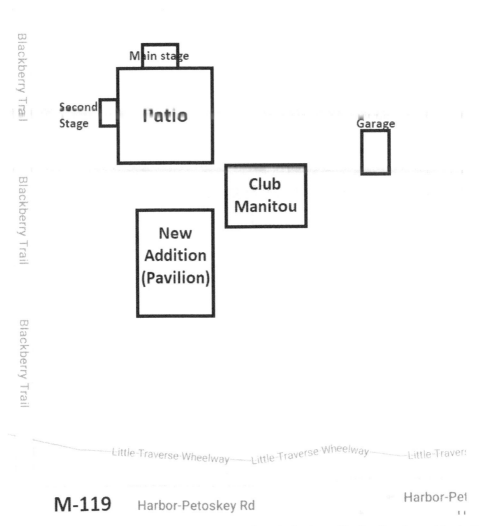

Venues of Club Ponytail, superimposed on 2022 roads and wheelway. The Pavilion burned in the fire that closed the club.

Motown signed many other artists who also played up north at the former Club Manitou, including the Supremes and Diana Ross, The Four Tops, Stevie Wonder, Marvin Gaye, the Miracles, the Temptations, and Martha and the Vandellas.

It is very possible that Motown identified Club Ponytail as a venue to get the word out to a diverse teen crowd early and may have even used the club to screen new artists. At any rate, the fortunes of Motown and Club Ponytail rose in tandem. Just as likely, Slim may have been an investor in the new venture. His contacts in Las Vegas may have clued him into the new and lucrative teen music scene emerging as the baby boomers started to reach their teen years.

It may well be, in the fine tradition of Prohibition, that Slim also saw an opportunity to provide booze where booze was not allowed. Teen-agers and their idols are notorious for their love of alcohol and other proscribed substances. Taking advantage of the black market was not new to Slim.

More prosaically – and equally likely – the Douglas's were simply keen businesspeople and realized that their purchase would provide an excellent summer venue for the bands. As always, the sweltering Heartland sought the cooler North. Bands were no different than other vacationers to Harbor Springs.

Historian Rick Wiles summarizes the tectonic shift in music in 1962:

> America was undergoing a Rock & Roll revolution. Radio stations were now playing the latest top 40 hits and 45 RPM records were flying off the shelves of music stores. American Bandstand, broadcast live on ABC television at 4pm each afternoon, was the rage of teenagers. It had debuted nationally in 1957 from

Philadelphia, Pennsylvania, with Dick Clark as the host. In March of 1962, the first teenage nightclub in the United States opened in Las Vegas, Nevada. ... The Teenbeat Club caught the attention of either Stan Douglas or, more likely, Al Gerhart.[210]

Club Ponytail, adjoining the former Club Manitou on the west. Photo courtesy Petoskey News.

Regardless of the genesis of the relationship, the Douglas's engaged the Detroit Federation of Musicians as their main booking agent (also used by Detroit's famous Roostertail nightclub).

Once again, business activity in Detroit was spilling over into Harbor Springs and, more particularly, the buildings on Pleasantview Road across from the Harbor Springs Airport. While in the 1930s Detroit was an epicenter of gang activity, now it was the mecca for music, a legitimate enterprise.

The Douglases at Club Ponytail.[211]

The Douglases, on left, welcome homecoming royalty at the club with a strong admonition on smoking.[212]

29 The Stage: 1962

The Hi-Notes were the first act at Club Ponytail, performing on the opening week in June 1962.

But, by July 4, and the beginning of the summer resort season, the Detroit-based Belvederes had become the house band for the remainder of the summer. A Grand Opening Special was held on July 7 with admittance set at 75 cents – hours set at 8:30 pm until 12:30 pm – with no minimum age.[213] The new pavilion featured moveable walls, allowing the dance floor to squeeze the dancers for better effect. The club also catered to the winter ski crowd that vacationed at Boyne Mountain and other smaller ski areas.

Belvederes

The first house band at Club Ponytail, the Belvederes were a Doo Wop band that may have had some occasional help from Smokey Robinson.

The bands that later played at Club Ponytail were a Who's Who of R&B, and American and British rock and roll.[214] Artists who eventually played at Club Ponytail and who were on Billboard's Hot-100 for 1962 included:[215]

№	Title	Artist(s)
3	"Mashed Potato Time"	Dee Dee Sharp
4	"Roses Are Red (My Love)"	Bobby Vinton
14	"Palisades Park"	Freddy Cannon
17	"Slow Twistin'"	Chubby Checker & Dee Dee Sharp
29	"Sealed with a Kiss"	Brian Hyland
38	"Twist and Shout"	The Isley Brothers
55	"Sherry"	The Four Seasons
65	"Dream Baby (How Long Must I Dream)"	Roy Orbison
72	"Uptown"	The Crystals
84	"Tell Me"	Dick and Dee Dee

90	"Gravy (For My Mashed Potatoes)"	Dee Dee Sharp
100	"Surfin' Safari"	The Beach Boys

The first protest against involvement in Vietnam came on August 2, 1962 when Youth Against War and Fascism set up a picket line in midtown Manhattan. "They were not supposed to be there in any combat role — there had been no vote in Congress to authorize a military action."[216]

Bob Dylan debuted a partially written *Blowin' in the Wind* in Greenwich Village in 1962 by telling the audience, "This here ain't no protest song or anything like that, 'cause I don't write no protest songs." *Blowin' in the Wind* went on to become possibly the most famous protest song ever, an iconic part of the Vietnam era.

30   The Stage: 1963

A keen deal was negotiated with Motown, and the acts started to roll in. On May 3, Bobby Vinton arrived for the first of two engagements at the club, well ahead of the summer tourist season.

Artists who eventually played at Club Ponytail and who were on Billboard's Hot-100 for 1963 included:[217]

No.	Title	Artist(s)
1	"Surfin' U.S.A."	The Beach Boys
5	"Blue Velvet"	Bobby Vinton
6	"Hey Paula"	Paul & Paula
7	"Fingertips"	Little Stevie Wonder
18	"Walk Like a Man"	The Four Seasons
26	"Heat Wave"	Martha and the Vandellas
39	"Candy Girl"	The Four Seasons
42	"Blue on Blue"	Bobby Vinton
44	"Two Faces Have I"	Lou Christie
49	"In Dreams"	Roy Orbison
53	"Mean Woman Blues"	Roy Orbison
56	"You've Really Got a Hold on Me"	The Miracles
60	"Baby Workout"	Jackie Wilson
61	"Pride and Joy"	Marvin Gaye
67	"The Night Has a Thousand Eyes"	Bobby Vee
83	"Come and Get These Memories"	Martha and the Vandellas
84	"Do the Bird"	Dee Dee Sharp
86	"Shut Down"	The Beach Boys
88	"Little Town Flirt"	Del Shannon

Bobby Vinton

Bobby Vinton from Philadelphia, then know for *Blue Velvet*, a minor hit for Tony Bennett in 1951 but which spent three weeks at the top of the Billboard charts in 1963 after Vinton's remake. Other songs included *Roses are Red*, *Rain Rain Go Away*, and *Over the Mountain*.

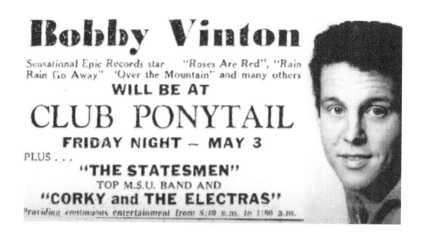

Bobby Vinton publicity photo, 1964.[218]

Corky and the Electras

Corky and the Electras layed alongside Bobby Vinton.

Bobby Vee

Bobby Vee arrived for a July 10-11 performance from Fargo, North Dakota. He had gained prominence when his hastily assembled band filled in for Buddy Holly after "The Day the Music Died," February 3, 1959. His recording of *Take Good Care of my Baby* hit the top of the Billboard chart in the summer of 1961,

Bobby Vee in 1962. https://commons.wikimedia.org

The Statesmen

This Michigan State University band played alongside Bobby Vinton.

The Beach Boys

No doubt, in retrospect, perhaps the most famous band to play at the club was The Beach Boys, formed in California in 1962, who played on August 8, 1963. They were then known for *Surfin' Safari* and *Surfin' U.S.A.*

The Beach Boys, in Pendleton outfits, performing at a local high school, late 1962. By The associated student body, Taft High School - yearbook of Taft High School, California,[219]

James Murphy recalls the Beach Boys' performance in his book:

On August 8, the Beach Boys, with Al filling in for Brian, earned $1,700 for a four-hour show and dance at the Club Ponytail in Harbor Springs, a quaint resort town on Little Traverse Bay, an inlet of Lake Michigan. To their growing repertoire of hits and covers, the guys added their own take on "Surf City." They played a forty minute set each hour followed by a twenty minute break during which the teen audience filed into the Hippocrene HideAway, a smaller area downstairs with its own stage to hear the Kingtones, local favorites since starting their six-night-a-week residency at Club Ponytail that May. Bruce Snoap, their keyboard player, recalled, "Stan Douglas, who owned Club Ponytail, had us play downstairs during the Beach Boys' breaks. Mike Love and another member, whom none of us can recall, surprised us by coming downstairs and playing sax with us. As a Top 40 cover band, we were in awe of the Beach Boys and thought they sounded very good. We later added "Surfin' U.S.A" to our show. They arrived around ten or eleven in the morning and we had lunch with them at the club. We watched them rehearse and, after 'Surfer Girl,' one of our members whispered to me, 'I don't have the heart to tell them, but that's a loser.' So much for that review."

The August 10 Petoskey, Michigan News-Review noted, "At first the Beach Boys appeared to be the biggest disappointment of the season. They were lacking in organization and harmony all during their first performance. However, they did seem to improve with time and by the end of the evening were sounding more like everyone expected them to. There is one thing that cannot be taken away from the Beach Boys – they really packed the house!"

The review heightened how detrimental Brian's absence could be to their reputation at a time when most people were getting their first glimpse of the band.[220]

Del Shannon

Del Shannon out of Grand Rapids, Michigan, was also an early act at the club. He released *Runaway* in early 1961. The single topped Billboard in April of that year. More popular in the U.K., Shannon became the first American to record a cover version of a Beatles song. His 1963 version of *From Me to You* charted before the Beatles' version.

The Kingtones

Michigan Rock-and-Roll legends vividly describes Michigan music in the late 1950s and early 60s:[221]

Grand Rapids was the second largest city in Michigan in 1957, but to Bob Major, one of the original Kingtones, it seemed like "a sleepy Dutch town". With its brick-paved streets, blocks of modest, well-kept homes, and its predominantly white population, Grand Rapids could very well have been the place where the television families on Leave It To Beaver or Father Know Best resided as they provided us with morally uplifting messages on a weekly basis.

In 1957, Gerald R. Ford was completing his eighth year of what would be a distinguished twenty-five year career serving the Grand Rapids congressional district in the House of Representatives. Nicknamed the "Furniture City", Grand Rapids was recognized world wide as a leader in the production of fine furniture and many of its citizens had jobs related to it.

The city was also famous for its churches. During the 1950's, there was a local radio show called Aunt Bertha's Bible Hour that presented religious songs for kids. Future Kingtones Phil and Dave Roberts could be heard harmonizing on the program early in the decade accompanied by Phil's ukulele.

Grand Rapids is generally thought to be a friendly city, but it is also known for being very conservative. The first Dutch settlers had arrived in Southwest Michigan in the middle of the 19th century, and they brought with them the strict doctrines of the Christian Reformed Church which frowned on playing musical instruments and dancing.

Although it seemed an unlikely place to form a Rock and Roll band, an invasion of sorts had been taking place on Grand Rapids' airwaves for the last year or so that was a harbinger of things to come. Local AM radio stations WGRD and WMAX had been broadcasting the sounds of Elvis Presley, Chuck Berry, Gene Vincent, and Fats Domino into the radios of Grand Rapids teens.

In September of 1957, the school year had just begun at Oakleigh Junior High School. Gil King, a cornet player in the school music program, urged some of his fellow 7th graders to start a Rock and Roll band. It didn't take a lot of convincing – what would be a better way of impressing the junior high girls and having a blast at the same time?

King recruited three sax players; Bob Major, Jim Hoeksma, and Jim Corsen; along with Jerry Gephart on piano, Tom Veenstra on trumpet, and Bob Green on drums. The fledgling group first started playing as a unit in the school's band lab. Classmate Bruce Snoap also wanted in, and offered to buy a guitar in order to join the band and provide the group with his Elvis imitation.

They first played an Oakleigh P.T.A. meeting, then at a YMCA dance where they got the kids dancing with their rendition of "Rock Around The Clock". The band played for free and the fun of performing instrumentals like "When The Saints Go Marching In" along with some of the hits of the day and Bruce's Elvis numbers.

In 1958, inspired by the "twangy" guitar of Duane Eddy, Gil King persuaded his parents to buy him an electric guitar. The line-up of the band also changed at this time. The horn section was dropped except for Bob Major on sax. Chuck Snoap (Bruce's brother) joined on bass, and Earl Hyde joined on guitar. Bruce Snoap, not a strong guitar player, offered to buy an organ in order to stay in the band.

The most important addition to the band, however, was vocalist Pete Mercerine. Not only did he possess an outstanding singing voice, but he was also handsome, a gifted athlete, and the most popular boy in school.

That same year, Gil King's father held a contest for the employees in his drafting firm to come up with a name for his son's band. The person with the winning suggestion would be presented a magnum of champagne. A list of 50 or 60 possible names was submitted to the band members to consider, and they chose the 'Kingtones' as their moniker.

The Kingtones went through some more personnel changes in 1959. The important additions were Mike King (Gil's cousin) on drums and Phil Roberts on guitar. Roberts, who was from across town in East Grand Rapids, had played for another local band, the Rocking Revels. The Kingtones were impressed with Phil's version of "Johnny B. Goode", and invited him to join the band.

The young Kingtones often rehearsed in Gil King's garage on Parmelee Avenue. The neighbors would keep their kids in the house and away from the 'bad influences' who were playing Rock and Roll. It had been reported that this new music was linked to juvenile delinquency and the parents were taking no chances.

By 1960 most of the Kingtones were attending Union High School with the exceptions being Phil Roberts who went to East Grand Rapids High and Mike King who attended Creston High School. Gil King got the band its first important gig by going to the WGRD studios and promoting the band. That led to an invitation to play dances sponsored by radio station for $15. After the Kingtones started drawing large groups of local teens to the hops, the dances became a regular booking.

Because of their ability to draw large crowds, Phil Roberts felt they were being underpaid. He told WGDR's management that the band wouldn't play anymore unless they gave the group a raise. Phil's demand doubled the Kingtones' pay at the dances and, as a result, established him as one of the leaders in the band.

That same year the Kingtones were taken under the wing of Doc Jorne, a professional musician and friend of Gil King's family. Jorne played a large theater organ and traveled with his own show called Orgarama, which featured the hundreds of sounds and effects that his organ could produce. Jorne was a show business veteran and he taught the boys how promote themselves with photos and posters, use makeup, and the art of doing comedic skits to liven up their sets.

It was during this time that the Kingtones began writing their own material in hopes of making their first record. The first two songs, "Wish For An Angel"[222] and "Don't Come Around" came from group jams during rehearsals at Mike King's garage. Phil Roberts claims that they got the beginning for "Wish For An Angel" from an old Floyd Collins song.

The band eventually cut the tunes in Doc Jorne's basement studio in 1961. The resulting single was released on Jorne's own Musitone label. "Wish For An Angel", featuring Pete Mervenne's impressive vocal, became a big hit on several West Michigan radio station charts including those of WGRD and WMAX. The 45 rpm even outsold Del Shannon's big hit "Runaway" in the Grand Rapids market.

Van logo painted by nationally-known artist Paul Collins

As described on their website[223]:

> The late 1950s was a time of innocence in West Michigan and around the country. Life was simple and hopes were high. The rock music scene was in its infancy and the dreams of teen groups were pinned on the willingness of someone's parents to

let their band practice in the garage. Small record labels were producing 45s for radio airplay and local fans to buy. Sharp-looking teen musicians with matching suits and neat haircuts played to huge crowds of teens at local dances on weekends, hoping to be part of the phenomenon sweeping the nation. In a garage in Grand Rapids, a group of young men were gathering their high hopes and starting a band, soon to be known throughout the Midwest as The Kingtones.

In 1961, The Kingtones hit the charts with "Wish for an Angel" and started a musical legacy that would last half a century. They raced up the charts and found local fame, while struggling to reach outside of Michigan. In the midst of the British Invasion, The Kingtones saw their records passed over in Detroit and Chicago.

Brian Hyland

Hyland played on August 13 as the summer season waned. As chronicled on Wikipedia:[224]

> Hyland was born in Woodhaven, Queens, New York City. He studied guitar and clarinet as a child and sang in his church choir. When aged 14 he co-founded the harmony group the Del-Fi's, which recorded a demo but failed to secure a recording contract. Hyland was eventually signed by Kapp Records as a solo artist, issuing his debut single, "Rosemary", in late 1959. ...
>
> In August 1960, Hyland scored his first and biggest hit single, at the age of 16, "Itsy Bitsy Teenie Weenie Yellow Polka Dot Bikini", written by Vance and Pockriss. It was a novelty song that reached No. 1 on the Billboard Hot 100 chart (No. 8 in the UK) and sold almost a million copies in the first two months of its release and over two million copies in total. It got awarded a RIAA certification as a golden disc.

Lou Christie

Luigi Alfredo Giovanni Sacco (born February 19, 1943), known professionally as Lou Christie, is an American pop and soft rock singer-songwriter known for several hits in the 1960s, including his 1966 US chart-topper "Lightnin' Strikes" and 1969 UK number-two "I'm Gonna Make You Mine":[225]

> While attending Moon Area High School, he studied music and voice, served as student conductor of the choir and sang solos at holiday concerts. His teacher, Frank Cummings, wanted him to pursue a career in classical music, but Sacco wanted to cut a record to get on American Bandstand. At age 15 he met and

befriended Twyla Herbert, a classically trained musician 20 years his senior, who became his regular songwriting partner and wrote hundreds of songs with him over the next 30 years until her death in 2009. Sacco performed with several vocal groups and between 1959 and 1962 released several records on small Pittsburgh labels, achieving a local hit with "The Jury" by Lugee & The Lions (a group consisting of Sacco, Twyla Herbert's daughter Shirley, and two others) released on the Robbee label. After graduating from high school in 1961, Sacco traveled to New York City and worked as a session vocalist.

In 1962, Sacco approached Nick Cenci with some demo tapes. One of the first things Cenci did was change the name Lugee Alfredo Giovanni Sacco to Lou Christie. Cenci told Sacco that there was only one great Italian singer and that he had to change his name. Sacco's father liked the name change because it had "Christ" in it.

Johnny & the Hurricanes

Johnny and the Hurricanes were an American instrumental rock band from Toledo, Ohio, United States. They specialized in adapting popular traditional melodies into the rock idiom, using organ and saxophone as their featured instruments. Between 1958 and 1963, the group had a number of hits in both the US and the UK, and the band developed a following in Europe. In 1962, they played at the Star-Club in Hamburg, where the Beatles, then a little-known band, served as an opening act.[226]

Freddy Cannon

The season drew to a close with Freddy "Boom Boom" Cannon playing on the patio.

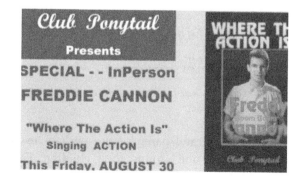

31 The Stage: 1964

On November 22, 1963, President John F. Kennedy, while starting a bid at a 1964 re-election via a motorcade in Texas, was assassinated, the symbolic end of Camelot. The U.S. plunged into a dark period, dominated by the Cold War and Vietnam War. Existential threats rocked the country. Children in America's grade schools rehearsed fall-out shelter drills, preparing for an Armageddon they knew nothing about. Dark indeed. The Doomsday Clock of the Bulletin of Atomic Scientists set the clock at 11:48pm – 12 minutes to disaster – in its April edition.

Doomsday Clock at 12 minutes before midnight.[227]

But summer would arrive as usual, and parents were perhaps even more interested in casting a veneer of normalcy over and around their children. Families headed out of Chicago, Detroit, and other Midwest locales to Northern Michigan.

Little is known of the 1964 line-up. Perhaps the 1963 acts returned, or maybe local bands were the entertainment. It is likely that the pressure for larger venues was impacting Club Ponytail. Later that year, the large outdoor patio – suitable for a Battle of the Bands – was started in the northwest portion of the property, directly north of the pavilion.

Battle of the Bands on the patio (previous) and dancers in Slim's Lounge (next).[228]

Artists who eventually played at Club Ponytail and who were on Billboard's Hot-100 for 1964 included:[229]

№	Title	Artist(s)
4	"Oh, Pretty Woman"	Roy Orbison
5	"I Get Around"	The Beach Boys
10	"Where Did Our Love Go"	The Supremes
17	"Dancing in the Street"	Martha and the Vandellas
24	"Rag Doll"	The Four Seasons
25	"Dawn (Go Away)"	The Four Seasons
28	"Dead Man's Curve"	Jan and Dean
30	"A World Without Love"	Peter and Gordon
33	"Baby Love"	The Supremes
38	"The House of the Rising Sun"	The Animals
53	"Remember (Walking in the Sand)"	The Shangri-Las
57	"Baby I Need Your Loving"	The Four Tops
63	"See the Funny Little Clown"	Bobby Goldsboro
69	"Leader of the Pack"	The Shangri-Las
70	"Funny How Time Slips Away"	Joe Hinton
71	"The Way You Do the Things You Do"	The Temptations
74	"It's Over"	Roy Orbison
75	"Ronnie"	The Four Seasons
86	"Money (That's What I Want)"	The Kingsmen
98	"There! I've Said It Again"	Bobby Vinton
99	"Louie Louie"	The Kingsmen

32   The Stage: 1965

A large outdoor patio – about the size of a tennis court – was added in 1965, allowing upwards of 2,500 teens to attend, drawn from across Michigan. A cement-block wall topped with barbed wire enclosed the space: there would be no party-crashing as the nation's top bands played inside the enclosure. The new venue, added to the existing pavilion and Slim's Lounge, was a strong draw for Motown acts.

Artists who eventually played at Club Ponytail and who were on Billboard's Hot-100 for 1965 included:[230]

No.	Title	Artist(s)
1	"Wooly Bully"	Sam the Sham and the Pharaohs
2	"I Can't Help Myself (Sugar Pie Honey Bunch)"	Four Tops
10	"My Girl"	The Temptations
11	"Help Me, Rhonda"	The Beach Boys
20	"Stop! In the Name of Love"	The Supremes
37	"Back in My Arms Again"	The Supremes
39	"The Jolly Green Giant"	The Kingsmen
49	"California Girls"	The Beach Boys
56	"Just a Little"	The Beau Brummels
58	"I'll Be Doggone"	Marvin Gaye
68	"Nowhere to Run"	Martha and the Vandellas
73	"It Ain't Me Babe"	The Turtles
75	"I Go to Pieces"	Peter and Gordon
78	"The Tracks of My Tears"	The Miracles
81	"Little Things"	Bobby Goldsboro
82	"True Love Ways"	Peter and Gordon
83	"It's the Same Old Song"	Four Tops
86	"We Gotta Get out of This Place"	The Animals
87	"Laugh, Laugh"	The Beau Brummels
93	"Ooo Baby Baby"	The Miracles
99	"Keep Searchin' (We'll Follow	Del Shannon

	the Sun)"	
100	"How Sweet It Is (To Be Loved by You)"	Marvin Gaye

The Iguanas

The Iguanas, led by Iggy Pop (Jim Osterberg), were a rock band out of Ann Arbor, Michigan, formed in 1963. Osterberg negotiated the band's residency at the Club Ponytail in mid-1965. At the venue, the Iguanas often shared the bill with acts like the Four Tops, the Shangri-Las, and the Kingsmen.[231] Iggy Pop joined the Prime Movers in 1965 at age 18, and earned the moniker "Iggy" for having played with the Iguanas. Gary Johnson writing for the Michigan Rock and Roll Hall of Fame described the Iguana's tenure at Club Ponytail[232]:

> Despite their rocky start, it wasn't long before the Iguanas developed into, as Cub Koda described them, "a great, greasy little rock and roll band." Their striped surf band shirts were replaced by matching sharkskin suits; and the sax-led instrumentals supplanted by the British Invasion songs of the Beatles, Rolling Stones, and Kinks. Sam Swisher proved adept at lining up gigs for the band; and for the next year and a half they played the local high schools, more U of M frat parties, monthly dance parties hosted by Robin Seymour at the Ann Arbor Fairgrounds, and a bevy of the teen nightclubs that had sprouted up throughout the state.

> Following the high school graduation of McLaughlin, Osterberg, and Swisher in 1965, the Iguanas scored their best gig yet when they secured a residency at Harbor Spring's Club Ponytail that summer. Don Swickerath remembers that idyllic summer fondly. "Club Ponytail was a big boost for us," he said. "I believe that Sam Swisher got us booked there for the summer. Harbor Springs in Northern Michigan was a favorite summer retreat for some of the wealthiest families in the Midwest."Club Ponytail's indoor stage

> "Mr. Douglas was the owner, and he paid us a couple hundred dollars per week each," Swickerath recalled. "He was a decent guy to work for. The venue used to be a hangout/speakeasy for Detroit's Purple Gang. It was located on a hill and had walls that moved and would expose part of the dancefloor when opened. It also had small gambling rooms. There was also a tunnel at the bottom of the place that went down into a field where cars were parked in case they were raided. The stage was on a wall that moved and would expose part of the dancefloor."

This work has been released into the public domain by its author, Merlewine at English Wikipedia

The Four Tops

The Four Tops out of Detroit, who started as backups for The Supremes while they got a foothold, attained their first top single in 1964 with *I Can't Help Myself (Sugar Pie, Honey Bunch*.

The Four Tops perform at New Rochelle High School in 1967. By Arnielee at the English-language Wikipedia, CC BY-SA 3.0, https://commons.wikimedia.org/w/index.php?curid=10543254

The Kingsmen

The Kingsmen, out of Portland, Oregon, played on July 20, 1965. They were best known for their 1963 recording of Richard Berry's *Louie Louie*.[233]

> *And now, the news*
>
> *Louie, Louie*
> *Oh baby, I gotta go now*
>
> *Louie, Louie*
> *Oh baby, I really gotta go now*

The communist world is fallin' apart
The capitalists are just breakin' hearts
Money is the reason to be
It makes me just wanna sing, Louie Louie

Louie, Louie
Oh baby, I gotta go now
Louie, Louie
Oh baby, I really gotta go now

And a fine little girl, she is waitin' for me
But I'm as bent as Dostoevsky
I think about the meaning of my life again
And I have to sing, Louie Louie again

Louie, Louie
Oh baby, I gotta go now
Louie, Louie
Oh baby, I really gotta go now
Oh, let's give it to 'em, right now

Alright

Oh man, I, I dunno like man like you know
I dunno like health insurance
And the homeless and world peace
And aids and education, I mean that
I'm tryin' to do right but hey
Life after Bush and Gorbachev
The wall is down but something is lost
Turn on the news, it looks like a movie
It makes me wanna sing, Louie Louie

Louie, Louie
Oh baby, I gotta go now
Louie, Louie
Oh baby, I really gotta go now
Said, I gotta go now
I gotta go now
I really gotta go now
Well, let's go

This band and their famous song caused the Douglas's to be castigated by the Harbor Springs clergy. *Louie Louie* had been banned in Indiana by its governor on February 1, 1965 for supposedly possessing lurid and obscene lyrics. In reality the song was nothing more than a calypso style tune recorded by the Kingsmen at a time when their lead singer had new braces on his teeth and was slurring his words. The song rose to No. 2 on the charts for six weeks in early 1964.[234]

The Kingsmen onstage at Club Ponytail.[235]

The Kingsmen 1963 "Louie Louie" line-up. L-R Don Gallucci, Jack Ely, Lynn Easton, Mike Mitchell, and Bob Nordby. © Gina Rossi[236]

The Nightwalkers

The Nightwalkers out of Raleigh, North Carolina, played in 1965.

The Nightwalkers play at Club Ponytail in 1966. Courtesy Club Ponytail Memories, Facebook

The Shangri-Las

The Shangri-Las circa 1965. Left to right: Betty Weiss, Mary Ann Ganser, Marge Ganser, Mary Weiss. Courtesy wikimedia. http://themusicsover.files.wordpress.com

The Shangri-Las, out of New York City, played on August 10, 1965 and were best known for their 1964 #1 single *Leader of the Pack*.

Iguanas back-up the Shangri-Las at Club Ponytail. Judith Landis collection.

The Supremes

The Supremes came out of Detroit's Brewster-Douglass Housing Projects, signing with Motown Records after the group's members graduated from high school in 1961. They joined the Motown pipeline to Club Ponytail, backed up by the Iguanas.

The Supremes in 1966 from the television program The Ed Sullivan Show. L-R: Florence Ballard, Mary Wilson, and Diana Ross. Public domain image courtesy of Wikimedia Commons.

33   The Stage: 1966

Artists who eventually played at Club Ponytail and who were on Billboard's Hot 100 for 1966 included:[237]

№	Title	Artist(s)
5	"Reach Out I'll Be There"	Four Tops
13	"You Can't Hurry Love"	The Supremes
16	"Li'l Red Riding Hood"	Sam the Sham and the Pharaohs
17	"Lightnin' Strikes"	Lou Christie
39	"Ain't Too Proud to Beg"	The Temptations
51	"Uptight (Everything's Alright)"	Stevie Wonder
53	"Sloop John B"	The Beach Boys
58	"Beauty Is Only Skin Deep"	The Temptations
72	"My World Is Empty Without You"	The Supremes
73	"Barbara Ann"	The Beach Boys
79	"Woman"	Peter and Gordon
80	"You Baby"	The Turtles
96	"Devil with a Blue Dress On/Good Golly Miss Molly"	Mitch Ryder & the Detroit Wheels
97	"Wouldn't It Be Nice"	The Beach Boys

The Animals

Throngs sardined in the outdoor stages for the Animals at Club Ponytail.

The Animals, formed in Newcastle upon Tyne in 1962, played at Club Ponytail on August 26, 1966. They were then known for *The House of the Rising Sun* and *We Gotta Get Out of This Place*.

The Animals at Club Ponytail in 1966. Courtesy Club Ponytail Memories, Facebook

The Animals posing for publicity in 1964: from left to right, Eric Burdon (vocals), Alan Price (keyboards), Chas Chandler (bass), Hilton Valentine (guitar), John Steel (drums)[238]

The Animals (above and next) share a meal with local fans at the Holiday House (less Eric Burdon).[239]

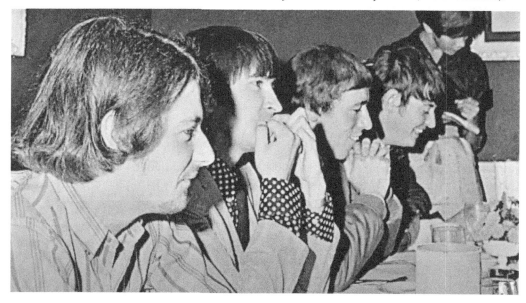

Animals on the Club Ponytail patio stage.[240]

The Shillings

The Shillings, from Arizona, played in 1966 alongside the Animals. They had appeared earlier in the year from July 1-5 along with Mitch Ryder and the Detroit Wheels.

Mitch Ryder and the Detroit Wheels

The Beau Brummels

The Beau Brummels played on July 28, 1966.

The Chancellors

The Chancellors, a Lansing, Michigan band active from 1965-1967. Chancellors rhythm guitarist Bruce Reinoehl wrote up a short history of the band:

> By late 1966, the Chancellors were becoming fairly well known in the mid Michigan area. We were playing jobs in Saginaw, Bay City, Jackson and as far away

as Harbor Springs. We played at nightclubs where the Byrds and Beach Boys had played a week or two previously. We also cut out second and final record around this time. This was the "Dear John" / "5 minus 3" record.[241]

The Chancellors stage in Slim's Lounge.

A concertgoer reflected:

> I was telling some people at work about the Ponytail and the groups that played there, I went to school in Indian River, The Ponytail was the place to be on the weekends, I saw a lot of the groups from 1963-1966. It was hard at times to save up the $8 to $10 to get in. It really was the best of times. I remember one group called The Lloyd's of London who was the summer band. I believe in 1966. The green river drink from the soda bar was my favorite. Stan was always everywhere, and I remember Linda, she was so popular at the time.[242]

The Chancellors at Band Canyon, a nightclub in Bay City, Michigan.
https://garagehangover.com/Chancellors/

Another wrote:

> I have tried to tell my friends and kids and family of the absolute fabulous times I spent there as a teenager. It was the highlight of my summers, along with Petoskey Bathing Beach??!! I saw Bobby Vinton and Roy Orbison and a mess of others.....too cool for words. I was there this fall and drove back in to take a look. Only the walls and the empty outdoor band shell.[243]

Sam the Sham and the Pharoahs

On Wednesday, August 17, 1996, the Texas group played at the club.

Sam the Sham and The Pharoahs were a 60s Tex-Mex rock 'n' roll band. The group was formed by lead singer Domingo "Sam" Samudio in 1961 in Dallas, Texas, USA. The other original members were Carl Medke, Russell Fowler, Omar "Big Man" Lopez, and Vincent Lopez. In a 2007 conversation with music writer Joe Nick Patoski, Samudio described his grandparents fleeing the Mexican Revolution and settling in Texas where his family supported themselves working in the cotton fields.[244]

Some of their top hits were *Wooly Bully* – their first and biggest hit in 1964 – and *Li'l Red Riding Hood*.

34   The Stage: 1967

Much like 1964, Club Ponytail perhaps could not get a contract with promoters in Detroit. Local bands vied in Battle of the Bands that summer.

The cultural clash between musicians and mainstream America widens. Pete Seeger released *Waist Deep in the Big Muddy* with a nameless narrator recalling an army patrol that almost drowns crossing a river in Louisiana in 1942 because of their reckless commanding officer, who is not so fortunate. Everyone understood the allusion to Vietnam, and CBS cut the song from a September 1967 episode of the Smothers Brother Comedy Show. Public protests eventually forced CBS to reverse course, and Seeger sang *Waist Deep in the Big Muddy* in a February 1968 episode of the show.[245]

A flurry of other protest songs came out in 1967 as hundreds of thousands of U.S. soldiers were shipped off to Vietnam. The disastrous Tet Offensive would start in January, 1968. Some of these songs included:[246]

- Arlo Guthrie, *Alice's Restaurant Massacree*. Who says that a protest song can't be funny? Guthrie's call to resist the draft and end the war in Vietnam is unusual in two respects: it's great length (18 minutes) and the fact that it is mostly a spoken monologue. For some radio stations it is a Thanksgiving tradition to play *Alice's Restaurant Massacree*.
- Nina Simone, *Backlash Blues*. Simone transformed a civil rights poem by Langston Hughes into a Vietnam War protest song. "Raise my taxes/Freeze my wages/Send my son to Vietnam."
- Joan Baez, *Saigon Bride*. Baez set a poem by Nina Duscheck to music. An unnamed narrator says goodbye to his Saigon bride—which could be meant literally or figuratively—to fight an enemy for reasons that "will not matter when we're dead."
- Country Joe & the Fish, *Feel Like I'm Fixin' to Die*. Sometimes called the "Vietnam Song," Country Joe & the Fish's rendition of *Feel Like I'm Fixin to Die* was one of the signature moments at Woodstock. The chorus is infectious: "and it's 1, 2, 3 what are we fighting for?/Don't ask me, I don't give a damn, next stop is Vietnam."

But for other Baby Boomers, sheltered from the draft by age or circumstance, the summer proceeded as though nothing was amiss. Those families left the sweltering cities of Illinois, Indiana, Michigan, and elsewhere and headed north to the cooling winds of Northern Michigan. But the teenagers among them twitched. They knew their turn was soon to come.

Author's family at Glen Lake, Michigan, 1967.

The market for entertainment for these teenagers and pre-teens was still alive, and Club Ponytail was there for many.

Artists who eventually played at Club Ponytail and who were on Billboard's Hot-100 for 1967 – but are likely not to have been at Club Ponytail that year – included:[247]

No.	Title	Artist(s)
8	"Happy Together"	The Turtles
11	"Little Bit O' Soul"	The Music Explosion
14	"I Was Made to Love Her"	Stevie Wonder
15	"Come Back When You Grow Up"	Bobby Vee
26	"Love Is Here and Now You're Gone"	The Supremes
29	"The Happening"	The Supremes
32	"Your Precious Love"	Marvin Gaye & Tammi Terrell
36	"Jimmy Mack"	Martha and the Vandellas
41	"Reflections"	The Supremes
43	"Please Love Me Forever"	Bobby Vinton
56	"You're My Everything"	The Temptations
78	"She'd Rather Be with Me"	The Turtles
82	"Bernadette"	Four Tops
87	"Ain't No Mountain High Enough"	Marvin Gaye & Tammi Terrell

35   The Stage: 1968

1968 is a tumultuous time in American history. In Vietnam, the spring Tet Offensive. In January, 1,100 Americans and other allied troops are killed, alongside 2,100 South Vietnamese troops and 14,000 civilians. A month later, these numbers are tripled.[248] Baby Boomers are getting slaughtered, and the body count is appearing on national TV. A massive culture war is developing as the veterans from World War II deal with their sons returning from Vietnam. The "Just Cause" is not apparent to many Americans, leading to massive protests. General Westmoreland considers use of nuclear weapons, an opinion quickly quashed by President Lyndon Johnson in the White House.

Throughout the U.S., the tragic news from abroad is being heard from a consistent and trusted source: Walter Cronkite of CBS News.

> In mid-February 1968, on the urging of his executive producer Ernest Leiser, Cronkite and Leiser journeyed to Vietnam to cover the aftermath of the Tet Offensive. They were invited to dine with General Creighton Abrams, the commander of all forces in Vietnam, whom Cronkite knew from World War II. According to Leiser, Abrams told Cronkite, "we cannot win this Goddamned war, and we ought to find a dignified way out."

> Upon return, Cronkite and Leiser wrote separate editorial reports based on that trip. Cronkite, an excellent writer, preferred Leiser's text over his own. On February 27, 1968, Cronkite closed "Report from Vietnam: Who, What, When, Where, Why?" with that editorial report:

> "We have been too often disappointed by the optimism of the American leaders, both in Vietnam and Washington, to have faith any longer in the silver linings they find in the darkest clouds. They may be right, that Hanoi's winter-spring offensive has been forced by the Communist realization that they could not win the longer war of attrition, and that the Communists hope that any success in the offensive will improve their position for eventual negotiations. It would improve their position, and it would also require our realization, that we should have had all along, that any negotiations must be that – negotiations, not the dictation of peace terms. For it seems now more certain than ever that the bloody experience of Vietnam is to end in a stalemate. This summer's almost certain standoff will either

end in real give-and-take negotiations or terrible escalation; and for every means we have to escalate, the enemy can match us, and that applies to invasion of the North, the use of nuclear weapons, or the mere commitment of one hundred, or two hundred, or three hundred thousand more American troops to the battle. And with each escalation, the world comes closer to the brink of cosmic disaster. To say that we are closer to victory today is to believe, in the face of the evidence, the optimists who have been wrong in the past. To suggest we are on the edge of defeat is to yield to unreasonable pessimism. To say that we are mired in stalemate seems the only realistic, yet unsatisfactory, conclusion. On the off chance that military and political analysts are right, in the next few months we must test the enemy's intentions, in case this is indeed his last big gasp before negotiations. But it is increasingly clear to this reporter that the only rational way out then will be to negotiate, not as victors, but as an honorable people who lived up to their pledge to defend democracy, and did the best they could."[249]

On cue, however, families from throughout the Midwest made their annual summer migrations to Northern Michigan, seeking some modicum of joy despite the deteriorating nation and international news. The families from Flint, Michigan, and Chicago suburbs all convened in the idyllic woodlands in and around Traverse City.

Baby boomers adrift in Northern Michigan, wondering about the news they are watching from Walter Cronkite.

And Club Ponytail shows its mojo, attracting national performers back to its pavilion and patio, including Bob Seger and THEM. Artists who eventually played at Club Ponytail and who were on Billboard's Hot-100 for 1968 included:[250]

No.	Title	Artist(s)
3	"Honey"	Bobby Goldsboro
22	"I Wish It Would Rain"	The Temptations
27	"Love Child"	The Supremes
57	"Ain't Nothing Like the Real Thing"	Marvin Gaye & Tammi Terrell
70	"Sky Pilot"	The Animals
80	"Elenore"	The Turtles
82	"You're All I Need to Get By"	Marvin Gaye & Tammi Terrell
85	"If You Can Want"	Smokey Robinson and the Miracles

Bob Seger

Bob Seger from Detroit, then known for *The Lonely One*, played on July 30, 1968.

Bob Seger ad. Judith Landis collection.

THEM (August, 1968)

Out of England, THEM was famous for *Here Comes the Night*.

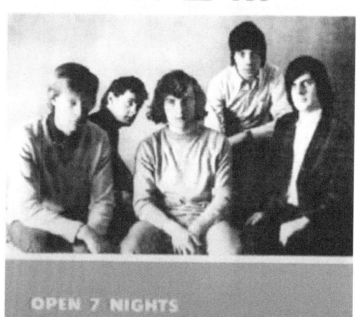

36   The Stage: 1969

The Amboy Dukes

Playing at the Douglas' nearby Golden Horseshoe Club after the Ponytail fire, The Amboy Dukes out of Detroit played a combination of hard rock and acid rock on July 3, 1969.

The Amboy Dukes
Greg Arama – K J Knight (top center) – Andy Solomon
Ted Nugent

Photo courtesy of theconcertdatabase.com.

The Turtles

The San Francisco band played on July 31, 1969, with the venue moved to the neighboring Golden Horseshoe Supper Club after the fire.

Poster for The Turtles at Club Ponytail. Photo by author, 2022.

MC5

Played on July 10, 1969 at the Club.

Playing almost nightly any place they could in and around Detroit, MC5 quickly earned a reputation for their high-energy live performances and had a sizeable local following, regularly drawing sellout audiences of 1000 or more. Contemporary rock writer Robert Bixby stated that the sound of MC5 was like "a catastrophic force of nature the band was barely able to control".[251]

MC5, short for "Motor City Five", was based on their Detroit roots. In some ways the group was similar to other garage bands of the period, composing soon-to-be historic workouts such as "Black to Comm" during their mid-teens in the basement of the home of Kramer's mother.[252] They led the hard rock revolution.

Under the "guidance" of John Sinclair (who dubbed his enterprise "Trans-Love Energies" and refused to be categorized as a traditional manager), MC5 were soon involved in left-wing politics: Sinclair was active with the White Panther Party and Fifth Estate.[15][16][17] In their early career, MC5 had a politically provocative stage show: They appeared onstage toting unloaded rifles, and at the climax of a performance, an unseen "sniper" would shoot Tyner. The band members were also all using the drugs LSD and marijuana.[253]

Mother Goose Spearmint

Back-up for MC5 on July 10, 1969.

The Pleasure Seekers

The all-girl band – renowned for *Stumbin In* – played in one of the final appearances for Club Ponytail, again at the Golden Horseshoe.

Our love is alive, and so we begin
Foolishly laying our hearts on the table
Stumblin' in
Our love is a flame, burning within
Now and then firelight will catch us
Stumblin' in

Wherever you go, whatever you do
You know these reckless thoughts of mine are following you
I've fallen for you, whatever you do
'Cause baby you've shown me so many things that I never knew
Whatever it takes, baby, I'll do it for you

Our love is alive, and so we begin
Foolishly laying our hearts on the table
Stumblin' in
Our love is a flame, burning within
Now and then firelight will catch us
Stumblin' in

You were so young, oh and I was so free
I may have been young
But baby, that's not what I wanted to be
Well, you were the one
Oh, why was it me
'Cause baby, you've shown me so many things that I never see
Whatever you need, baby, you've got it from me

Our love is alive, and so we begin
Foolishly laying our hearts on the table
Stumblin' in
Our love is a flame, burning within
Now and then firelight will catch us stumblin' in
Stumblin' in, stumblin' in
Foolishly laying our hearts on the table
Stumblin' in

Ah, stumblin' in
Mm, stumblin' in
Now and then firelight will catch us
Stumblin' in

Oh, stumblin' in
I'm stumblin' in
Foolishly laying our hearts on the table
Stumblin' in
Oh, stumblin' in
Ah, stumblin' in
I'm stumblin' in
Keep on stumblin' in
Now and then firelight will catch us, stumblin' in[254]

37   Other performers

The following bands played at Club Ponytail, but their exact dates are elusive.

Bobby Goldsboro

Chad and Jeremy

Conway Twitty out of Hamilton, Ontario

The Crystals

Dawn

Dee Dee Sharp

Dee Dee Sharp out of Philadelphia. Her 1962 hits included *Mashed Potato Time* and *Ride!* Her career had started 4 years earlier when she sought out back-up vocals jobs to support her family while her mother recovered from an auto accident.

Dee Dee Sharp, courtesy Cameo Records, http://vinylphilly.squarepins.org/

Dick & DeeDee

The Guess Who's

Jan & Dean

Jan & Dean were pioneers of the California Sound and vocal surf music styles popularized by the Beach Boys.[255] Among their most successful songs was 1963's "Surf City", the first surf song to ever reach the #1 spot. They met while both were students at Emerson Junior High School in Westwood, Los Angeles, and both were on the school's football team. By 1957, they were students in the class of 1958 at the nearby University High School, where again they were both on the school's football team, the Warriors.[11] Berry and Torrence had adjoining lockers, and after football practice, they began harmonizing together in the showers with several other football players, including future actor James Brolin

Jan and Dean in 1964. By WWDC Radio - eBaysurvey, Public Domain, https://commons.wikimedia.org/w/index.php?curid=30627170

The Lloyds of London

Martha and the Vandellas

Martha Reeves (Martha and the Vandellas) from Detroit, *Heat Wave* became the group's first million-seller.

Martha and the Vandellas in 1965. (L-to-R) Rosaland Ashford, Martha Reeves, and Betty Kelley. Public domain photo courtesy https://commons.wikimedia.org

Marvin Gaye

Marvin Gaye of Washington, D.C. signed with Tamla Records (later to become Motown) in 1960. *Pride and Joy* became Gaye's first top ten single after its release in 1963.

Marvin Gaye in 1966. Public domain photo courtesy https://commons.wikimedia.org

The Music Explosion

Poster for The Music Explosion. Author photo, 2022.

Paul and Paula

Peter & Gordon

Roy Orbison

Coming from Texas, Orbison wrote or co-wrote almost all of his own Top 10 hits, including *Only the Lonely* (1960), *Running Scared* (1961), *Crying* (1961), *In Dreams* (1963), and *Oh, Pretty Woman* (1964).

Roy Orbison playing "Pretty Woman" in the Netherlands, 1965. Courtesy of Netherlands Nationaal Arhief.[256]

Smokey Robinson

Smokey Robinson and the Miracles, out of Detroit. This is the direct connection to Motown.

The Miracles in 1962. Clockwise from top left: Bobby Rogers, Marv Tarplin, Ronald White, Claudette Robinson, and Smokey Robinson. Public domain image courtesy of Wikimedia Commons.

Stevie Wonder

Stevie Wonder, blind from birth, was a child wonder who signed with Tamla Records (later Motown) in 1961 at the age of 11. His single *Fingertips* topped the Billboard chart in 1963, making him the youngest artist ever to top the charts.

The Temptations

The Temptations came out of Detroit alongside the Supremes, and followed their ascent, but not with nearly as much success.

A promotional image of the original early 1960s Temptations lineup. Clockwise from top right: Otis Williams, Paul Williams, Melvin Franklin, Eddie Kendricks, and Elbridge "Al" Bryant. Public domain image courtesy of Wikimedia Commons.

Club Ponytail

"MICHIGAN'S ONLY
TEEN-COLLEGIATE NITE CLUB"
HARBOR SPRINGS, MICHIGAN

FRIDAY, DECEMBER 27
"Holiday Shower of Stars"
JOHNNY TILLOTSON, PAUL & PAULA
RONNIE COCHRANE, THE KASUALS

SATURDAY, DECEMBER 28
"Kris Kringle Stomp"
CROWNING MISS PONYTAIL

SUNDAY, DECEMBER 29
"Mistletoe Hop"

MONDAY, DECEMBER 30
"Holly Sock Dance"

TUESDAY, DECEMBER 31
"New Year's Eve Party"

WEDNESDAY, JANUARY 1
"Popcorn Party"

THURSDAY, JANUARY 2
"Holiday Sadie"

FRIDAY, JANUARY 3
"Snowflake Frolic"
DANCE CONTEST - PRIZES

SATURDAY, JANUARY 4
"Holiday Ball"

**DOOR PRIZES EVERY NIGHT
CASUAL DRESS**

Club Ponytail winter line-up. Judith Landis collection.

38 Top artists and songs

The top musical artists of the 1960s were well represented at Club Ponytail.

Act	Number of Songs on Top of the Billboard Hot 100	Duration on Top of the Billboard Hot 100 (in weeks)
The Beatles	18	55
The Supremes	12	21
Elvis Presley	6	20
Frankie Valli and The Four Seasons	4	15
The Rolling Stones	4	13
The Monkees	3	12
Bobby Vinton	3	10
The Young Rascals	3	10
The 5th Dimension	2	9
Ray Charles	3	8

Appearances on the Billboard-100.[257]

Based on chart performance on the Billboard Hot 100 from 1960-1969,[258] the top 100 songs from the 1960s were as follows (those groups which played at Club Ponytail are bolded):

1. The Twist - Chubby Checker
2. Hey Jude - The Beatles
3. Theme From "A Summer Place" - Percy Faith
4. Tossin' and Turnin' - Bobby Lewis
5. I Want to Hold Your Hand - The Beatles
6. Aquarius/Let the Sunshine in - The 5th Dimension

7. I'm a Believer - The Monkees
8. Are You Lonesome Tonight? - Elvis Presley
9. Sugar Sugar - The Archies
10. I Heard It Through the Grapevine - **Marvin Gaye**
11. I Can't Stop Loving You - Ray Charles
12. Love Is Blue - Paul Mauriat
13. Cathy's Clown - The Everly Brothers
14. It's Now or Never - Elvis Presley
15. Honky Tonk Women - The Rolling Stones
16. Big Bad John - Jimmy Dean
17. Lulu - To Sir With Love
18. People Got to Be Free - The Rascals
19. Everyday People - Sly & the Family Stone
20. Big Girls Don't Cry - **The Four Seasons**
21. (I Can't Get No) Satisfaction - The Rolling Stones
22. She Loves You - The Beatles
23. Stuck on You - Elvis Presley
24. Love Child - **Diana Ross & the Supremes**
25. Get Back - The Beatles
26. Groovin' (1967) - The Young Rascals
27. Roses Are Red - **Bobby Vinton**
28. Runaround Sue - Dion
29. I'm Sorry - Brenda Lee
30. Ode to Billie Joe - Bobbie Gentry
31. Honey - **Bobby Goldsboro**
32. In the Year 2525 - Zager & Evans
33. Wonderland by Night - Bert Kaempfert
34. (Sittin' On) the Dock of the Bay - Otis Redding
35. Runaway - **Del Shannon**
36. The Letter - The Box Tops
37. The Four Seasons - Sherry
38. The Monkees - Daydream Believer
39. Peppermint Twist - Joey Dee & the Starliters
40. Jimmy Gilmer & the Fireballs - Sugar Shack
41. This Guy's in Love With You - Herb Alpert
42. The Singing Nun - Dominique
43. Crimson and Clover - Tommy James & the Shondells
44. Happy Together - **The Turtles**
45. Ballad of the Green Berets - S/Sgt. Barry Sadler
46. El Paso - Marty Robbins
47. The New Vaudeville Band - Winchester Cathedral

48. He'll Have to Go - Jim Reeves
49. You've Lost That Lovin' Feelin' - The Righteous Brothers
50. Running Bear - Johnny Preston
51. My Heart Has a Mind of Its Own - Connie Francis
52. Hey Paula - **Paul and Paula**
53. Everybody's Somebody's Fool - Connie Francis
54. Pony Time - Chubby Checker
55. Somethin' Stupid - Nancy Sinatra & Frank Sinatra
56. Windy - The Association
57. Louie Louie - **The Kingsmen**
58. Blue Velvet - **Bobby Vinton**
59. Light My Fire - The Doors
60. Where Did Our Love Go? - **The Supremes**
61. There I've Said It Again - **Bobby Vinton**
62. Dizzy - Tommy Roe
63. He's So Fine - The Chiffons
64. Calcutta - Lawrence Welk
65. Last Date - Floyd Cramer
66. Stranger on the Shore - Mr Acker Bilk
67. Mrs. Robinson - Simon and Garfunkel
68. I Will Follow Him - Little Peggy March
69. I Can't Help Myself (Sugar Pie, Honey Bunch) - **The Four Tops**
70. Baby Love - **The Supremes**
71. Soldier Boy - The Shirelles
72. Can't Buy Me Love - The Beatles
73. Mrs. Brown You've Got a Lovely Daughter - Herman's Hermits
74. Fingertips, Pt. 2 - **Stevie Wonder**
75. Leaving on a Jet Plane - Peter, Paul & Mary
76. Yesterday - The Beatles
77. Hello Dolly, Louis Armstrong
78. Come See About Me - **The Supremes**
79. Downtown - Petula Clark
80. Shelley Fabares - Johnny Angel
81. Return to Sender - Elvis Presley
82. Turn! Turn! Turn! - The Byrds
83. I Get Around - **The Beach Boys**
84. We Can Work It Out/Day Tripper - The Beatles
85. I Feel Fine - The Beatles
86. Duke of Earl - Gene Chandler
87. Judy in Disguise With Glasses - John Fred and His Playboy Band
88. The Tornados - Telstar

89. Bruce Channel - Hey Baby
90. Kyu Sakamoto - Sukiyaki
91. Do Wah Diddy Diddy - Manfred Mann
92. Save the Last Dance for Me - The Drifters
93. Wedding Bell Blues - The 5th Dimension
94. Stop! in the Name of Love - **The Supremes**
95. Someday We'll Be Together - **Diana Ross & the Supremes**
96. (You're My) Soul and Inspiration - The Righteous Brothers
97. Mark Dinning - Teen Angel
98. Jeannie C Riley - Harper Valley PTA
99. Chapel of Love - The Dixie Cups
100. The Lion Sleeps Tonight - The Tokens

The durability of the performers who played at Club Ponytail is evident in a list of best-remembered songs from the 1960s (those groups which played at Club Ponytail are bolded):[259]

1. "Respect," Aretha Franklin
2. "Dancing in the Street," **Martha Reeves and the Vandellas**
3. "My Girl," **The Temptations**
4. "Kick Out the Jams," **MC5**
5. "The Tracks of My Tears," **Smokey Robinson & the Miracles**
6. "Ain't No Mountain High Enough," **Marvin Gaye & Tammi Terrell**
7. "Stop! In the Name of Love," **The Supremes**
8. "Chain of Fools," Aretha Franklin
9. "I Heard it Through the Grapevine," **Marvin Gaye**
10. "I Heard it Through the Grapevine," Gladys Knight & the Pips
11. "(Your Love Keeps Lifting Me) Higher and Higher," Jackie Wilson
12. "I Wanna Be Your Dog," **Iggy Pop** and the Stooges
13. "96 Tears," Question Mark & the Mysterians
14. "Devil With a Blue Dress On/Good Golly Miss Molly," **Mitch Ryder & the Detroit Wheels**
15. "I Can't Help Myself (Sugar Pie Honey Bunch)," **Four Tops**
16. "My Cherie Amour," **Stevie Wonder**
17. "Reach Out I'll Be There," **Four Tops**
18. "For Once in My Life," **Stevie Wonder**
19. "(You Make Me Feel Like) A Natural Woman," Aretha Franklin
20. "Baby Love," **The Supremes**
21. "Uptight (Everything's Alright)," **Stevie Wonder**
22. "Boom Boom," John Lee Hooker

23. "You Can't Hurry Love," **The Supremes**
24. "You Keep Me Hanging On," **the Supremes**
25. "My Guy," Mary Wells
26. "Shop Around," **The Miracles**
27. "Runaway," **Del Shannon**
28. "I Second That Emotion," **Smokey Robinson & the Miracles**
29. "Heavy Music," **Bob Seger & the Last Heard**
30. "Ooo Baby Baby," **The Miracles**
31. "Please Mr. Postman," **The Marvelettes**
32. "Baby I Need Your Loving," **Four Tops**
33. "Nowhere to Run," **Martha and the Vandellas**
34. "Ain't Too Proud to Beg," **The Temptations**
35. "Ramblin' Gamblin' Man," **Bob Seger**
36. "Get Ready," **The Temptations**
37. "The Way You Do the Things You Do," **The Temptations**
38. "(Love is Like A) Heat Wave," **Martha and the Vandellas**
39. "Bernadette," **Four Tops**
40. "Someday We'll Be Together," **Diana Ross & the Supremes**
41. "Shotgun," Junior Walker & the All-Stars
42. "What Becomes of the Brokenhearted," Jimmy Ruffin
43. "Cool Jerk," the Capitols
44. "How Sweet It Is (To Be Loved By You)," **Marvin Gaye**
45. "Think," Aretha Franklin
46. "You've Really Got a Hold on Me," **The Miracles**
47. "Do You Love Me," the Contours
48. "Ain't Nothing Like the Real Thing," **Marvin Gaye & Tammi Terrell**
49. "Fingertips -- Pt. 2," **Stevie Wonder**
50. "Respect," the Rationals

39 Competition

Local

Interlochen

In 1962 – the year Club Ponytail launched – Interlochen Arts Academy, the country's first independent fine arts boarding high school, opened with 132 students.

But Interlochen had built its Interlochen Bowl in 1928, the year Slim started construction of Club Manitou. Large outdoor venues were plentiful in the first half of the 20th century. The competition for the emerging music genres would be fierce.

Postcard.

In 1961, internationally acclaimed pianist Van Cliburn had visited the National Music Camp to perform a benefit concert. Inspired by the success of Cliburn's performance, the Camp arranged for future performances by Cliburn and other high-profile artists. In 1964, a visit from the Philadelphia Orchestra inaugurated the Interlochen Arts Festival, a summer-long series of performances by acclaimed artists in both classical and contemporary genres.[260] Among those artists were Diana Ross and other performers from Motown.

In 1964, Kresge Auditorium is re-opened after a major expansion of the original 1948 building, including a full roof and new seating,[261] Over 4,000 people could watch a single performance. However, concerts at the outdoor stage were primarily if not entirely limited to classical music. The record of pop and other "controversial" music at Interlochen is sparse; classical music was its focus and its bread-and-butter. The 1972 performance of Lloyd Weber's "Jesus Christ: Superstar" at Interlochen is lost in history[262], yet the author traveled there with other teenagers visiting Northern Michigan for the summer in 1972 or thereabouts.

An equally important hurdle, accommodations near Interlochen were few and far between. Travel there meant a road-trip with the precarious return trip always in the teenager's parents' minds. Parents could not simply pick their children up after a concert without having gone there themselves. To do so would be highly inconvenient for parents who, perhaps, were not exactly fond of the new music genres emerging in the 1960s.

And so, Interlochen was perhaps not a direct competitor to Club Ponytail, the former shying away from edgier music. Nonetheless, the presence of large, outdoor music venues for summer concerts got promoters licking their chops: more room meant more ticket sales. Summers did not require roofs over patrons.

The Grande Ballroom.

Grande Ballroom

The Grande Ballroom was a two-story music venue built in 1921 on Grand River Street in Detroit. The Grande had a retail space on the first floor, with the ballroom being on the second floor.

The Who at the Grande Ballroom, Image – Thomas Weschler

Of all the legendary music, few are as storied as the Grande Ballroom. If only because it is the site within which what is perhaps the quintessential Detroit album – MC5's Kick out the Jams – was recorded. The Grande Ballroom was the Detroit headquarters of John Sinclair and the MC5's White Panther movement, hosting the Stooges as their house band, before increasing violence in the area forced Iggy and co to flee to Ann Arbor. Today, the once magnificent space and birthplace of Detroit psychedelia is, like so many local historic landmarks, a ruin.[161]

National

In nearby Chicago, teen-ager entertainment budgets were being drained by large concerts at Grant Park and, north of the city, Ravinia Festival.

Grant Park, Chicago, 1951.

40 Demise

President Richard Nixon was inaugurated on January 20, 1969. He begins troop withdrawals from Vietnam.

> The anti-war movement was gaining strength in the United States. Nixon appealed to the "silent majority" of Americans who he said supported the war without showing it in public. But revelations of the 1968 My Lai Massacre, in which a U.S. Army unit raped and killed civilians, and the 1969 "Green Beret Affair", where eight Special Forces soldiers, including the 5th Special Forces Group Commander, were arrested for the murder of a suspected double agent, provoked national and international outrage.[264]

Club Ponytail went up in a blaze of fire on March 18, 1969. Rumors circulated that Stan Douglas lit the match as the club began to lose money[265], though the fire department concluded that a gas leak was to blame.

Club Ponytail burns. Photo courtesy Rick Wiles and Mackinac Journal, February/March 2014.

While the Douglases originally declared their intent to rebuild the pavilion and re-open Club Ponytail, they did get there.

Record sales were taking off, and concert attendance rose in tandem. The demand for large venues near large population areas soared.

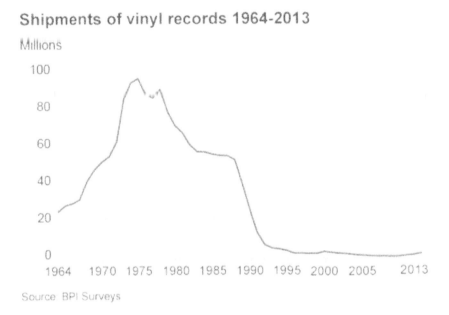

Record sales skyrocket in the late 1960s.[266]

At the same time, the relatively innocuous lyrics of the 1960s were giving way to the more rebellious lyrics that accompanied the Vietnam War protests. The innocence of a revived Club Ponytail would have difficulty adjusting to the increasingly rebellious Baby Boomers. If the conservative Northern Michigan culture had difficulty with The Kingsmen's *Louie Louie* – which was actually quite innocent – the new lyrics and their singers would be dead on arrival.

> Woodstock Music and Art Fair, commonly referred to simply as Woodstock, was a music festival held August 15–18, 1969, on Max Yasgur's dairy farm in Bethel, New York .... Billed as "an Aquarian Exposition: 3 Days of Peace & Music" and alternatively referred to as the Woodstock Rock Festival, it attracted an audience of more than 400,000. Thirty-two acts performed outdoors despite sporadic rain.
>
> The festival has become widely regarded as a pivotal moment in popular music history as well as a defining event for the counterculture generation. The event's

significance was reinforced by a 1970 documentary film, an accompanying soundtrack album, and a song written by Joni Mitchell that became a major hit for both Crosby, Stills, Nash & Young and Matthews Southern Comfort.[267]

The Douglases were arguably shrewd in avoiding this confrontation, instead devoting themselves to their 2-year-old Golden Horseshoe Supper Club just a few hundred yards to the north of Club Ponytail, eventually selling that in 1971.

41 Club Ponytail's place in history

While a short-lived, small venue in a remote Northwoods locale, Club Ponytail nonetheless played an out-sized role in fostering the musical talent coming out of Detroit and other parts of Michigan as well as other parts of the country. Smaller bands found an enthusiastic crowd with which to share new and often bleeding-edge music. It was a test stage for Motown and its performers, while providing a strong venue for lesser-known groups.

42 Golden Horseshoe Supper Club

The Douglases did not forsake their adult customer base. A few hundred feet north of Club Ponytail they opened Golden Horseshoe Supper Club in 1967. After Club Ponytail burned in 1969, the new venue was used for concerts that had already been booked.

Was Slim involved in the Golden Horseshoe? Perhaps as an early advisor, but from White Sulphur Springs. He would need to keep a very low profile so that the Golden Horseshoe would not lose its liquor license as Club Manitou had.

Interestingly, there is a building just north of Club Manitou and built decades later. Underground storage and tunnels have been found there as well. Was it supplying Golden Horseshoe with cut-rate, tax-free liquor?

Regardless of Slim's involvement, the Golden Horseshoe carried on the edgy adult offerings of its predecessor. The following memoir of "Lottie the Body" is most intriguing, written for Coastal Connecticut Magazine and repeated by Bebe Bardot[268]:

> The name "Lottie the Body" came early on when a sculptor, who was with a college in New York, made a sculpture of me. He named his creation Lottie the Body and the name stuck to the real thing.
>
> At this age, I can admit that I was blessed with a great body. I was even known as the "Gypsy Rose Lee of Detroit" for the town where I eventually settled down. But although I loved the costumes and glamour and attention and fame, that wasn't what was most important to me. I wanted to entertain men and women through my love of dance. I wanted them to experience the joy of life that I felt. It was my love of people that made me want to make them happy. I know that sounds too simple to be true, but it is. I think that's the truth for many performers. In the 1950s, after Whitey's Lindy Hoppers ran its course and closed, there was only one place for me to dance, only one place for a professionally-trained black dancer to make a living. Burlesque. It was either take off my clothes while dancing or don't dance at all. So I took it off.
>
> However, back then it wasn't like it is today. "Stripping" meant ending up in a bikini bottom and pasties, more than a lot of women wear to the beach these days. In my kind of exotic dancing, it wasn't the attitude that dancers have today: "Look at what I've got that you can have." It was more like: "Look at what I've got that you can't have." That's what drove men wild.

By the early 1970s, Idlewild's popularity waned because blacks could get into other places they had been barred from before. Then I often performed at the Golden Horseshoe club in Harbor Springs, Michigan. You can probably tell that the club had a western theme. I really liked the owners, kind people who were good to their workers. Harbor Springs is a resort town on Lake Michigan that has a long history of wealthy vacation homeowners from Detroit and Chicago. That area is popular in the summer with boaters, golfers, and lake lovers; and in the winter with skiers and snow lovers.

The Golden Horseshoe was popular with everybody. On any given night customers might include high-rolling big city businessmen, a famous singer or actor or two, a celebrity athlete, a few mobsters, politicians, fraternity boys, couples, locals, a bridal shower or bachelor party, a doctors' convention, and Vietnam veterans just returned from war…. You name it, they came. …

The most fun night of the week at the Golden Horseshoe was Thursday night because it was "butler and servant's night" off from work. House workers, almost all black, who came with their wealthy employees to their summer residences, came to the club to hear good music, dance, and watch a good performance. The Dixieland Band had some Lawrence Welk musicians on summer break from filming their popular TV shows. They were great musicians. The energy in the place was electric! It was so much fun. The waitresses at the club said the butlers, maids, and servants tipped better than anybody else. I told them that's because they knew what it was like to serve other people and they appreciated their chance to be served.

Performers, including me, stayed in the servants' quarters of the Fisher mansion. It was the vacation residence of the Fisher family of Fisher Body, the automobile company that merged with GM. In Harbor Springs there were, and still are, fabulous vacation homes owned by wealthy families, mostly from Detroit with connections to the auto industry, passed down from generation to generation. The Fisher home was a beautiful place to stay.

Lottie was not the first nor the last to carry on the fine traditions of Club Manitou and its offspring. The Golden Horseshoe eventually closed in 1970 and with it the long shadow of Club Manitou, long fading, finally disappeared.

Judy Landis at Club Manitou (ca. 1990) working on the archives.

43 Epilogue

On July 26, 1974, Keehn and Mary Landis purchased an old run-down home on the eastern edge of Harbor Springs, Michigan for the price of the land and started extensive renovations. They did not touch the basement except to run wiring and plumbing for the main floor. Appendix A shows their plans for the main level.

But local kids knew what lay underground. The basement and its tunnels were haunting and intriguing. Adventurers took advantage of the easy access to the basement; a newer door to the lounge entrance – not part of the original barriers – was quickly jimmied.

The renovations took their toll. Keehn and Mary Landis divorced and, in 1984, Keehn married Judith Mallen. They continued to occupy and improve what was once Club Manitou.

Slim died on December 16, 1987, and is buried in Gaylord, Michigan. A sketchy and inaccurate obituary read:

> William A. (Al) Gerhart and his wife, Jeanette Kenich Gerhart, owned and operated Al's Place (now Harbor Springs Pier Restaurant) and the Club Manitou, a popular nightclub in the forty's and fifty's. In 1959 Club Manitou was sold to Jean and Stanley Douglas. They turned it into a teenage nightclub called the "Pony Tail." The club was enormously popular and featured the biggest rock'n'roll stars of the day. Prior to the Douglases ownership, there were rumors the Gerhart night clubs had been connected to the prohibition era's organized crime. Nothing was ever proven, but after 70 years, the gangster tales and evidence of secret tunnels continue to fuel imaginations of locals and tourists alike.[269]

Judy Landis was busy keeping Club Manitou standing in 2023 at age 92, having had to fill in some of the tunnels as they collapsed. Earlier, in her 80s, she had been known to climb onto the roof to repair caulk and clear gutters, at one point kicking her ladder almost out of reach. She died in August of 2023, likely with several home projects in mind.

Appendix A: 1970s plans

The possibilities of the dilapidated Club Manitou Keehn Landis and his wife Mary purchased in 1974 continued the club's tradition of skirting disaster. Leveraging the open spaces enabled by the 12 massive steel beams traversing the building east-to-west – 3 lined up 10' from the south wall and 3 more 10' further in, a set supporting the main floor and a set supporting the second floor – they envisioned a duplex arrangement with Mary's father in the western wing.

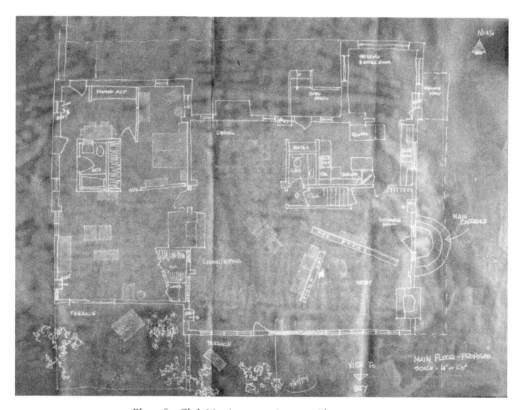

Plans for Club Manitou as private residence, ca 1975.

As well, bookshelves would dominate the former lounge area in the southeast corner, separating it from the living and dining area in the middle of the main floor.

The plans for the west apartment and a new north-facing entrance never came about, but a much-needed bathroom and the bookshelves were built.

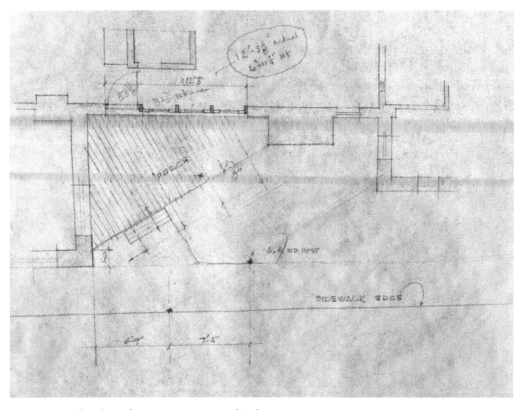

The planned new entrance, unrealized.

Appendix B: Exterior photos

Southern windows outside former dining room, ca.2002

View from the southeast. 2016

View from the north, 2021

Appendix C: 2022 Exhibit

The Harbor Springs Area Historical Society featured Club Manitou in its exhibit, "Dry Harbor: Prohibition, Gambling and Gangsters in Harbor Springs", which opened on May 28, 2022.

Author Judith Landis at the Exhibit, July 12, 2022.

Appendix D: Miniaturization

Judy Landis' great-granddaughter first visited Club Manitou on July 10, 2021. That year, construction began on "Club Manitou: the dollhouse". The 1:24 model was based off dimensions taken by the author that year.

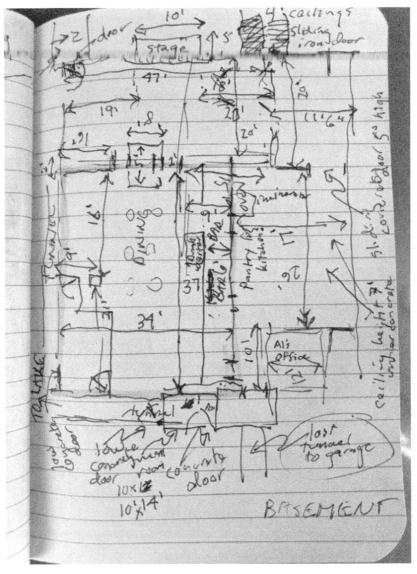

Basement dimensions, approximate.

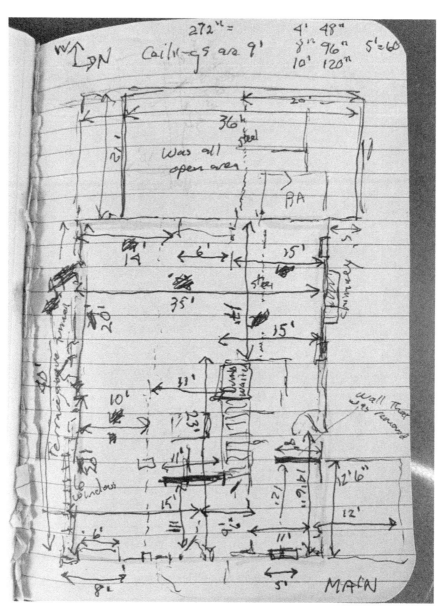

Main floor dimensions, approximate.

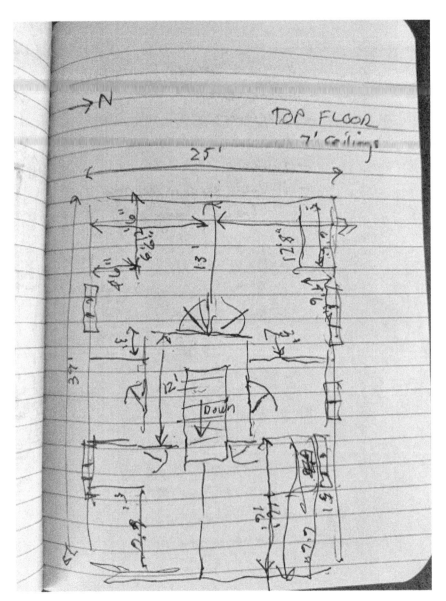

Top floor dimensions, approximate.

Club Manitou, 2nd Edition

Left to right: Keehn Landis and authors, Judith Landis and Mark Huck. Sarajevo, 1984.

About the authors

Mark Huck grew up north of Chicago, graduating from New Trier High School, Princeton University, and the University of Washington. He lives on Washington's Pacific coast with his wife, Nadine, and their two dogs, Stan and Bell.

Judith Mallen Landis grew up north of Chicago, graduating from New Trier High School and Carleton College. She lives in Club Manitou with her cat, Duncan.

Other books by Mark Huck (available on Amazon):
- Ron's Hollow: Operating Manual for the Wet Woods
- Bull Beaches: A Dog's Guide to the Olympic Coast
- Olympics via the Pacific: Four Epic Hikes through the Wet Woods to the Glaciers
- Salmon, Ghosts, and Bugs: Suffering in the Wet Woods
- Olympic Approaches: Four Guides to the Pacific Northwest Coast and its Beaches
- Darkest Winter: Journal of a Pandemic
- Flying Blind: 20 Days as Data Analyst during the COVID-19 Pandemic of 2020

Index

126th Infantry, 45
1784, 27
1873, 33
1876, 26
1878, 59
1880, 29
1882, 29
1886, 28
1887, 27, 117
1893, 27, 31, 38, 339
1895, 41, 153
1899, 31
18th Amendment, 17, 205
1900, 30, 33
1905, 29
1906, 29, 38
1912, 59, 205
1916, 27, 32, 34, 175
1918, 15, 20, 27, 40, 41, 49
1919, 20, 40, 45, 46, 201
1920, 29, 38, 60
1927, 42, 49, 52, 55, 69, 148, 201
1928, 20, 55, 69, 70, 74, 117, 122, 145, 176, 197, 198
1929, 52, 60, 79, 171, 179
1931, 215
1932, 215
1933, 17, 21, 55, 71, 126, 158, 159, 183
1935, 21, 32, 55, 79, 156, 179, 183, 189, 197, 215
1936, 21, 38, 145, 162, 179, 188, 189, 197
1937, 206, 215
1938, 42, 149, 197, 201
1945, 150, 186
1949, 217, 219, 224, 226
1950, 222, 223, 245
1954, 190, 216, 219, 220, 225
1957, 219, 221, 224, 232, 235, 245, 291
1958, 217, 219, 224, 232, 246, 249, 291
1959, 21, 224, 242, 246, 248, 249, 317
1960, 226, 232, 246, 248, 293, 296
1961, 227, 228, 242, 244, 247, 248, 249, 264, 275, 296, 297, 306
1962, 192, 194, 195, 205, 226, 230, 232, 235, 236, 238, 239, 242, 243, 249, 267, 289, 297, 305
1963, 21, 192, 193, 194, 195, 224, 232, 240, 241, 243, 244, 249, 251, 254, 257, 260, 274, 291, 293, 296, 297
1964, 216, 217, 241, 250, 251, 256, 259, 262, 269, 276, 277, 291, 296, 306
1965, 253, 254, 262, 273, 292, 296
1966, 248, 261, 265, 266, 267, 268, 272, 273, 274, 293
1967, 193, 256, 273
1968, 280, 282, 283
1969, 206, 248, 284, 285, 286, 309
1974, 15, 317, 319
Abe, 34, 48, 52
airflow, 98
airplanes, 62
Al Gerhart, 16, 20, 34, 47, 51, 56, 193
Alabama, 228
Alan Freed, 220
alcohol, 16, 25, 26, 27, 50, 51, 69, 70, 125, 158, 175, 201, 232, 235, 339
Allah, 16, 20, 34, 38, 40, 41, 42, 44, 45, 47, 51, 179
Amboy Dukes, 284
American Bandstand, 232, 235, 248
American Culinary Federation, 171
Animals, 267, 268, 269, 271, 272
Ann Arbor, 254
Anti-Saloon League, 20, 27
Arizona, 272
Armstrong, 147, 148
auto industry, 20, 31, 33, 52, 212, 314
B&O, 44
Babe Ruth, 47
Baby Boom, 216

Baldwin County, 214
basement, 15, 81, 83, 97, 100, 107, 134, 150, 177, 186, 317
Battle of the Bands, 251, 277
Bay View, 33
Beach Boys, 243, 244, 274, 291
Beatles, 232, 244, 254
Beau Brummels, 273
Belvedores, 238
Benny Goodman, 148
Bernstein, 16, 20, 29, 34, 48, 52
Berry Gordon, 223
Berry Gordy, 213, 214, 232
Berry Gordy I, 213
Berry Gordy II, 213, 214
Berry Gordy III, 214
Berry Gordy, Sr, 213
Billboard, 219, 241, 242, 244, 248, 297
Billups, 211, 212
blind pigs, 34
Bob Major, 245, 246
Bob Seger, 282, 304
Bobby Vee, 242
Bobby Vinton, 240, 241, 242, 275
Booker T. Washington Grocery Store, 214
Boston, 29
Boynton v. Virginia, 228
Brian Hyland, 273
Broadway Limited, 42, 43, 44
brothers, 20, 34, 38, 46, 47, 197, 198, 205
Burt Lake, 59
California, 243
Canada, 29, 123, 175, 176
Canadian Club, 49, 123, 163, 164
Capone, 49, 124, 175, 176
caster, 25, 26
casters, 25, 26, 339
Chancellors, 273, 275
Charles Dahlstrom, 81
Charlevoix, 175, 179
Chicago, 29, 33, 51, 59, 124, 175, 176
Chickasaw, 211
chimney, 86
Civil Rights Movement, 227

Cleaners and Dyers War, 49
Cleveland, 32, 59
Club Manitou, 1, 5, 17, 20, 21, 25, 34, 52, 53, 55, 56, 61, 62, 69, 70, 72, 74, 97, 116, 117, 123, 124, 128, 129, 132, 133, 135, 145, 147, 149, 170, 171, 175, 176, 179, 182, 190, 195, 197, 198, 201, 225, 226, 232, 233, 234, 236, 305, 312, 314, 316, 317, 319, 326, 331
Club Ponytail, 21, 232, 233, 235, 236, 238, 244, 254, 261, 263, 264, 267, 268, 299, 309, 312
Coast Guard, 175, 176
cocaine, 207
Cold War, 227
Collingswood Manor Massacre, 201
Colonial Club, 21, 175, 192, 193, 194, 195, 226, 232
Columbia Records, 218
concrete, 81, 83, 84, 85, 89, 98, 100
Controlled Substances Act, 206
convection, 97, 99, 150, 151
Conway Twitty, 289
counterfeit, 55
Crooked Lake, 59
Crystals, 289
Cuba, 227, 229
Dahlstrom Metallic Door Co, 81
Dawn, 289
Dearborn, 20, 200
death rate, 41
Dee Dee Sharp, 289, 290
Del Shannon, 244
depression, 32
Detroit, 16, 20, 31, 32, 33, 34, 37, 40, 42, 43, 44, 45, 46, 47, 49, 50, 51, 52, 56, 59, 61, 62, 69, 123, 124, 148, 163, 175, 176, 177, 179, 183, 196, 197, 198, 199, 201, 205, 211, 214, 223, 224, 226, 232, 236, 238, 248, 254, 256, 264, 272, 273, 277, 282, 284, 286, 292, 297, 298, 303, 307, 308, 311, 312, 313, 314
Dewey Phillips, 220
Dick & DeeDee, 256

Dick Clark, 220, 236
dining room, 117, 133, 134, 135
disc jockey, 220
door, 81, 82, 83, 85, 86, 97, 98, 100, 107, 108, 140, 158, 186
doors, 78, 79, 81, 83, 90, 98, 99, 100, 135
Douglas, 21, 195, 235, 236, 244, 254, 259, 284, 309, 317
Duke Ellington, 149
Duryea Motor Company, 37
Edict of Expulsion, 28
Edwin, 38
electric guitar, 215, 246
Eliza Mae, 211, 223
Elvis, 226, 245, 246
Elvis Presley, 245
England, 283
Esther Johnson, 213
Ever Ready Gospel Singers Group, 223
Falcons, 223
Fatty, 52
FBI, 21, 79, 101, 195, 232
Federal Reserve, 189, 194
Feds, 97, 98, 101
fentanyl, 206
fireplace, 97, 98, 134, 135, 136, 143, 147, 150, 151, 152, 153, 158
Fisher, 26, 195
Flame Show Bar, 223
Fleisher, 197, 198, 205
Ford, 20, 31, 32, 38, 42, 44, 51, 205, 214
Ford Motor Company, 20, 31, 38
Four Tops, 234, 254, 256
Freddy "Boom Boom" Cannon, 249
Freddy Cannon, 254
Frederick, 38, 40, 44, 45
French Lick, 172
gang, 34, 49, 52, 55, 205
gangster, 51, 69, 75, 176, 198, 201, 202, 317
gangsters, 49, 79, 205
Georgia, 213, 214, 227
Gerald R. Ford, 245
Gerhart, 69, 135, 193, 194, 236, 317
Gil King, 245, 246

Glanzrock, 197
Golden Horseshoe, 284, 285, 287
Golden Horseshoe Supper Club, 312
Gordy, 213, 214, 223, 224, 226, 232
Graceland Ballroom, 176
Grand Hotel, 117, 175, 176, 201
Grand Rapids, 33, 59, 244, 245, 246, 247, 248
Grand Rapids and Indiana Railroad, 33, 59
Great Depression, 79, 179, 216
Greatest Generation, 216
Greenbrier Resort, 192
guests, 90, 99, 105, 135, 145, 151, 171, 175, 176, 201
guitar, 215, 245, 246, 248, 269
Gwen Gordy, 224
Harbor Springs, 5, 15, 20, 33, 52, 55, 58, 59, 60, 61, 62, 69, 70, 74, 123, 124, 129, 134, 175, 176, 235, 236, 244, 254, 259, 274, 313, 314, 317
Harbor Springs Airport, 61
heroin, 206
Hiram Walker, 163
Hooper, 197
Hyland, 248
Idlewild, 313
Iggy Pop, 254, 303
Iguanas, 254, 263
immigrants, 27, 29, 30
incinerator, 86
Indian River, 274
Industrial Revolution, 17, 26
industrialization, 26
investment, 70, 74
Irwin, 38, 40, 44, 45
jazz, 147, 148, 149
Jewish, 28, 29, 30, 31, 34, 47
Jews, 28, 29, 31
jitterbug, 148
John F. Kennedy, 227
Johnny & the Hurricanes, 257
Johnny and the Hurricanes, 249
Kiev, 28

Kingsmen, 254, 257, 260
Kingtones, 244, 245, 246, 247, 248
kitchen, 74, 84, 85, 86, 87, 98, 103, 135, 143, 145, 167
Landis, 1, 5, 15, 21, 59, 263, 282, 299, 316, 317, 319, 326, 330, 331
Lansing Correctional Institute, 223
law enforcement, 55, 62, 81, 97, 99, 125, 148, 175, 189, 201, 202, 207
Lee's Sensation Club, 223
Lindy Hoppers, 312
liquor, 16, 49, 51, 56, 69, 70, 101, 123, 124, 125, 130, 159, 163, 176, 190, 197, 201, 225, 312
Little Traverse Bay, 33, 59, 132, 133, 134, 175
Los Angeles, 215, 291
Lottie, 312
Lou Christie, 248, 249, 292
Love, 46, 232, 244
Lowndes County, 211
Lupton, 176, 177
Mackinac Island, 175, 176
Mallen, 317
marijuana, 206
Marijuana Tax Stamp Act, 206
Martha and the Vandellas, 234, 292
Martha Reeves, 292
Martin Luther King, Jr., 227
Marvin Gaye, 234, 293
Mary Wells, 226, 304
Max, 20, 36, 37, 38, 39
MC5, 286, 303, 308
Michigan, 15, 20, 27, 34, 38, 40, 42, 44, 45, 49, 51, 59, 69, 74, 100, 122, 124, 126, 163, 175, 176, 179, 183, 190, 197, 201, 225, 244, 253, 254, 273, 275, 313, 317, 339
Michigan Liquor Control Board, 190, 225
Michigan State University, 242
Milaflores Massacre, 55, 201
Miracles, 224, 226, 232, 234, 297, 303, 304
Mississippi, 211
Mitch Ryder, 273
Model T, 31, 49

Mosler Safe Company, 71
Motown, 213, 223, 226, 232, 234, 235, 240, 253, 264, 293, 297, 306, 311
Motown Records, 232, 264
Munich, 37
murder, 49, 52, 55
National Cash Register, 143, 144, 145
National Labor Relations Act, 32
New Jersey, 27
New York, 27, 28, 29, 30, 31, 32, 34, 41, 171, 194, 339
New York City, 10, 29, 30, 34, 37, 38, 179, 248, 249, 262
Nighwalkers, 261
North Dakota, 242
Oakland Sugar House Gang, 49, 197
Ohio, 32, 42, 44, 68, 71, 72, 175
Old Bishop School, 47
Ontario, 49
opioid, 206, 207
patent, 37, 40, 68, 155, 188, 189, 339
patio, 233, 249, 251, 253, 272
Paul and Paula, 296
pavilion, 233, 238, 251, 253
Pennsylvania, 16, 20, 31, 37, 38, 39, 41, 42, 194
Pepper, 79, 130, 131
Peter & Gordon, 296
Petoskey, 5, 20, 33, 59, 71, 123, 129, 187, 195, 236, 244, 275
Philadelphia, 37, 40, 42, 44, 241, 289
Philips, 219
pogroms, 28, 29
poker, 186, 192, 194, 195
police, 49, 52, 62, 63, 79, 98, 177, 198, 232
Portland, 257
prohibition, 27, 55, 317
Prohibition, 15, 16, 17, 20, 21, 27, 28, 50, 51, 62, 69, 70, 124, 126, 133, 163, 176, 183, 197, 204, 205, 235, 339
Purple Gang, 20, 34, 42, 47, 48, 49, 50, 52, 55, 59, 60, 69, 70, 75, 79, 117, 124, 126, 175, 176, 177, 179, 183, 192, 196, 197, 198, 199, 201, 205, 254

raid, 51, 62, 79, 85, 98, 99, 100, 101, 125, 126, 153, 158, 193, 195, 200, 201
Ramona, 21, 60, 175
Ramona Park, 60, 175
Ramona Park Hotel, 60, 175
Ravinia Festival, 308
RCA, 218
Reading, 16, 20, 31, 37, 38, 40, 44
Reed Landis, 17, 59
Reinoehl, 273
rhythm and blues, 149
Richard Berry, 257
Rick Wiles, 235
Rickenbacker Electro Stringed Instrument Company, 215
Roaring Brook, 33
Roaring Twenties, 42, 47, 214
rock and roll, 149, 232, 238, 254
Rol-A-Top, 153, 154, 156
roulette, 126, 153, 186, 193, 195
Roy Orbison, 232, 275, 296
Russia, 16, 20, 28, 29, 30, 34
Sam, 52, 53, 54, 55, 75, 143, 145, 197, 198, 254
Sam the Sham, 275
San Francisco, 285
Schwendner, 16, 20, 31, 34, 36, 37, 38, 39, 47, 51, 179
Secret Service, 55, 179
Shangri-Las, 254, 262, 263
sheriff, 79
Shillings, 272
Sisters of Christian Charity, 39
Skater, 33
Slim, 16, 20, 21, 25, 37, 46, 47, 48, 49, 51, 52, 55, 56, 59, 61, 70, 73, 78, 79, 81, 84, 87, 98, 99, 105, 117, 123, 126, 128, 135, 140, 142, 143, 145, 150, 153, 156, 171, 175, 176, 179, 183, 186, 190, 192, 195, 197, 198, 205, 226, 232, 233, 235, 251, 253, 274, 305, 312, 317
slot machines, 126, 153, 154, 194, 195
Smokey Robinson, 224, 226, 232, 238, 297, 303, 304

Sonje Henie, 145, 146
Sony, 221
Soviet, 229
Soviet Union, 229
Spanish Flu, 16, 40
speedboats, 176
St. Louis, 51, 59
St. Paul's Church, 39
staff, 39, 98, 126, 150, 167, 170, 171, 175
State Police, 190, 201, 225
steel, 81, 82, 83, 84, 85, 89, 97, 99, 117, 139, 186, 319
Stevie Wonder, 234, 297
Stock Market crash, 20
submachine gun, 49
Supremes, 234, 256, 264, 265, 298
swing, 42, 148, 149
Swing, 147, 148
Tamla Records, 224, 293, 297
Tammy Records, 224
Temperance, 27, 339
Temple Malleable Iron and Steel Company, 39
Temptations, 234, 298
tenements, 27, 30, 32
Texas, 296
the Great Northern Railroad, 59
The Pharaohs, 275
THEM, 282, 283
Tigers, 46, 47
Todd Storz, 219
Top 40, 244
transistor, 220, 221, 222, 226
transistor radio, 220, 221, 222
Tsar Alexander III, 28
tunnel, 51, 71, 74, 81, 84, 89, 98, 99, 100, 101, 102, 103, 105, 108, 114, 117, 124, 125, 143, 153, 158, 189, 254
tunnels, 15, 16, 17, 26, 50, 79, 81, 97, 98, 99, 100, 101, 102, 107, 114, 117, 126, 143, 177, 312, 317
TV, 220, 222
U.S. Fair Labor Standards Act, 42
U.S.S.R., 229

Union Depot, 42, 43
Vatel Club, 171
ventilation, 97, 98
Victor Lustig, 55
Vietnam, 227, 239
vinyl, 218, 219
Vivian Welch, 55, 201
waiters, 135, 149, 150
walkie-talkie, 189
Washington, D.C., 293

Watling, 153, 154, 155, 156
Watling Manufacturing Company, 153
Wertheimer, 60
whiskey, 25, 27, 163, 175, 176, 179, 339
White Sulphur Springs, 192, 193, 194
Wiles, 5, 309
Wilson, 211, 223, 224, 265, 303
Wolfman Jack, 220
World War I, 13, 17, 205
World War II, 15, 206

Notes

[1] 18th Amendment, Section 1: "After one year from the ratification of this article the manufacture, sale, or transportation of intoxicating liquors within, the importation thereof into, or the exportation thereof from the United States and all territory subject to the jurisdiction thereof for beverage purposes is hereby prohibited."

[2] Quoted in Barbara Tuchman, Practicing History: Selected Essays, Random House: 1981.

[3] Tuchman, Barbara. "In Search of History" in Practicing History: Selected Essays, Random House: 1981.

[4] https://patents.google.com/patent/US174794

[5] Monroe Engineering, Rochester Hills, Michigan, "A Short History of Casters," January 5, 2021. https://monroeengineering.com/blog/a-short-history-of-casters/ This section of the prologue is heavily indebted to this history.

[6] Charles H, Patrick; Durham, NC (1952). Alcohol, Culture, and Society. Duke University Press (reprint edition by AMS Press, New York, 1970). pp. 26–27. ISBN 9780404049065.

[7] Kahn, Jeffry P. (15 March 2013). "How Beer Gave Us Civilization". The New York Times. Quoted from Wikipedia.

[8] Centers for Disease Control. A Century of U.S. Water Chlorination and Treatment: One of the Ten Greatest Public Health Achievements of the 20th Century. Morb Mortal Wkly Rep. 1999;48 (29):621-9. https://www.cdc.gov/mmwr/preview/mmwrhtml/mm4829a1.htm

[9] In 1914 the U.S. Public Health Service (PHS) published a set of drinking water standards, pursuant to existing federal authority to regulate interstate commerce, and in response to the 1893 Interstate Quarantine Act. United States. "An act granting additional quarantine powers and imposing additional duties upon the Marine-Hospital Service." (Commonly known as the "Interstate Quarantine Act of 1893.") 27 Stat. 449-452 52nd Congress, 2nd session, Chapter 114. February 15, 1893.

[10] David Von Drehle (May 24, 2010). "The Demon Drink". Time. New York. p. 56. Archived from the original on May 15, 2010.

[11] Rush judged the excessive use of alcohol injurious to physical and psychological health. Influenced by Rush's Inquiry, about 200 farmers in a Connecticut community formed a temperance association in 1789 to ban the making of whiskey.
https://en.wikipedia.org/wiki/Temperance_movement_in_the_United_States

[12] https://en.wikipedia.org/wiki/Prohibition_Park#/media/File:National_Prohibition_Park,_Staten_Island,_N.Y._NYPL_5376736.jpg This image is available from the New York Public Library's Digital Library under the digital ID 5376736

[13] Lewin, Rhoda G. (1979). "Stereotype and reality in the Jewish immigrant experience in Minneapolis" (PDF). Minnesota History. 46 (7): 259. Archived (PDF) from the original on July 21, 2020. Retrieved

January 20, 2017.

[14] https://reimaginingmigration.org/pogroms-and-russian-jewish-immigrants Cowen's report on the Kalarash pogrom in its entirety: https://www.docsteach.org/documents/document/kalarash-pogrom

[15] https://en.wikipedia.org/wiki/Catholic_Church_in_Germany

[16] Diner, Hasia R.. "German Immigrant Period in the United States." Shalvi/Hyman Encyclopedia of Jewish Women. 31 December 1999. Jewish Women's Archive. (Viewed on November 10, 2021) https://jwa.org/encyclopedia/article/german-immigrant-period-in-united-states

[17] Ciwek, Sarah (January 27, 2014). "The Middle Class Took Off 100 Years Ago ... Thanks To Henry Ford?". NRP.org. Retrieved July 29, 2021. https://en.wikipedia.org/wiki/Henry_Ford

[18] http://www.michiganrailroads.com/railroads-in-history/461-g-h/3478-grand-rapids-indiana-railroad

[19] Paul R. Kavieff, The Purple Gang: Organized Crime in Detroit 1910 – 1945. Barricade Books, 2000. Page 69. ISBN 1-56980-494-X (pb)

[20] Rockaway, Robert A. "The Notorious Purple Gang: Detroit's All-Jewish Prohibition Era Mob." Shofar, vol. 20, no. 1, Purdue University Press, 2001, pp. 113–30, http://www.jstor.org/stable/42944836
[21] Idem.

[22] Rockaway, op. cit., page 122.

[23] U.S. Patent and Trademark Office
https://pdfpiw.uspto.gov/.piw?PageNum=0&idkey=NONE&SectionNum=3&HomeUrl=&docid=0864806

[24] Wiles, Rick, Freedom of Information Act request, received back on May 13, 2014. The link of Al Gerhardt with Allah Schwendner is made by the Social Security number 367-14-1835 being assigned to both those names. The Social Security application of Allah Schwendner references Club Manitou and Harbor Springs, and so is not a Social Security Administration clerical error. Copy in the files of Judith Landis.

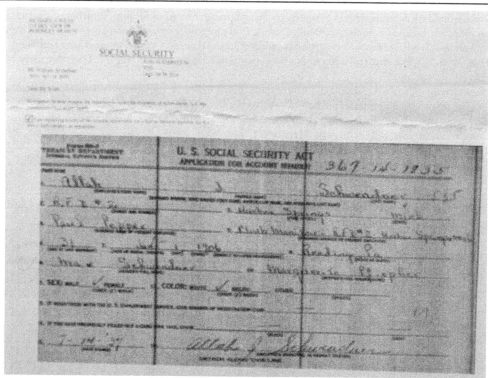

Social Security records for 367-14-1835.

[25] https://www.ancestry.com/genealogy/records/max-schwendner-24-5qpwz2

[26] In the U.S. Census of 1910 (and 1920) Max reports his year of immigration as 1877.

See Year: 1910; Census Place: Reading Ward 15, Berks, Pennsylvania; Roll: T624_1315; Page: 2B; Enumeration District: 0102; FHL microfilm: 1375328 Source Information Ancestry.com. 1910 United States Federal Census [database on-line]. Lehi, UT, USA: Ancestry.com Operations Inc, 2006. Original data: Thirteenth Census of the United States, 1910 (NARA microfilm publication T624, 1,178 rolls). Records of the Bureau of the Census, Record Group 29. National Archives, Washington, D.C. For details on the contents of the film numbers, visit the following NARA web page: NARA.

This earlier date accords with the August 9, 1892 marriage record of St. John's Lutheran Church in Reading, PA. Historical Society of Pennsylvania; Philadelphia, Pennsylvania; Historic Pennsylvania Church and Town Records; Reel: 577 Source Information Ancestry.com. Pennsylvania and New Jersey, U.S., Church and Town Records, 1669-2013 [database on-line]. Lehi, UT, USA: Ancestry.com Operations, Inc., 2011.
Original data: Historic Pennsylvania Church and Town Records. Philadelphia, Pennsylvania: Historical Society of Pennsylvania.
Methodist Church Records. Valley Forge, Pennsylvania: Eastern Pennsylvania United Methodist Church Commission on Archives and History.

There is a ship's manifest for the year 1900, but does not list any family members. Perhaps Max made a business or personal trip back to Germany.

Staatsarchiv Hamburg; Hamburg, Deutschland; Hamburger Passagierlisten; Volume: 373-7 I, VIII A 1 Band 114; Page: 2204; Microfilm No.: K_1767

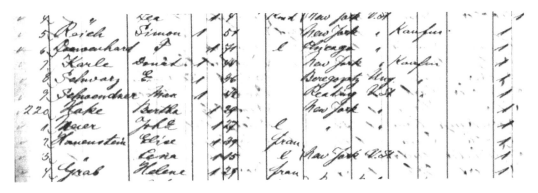

Source Information: Staatsarchiv Hamburg. Hamburg Passenger Lists, 1850-1934 [database on-line]. Provo, UT, USA: Ancestry.com Operations, Inc., 2008. Original data: Staatsarchiv Hamburg, Bestand: 373-7 I, VIII (Auswanderungsamt I). Mikrofilmrollen K 1701 - K 2008, S 17363 - S 17383, 13116 - 13183.

[27] Max's death in Reading, Pennsylvania, means he returned there. It may well have been because of troubles his children created in Detroit. Reading may have been safe from the Purple Gang and those seeking to level scores with it.

[28] Pennsylvania Historic and Museum Commission; Harrisburg, PA; Pennsylvania (State). Death Certificates, 1906-1968; Certificate Number Range: 030001-033000. Source Information Ancestry.com. Pennsylvania, U.S., Death Certificates, 1906-1968 [database on-line]. Lehi, UT, USA: Ancestry.com Operations, Inc., 2014. Original data: Pennsylvania (State). Death certificates, 1906–1968. Series 11.90 (1,905 cartons). Records of the Pennsylvania Department of Health, Record Group 11. Pennsylvania Historical and Museum Commission, Harrisburg, Pennsylvania.

[Certificate of Death — Commonwealth of Pennsylvania, Department of Health, Bureau of Vital Statistics. File No. 30292. Registration District No. 233. Primary Registration District No. 49. Registered No. 407. County of Berks, City of Reading, 824 N. Front St., 15 Ward. Full Name: Max Schwendner. Sex: Male. Color or Race: White. Married. Husband of Marguerite Schwendner. Date of Birth: April 11, 1854. Age: 69 years, 10 months, 23 days. Occupation: Garage Owner. Date of Death: March 4, 1924, at 6:30 a.m. Cause of Death: acute cardiac dilatation.]

[29] Reading Times, March 5, 1924, page 2.

[30] https://www.garagejournal.com/forum/threads/the-ancient-and-independent-order-of-oddfellows-adjustables-that-is.435464/page-4#post-9274738

Comments on thread:

"There is a set screw on the back of the (lower) dynamic jaw, I guess to allow adjustment of fit to the fine ridges on the shank. No branding I could see, which seemed strange for such an original design."

"The earlier "PAT APL" state of the Schwendner nut wrench. [https://www.datamp.org/patents/displayPatent.php?number=864806&typeCode=0 } is the patent. The Schwendner wrenches are not all that common. The pipe wrench version of this patent is visually interesting because of the curved, textured handle."

[31] Ancestry.com. Philadelphia, Pennsylvania, U.S., Marriage Index, 1885-1951 [database on-line]. Provo, UT, USA: Ancestry.com Operations, Inc., 2011. Original data: Pennsylvania, Philadelphia Marriage Index, 1885–1951." Index. FamilySearch, Salt Lake City, Utah, 2009. Philadelphia County Pennsylvania Clerk of the Orphans' Court. "Pennsylvania, Philadelphia marriage license index, 1885-1951." Clerk of the Orphans' Court, Philadelphia, Pennsylvania.

[32] Pennsylvania Historical and Museum Commission; Harrisburg, Pennsylvania; Pennsylvania (State). Birth certificates, 1906–1913; Box Number: 2; Certificate Number Range: 003001-006000

Source Information
Ancestry.com. Pennsylvania, U.S., Birth Certificates, 1906-1913 [database on-line]. Lehi, UT, USA: Ancestry.com Operations, Inc., 2015.

Original data: Pennsylvania (State). Birth certificates, 1906–1913. Series 11.89 (50 cartons). Records of the Pennsylvania Department of Health, Record Group 11. Pennsylvania Historical and Museum Commission, Harrisburg, Pennsylvania.

[33] Reading Times, November 20, 1930, page 18.

[34] Reading Times, March 5, 1924, page 2.

[35] However, Frederick was baptized at St. John's Lutheran Church in Reading on July 22, 1895. It may well be that his mother, Emilie, was Lutheran and so the family leaned Protestant. However, after her death, the Catholic Church held sway.

[36] Reading Times, August 28, 1920, page 16.

37 https://goreadingberks.com/history-of-st-pauls-church/

38 United States Bureau of the Census figures presented in Child Welfare Magazine, Volume VIII, September, 1918 to August, 1919, Lancaster, Pennsylvania: Press of The New Era Printing Company, page 298.

39 http://www.edwardianpromenade.com/health-2/living-with-enza-the-spanish-flu-pandemic-1918-1919/

40 https://www.psea.org/about-psea/mission--history/psea-a-timeline/

41 Eisenberg, Martin Jay, "Compulsory attendance legislation in America, 1870 to 1915" (1988). Dissertations available from ProQuest. AAI8824730.
https://repository.upenn.edu/dissertations/AAI8824730

42 Davis, Ann, "Report of the Vocational Bureau in Chicago" in Child Welfare Magazine, Volume VIII, September, 1918 to August, 1919, Lancaster, Pennsylvania: Press of The New Era Printing Company, page 6.

43 "{M}any owners of the Model T didn't have to just learn how to drive it, but also how to repair it out on the road, serving as their own mechanics when a part broke or a tire popped when bounding down the lane." Doran, Nick, "We Learn How to Drive a Model T and Somehow Live to Tell about It"
https://performance.ford.com/enthusiasts/newsroom/2018/11/drive-a-ford-model-t.html

44 https://www.ushistory.org/Us/46a.asp Estimate based on registrations of 8 million in 1920.

45 https://worldhistory.us/american-history/cars-in-the-1920s-the-early-automobile-industry.php

46 Gross, Daniel, "Greatest Business Stories of All Time" Forbes, at
https://www.wiley.com/legacy/products/subject/business/forbes/ford.html

47 https://www.railserve.com/stats_records/railroad_route_miles.html

48 Michigan Department of Transportation, Michigan's Railroad History: 1825-2014, pdf at
https://www.michigan.gov/documents/mdot/Michigan_Railroad_History_506899_7.pdf referenced at http://www.michiganrailroads.com/timeline/474-1920-1929/3647-timeline-1920

49 Detroit Free Press, January 12, 1919, page 4.

50 https://www.worldwar1centennial.org/index.php/michigan-in-ww1-articles/1796-the-story-of-the-126th-infantry-regiment.html

> After the relief from the line here the Regiment was ordered back for a rest, and the days from September 10 to September 20 [1918] were spent at Joinville, France, out of the battle area. This was the only real rest the Regiment received from May to November; the balance of the time it was under fire. On September 20 the Regiment enbussed at Joinville for the Argonne-Meuse front. After being carried as far as trucks could go and then hiking, the Regiment entered the front line on September 30 before

the Kriemhilde Stellung (Kriemhilde Stellung) near Romagne-sons-Montfancon.

In a series of desperate attacks during the next three weeks the Division succeeded in completely breaking the German line and penetrating the enemy position to a depth of 8 1/2 kilometers.

For 20 consecutive days the Division remained in the front line, continually fighting, and the 126th during all of this time was either in the front or support lines. It is a record for endurance that can be equaled by very few outfits. (Kriemhilde Stellung) was the Cote' Dann Marie, which hill was directly to the front of the sector occupied by the 126th. Officers and men from this regiment in a daring daylight attack succeeded in taking this formidable position, and it was then the Division, headed by the 126th, first penetrated this strongly fortified line of resistance.

During these 20 consecutive days of fighting the Division was opposed by 11 German Divisions, including the 5th Prussian Guards, the 3rd Prussian Guards, and the 28th Division, known as the "Kaiser's Own." During this long period in the line the sector on our right was occupied by the 79th, 3rd, 5th U.S. Divisions and the sector on our left by the 91st, 1st and 42nd Divisions. The 32nd Division losses during this action were as follows:

Killed, 39 officers and 860 men; severely wounded, 32 officers and 1,176 men; slightly wounded, 83 officers and 2,784 men; gassed, 17 officers and 53 men; missing 9 officers and 140 men; died of wounds, 10 officers and 200 men; total loss from all causes 5,950.

The Regiment was moved back to the Bois de Montfancon on October 21 for a period in which to reorganize and rest up. The woods at the time was a sea of mud and under shell fire from the east of the Nunse. It is doubtful if anyone received any rest, but owing to a lack of troops it was not possible to move us back to a real rest area. About the 1st of November we again moved up and took reserve position near Aincreville. It was here on November 7 that Colonel Westnedge left us to go to the hospital. For several days the doctor and other officers had been urging him to go back but he had steadily refused. He had tonsilitis (Tonsillitis), which developed into quinsy, and at last he was made to see that he was in serious condition. This was the last sight any of us at headquarters had of our beloved Colonel and it was some six weeks after his death before we learned of it.

On the afternoon of the same day on which the Colonel left us, under the command of Lieutenant Colonel Meyer, the regiment crossed the Meuse River at Dun-sur-Meuse and entered the Dun-sur-Meuse bridgehead, where we were in support position on November 11 when the Armistice was signed.

The total Division losses during this period of five days, from all causes, was 687 men.

During our eight months in France we had spent six months under fire with but 10 days in a rest area. The Regiment had fought on five fronts, in three major offensives- Aisne-Marne, Oise-Aisne, and Meuse-Argonne. The Division had losses of 14,000 men killed, wounded and missing in action; had captured 2,000 rifles, 200 machine guns, 100 pieces of artillery, and thousands of rounds of ammunitions of all kinds; had gained 380 kilometers in four attacks and repulsed without loss of ground, every counter attack of the enemy; were the first American troops to set foot on German soil in Alsace; captured Fismes in Aisne-Marne offensive; fought as the only American unit in General Mangin's famous 10th French Army in Oise-Aisne offensive; twice in the line of Argonne-Meuse offensive, fighting continuously for 20 days and penetrating the Kreimhilde Stellung (Kriemhilde Stellung); in action when the Armistice was signed.

On November 17, as a part of the 3rd Army, the Division started its march to Germany. After crossing the Sauer River into German territory on December 1, 1918.

On December 13 the Division crossed the Rhine River after marching 300 kilometers in winter weather. It was a hike such as would try the strongest heart. It is an actual fact that it was sheer American grit that carried the average soldier through it. Many a man tramped along with his bare feet leaving blood-stains on the snow. The Army did all in its power to keep up with supplies, but at times it simply could not be done.

The 126th Infantry entered the front line of the Coblenz bridge-head and held it until relieved by the 125th Infantry, which Regiment held it until the Division was relieved to return to the States.

The troops of the Division held the center sector between the 1st Division on the right and the 2nd Division on the left.

It is significant that the 32nd was the only former National Guard Division to cross the Rhiine, and it was an honor which the Regiment fully appreciated.

[51] The National Archives at College Park; College Park, Maryland; Record Group Title: Records of the Office of the Quartermaster General, 1774-1985; Record Group Number: 92; Roll or Box Number: 134. Source Information Ancestry.com. U.S., Army Transport Service Arriving and Departing Passenger Lists, 1910-1939 [database on-line]. Lehi, UT, USA: Ancestry.com Operations, Inc., 2016. Original data: Lists of Incoming Passengers, 1917-1938. Textual records. 360 Boxes. NAI: 6234465. Records of the Office of the Quartermaster General, 1774-1985, Record Group 92. The National Archives at College Park, Maryland. Lists of Outgoing Passengers, 1917-1938. Textual records. 255 Boxes. NAI: 6234477. Records of the Office of the Quartermaster General, 1774-1985, Record Group 92. The National Archives at College Park, Maryland.

[52] Walter P. Reuther Library, Wayne State University, "Subject Focus: the Purple Gang", July 30, 2012. http://reuther.wayne.edu/node/8731

[53] Detroit Free Press, January 29, 1911, page 1.

[54] Edwin, two years older than Allah, was listed as 5'8" and 100 lbs. on his draft card. However, this seems an impossibly light weight. It may well have been that the weight listed was to avoid being drafted to fight his parents' homeland.

[55] Knapp, Robert. Gangsters Up North: Mobsters, Mafia, and Racketeers in Michigan's Vacationlands. 2020: Cliophile Press.Kindle Edition, page 167.

56 https://fornology.blogspot.com/2018/03/the-rise-and-fall-of-detroits-purple.html

57 Much of this story is told in Kavieff, op. cit., location 245 in the Kindle edition.

58 Knapp, op. cit., page 166.

59 Nicole Jankowski, "Detroit Returns to its Prohibition-Era Whiskeytown Roots and Finds New Life," November 30, 2016, National Public Radio. https://www.npr.org/sections/thesalt/2016/11/30/503617821/detroit-returns-to-its-prohibition-era-whiskeytown-roots-and-finds-new-life

60 Nolan, Jenny, "Detroit during Prohibition: Bootlegger's dream town," February 3, 2018. The Detroit News. http://blogs.detroitnews.com/history/1999/06/14/how-prohibition-made-detroit-a-bootleggers-dream-town/ See also http://reuther.wayne.edu/node/8731

61 Christensen, Erik, "14 American Cities with Crazy Tunnel Systems," September 8, 2015.https://www.thrillist.com/travel/nation/14-american-cities-with-crazy-underground-tunnel-systems-chicago-boston-new-york
62 http://reuther.wayne.edu/node/8251

63 Port Huron Times-Herald, August 28, 1925, page 7 referenced in Knapp, op. cit., page 166.

64 Knapp, op. cit., page 167.

65 Richard Wiles quoted in Kristi Kates, "Rockin' and Rollin' in Harbor Springs", May 27, 2017. https://www.northernexpress.com/news/feature/rockin-and-rollin-in-harbor-springs/

66 Kavieff, op. cit., Chapter 3, location 462 in Kindle edition.

67 Nolan, op. cit.

68 Newton, Michael, <u>Mr. Mob: The Life and Crimes of Moe Dalitz</u>. 2009: McFarland & Co. Page 11.
69 FBI file, notes from October 12, 1932. Freedom of Information Act file. Purple Gang (aka Sugar House Gang)02.pdf location 44/97. https://archive.org/details/PurpleGangAKASugarHouseGang/Purple%20Gang%20%28aka%20Sugar%20House%20Gang%29%2002/page/n43/mode/2up

70 Entry from Sam Bernstein, grandson of Sam "Fatty" Bernstein, on December 25, 2002 at https://www.albionmich.com/purplegang/index.html

71 http://reuther.wayne.edu/node/13044

72 A birthdate of 12/22/1902 is gathered from a U.S. Naturalization Record for a "Sam Burns *Sam Bernstein" in Detroit. This Sam died in November of 1958 of, likely, natural causes. The "older" Sam is inferred from a World War II draft card issued to a Sam Bernstein in 1942 listing his age as 44 and born on 10/1/1897, height 5'10", weight 200 lbs., born in Russia. This sounds like the Sam of the Purple Gang. A World War I draft record has a Sam Bernstein born 10/1/1898 but with a medium build. This

may be the Sam of the World War II registration based on the similarity of birthdates, despite the exactly one year difference. Sam was perhaps gaining weight over the years. All records were retrieved from ancestry.com.

[73] Idem.

[74] Kavieff, op. cit., Chapter 4, location 579 in Kindle edition.

[75] https://www.secretservice.gov/about/history

[76] New York Times, March 3, 1920, "Counterfeiting has doubled." https://timesmachine.nytimes.com/timesmachine/1920/03/03/118265308.html?pageNumber=2

[77] https://en.wikipedia.org/wiki/Victor_Lustig Lustig also sold the Eiffel Tower twice for scrap metal, in 1925 and 1926.

[78] Nolan, op. cit., page 172.

[79] Wendy Morris received the pictures of Club Manitou from Walt Baker who, in turn, had received them from the widow of Al Gerhart

[80] Powers, Perry F., "A History of Northern Michigan", 1912, quoted in Alan Teelander, Early History of Harbor Springs, Michigan, February 24, 2011. https://www.imagesofmichigan.com/early-history-of-harbor-springs-michigan

[81] Powers, op. cit.

[82] https://greatlakesecho.org/2020/07/09/mobsters-in-the-vacationlands/

[83] https://janeshistorynook.blogspot.com/2013/03/miami-beach-mert-wertheimer-gambling-and.html?m=1

[84] Judith Landis notes.

[85] Connor, Richard, "Rum Runners to Cocaine Cowboys: Barry Seal and the Legacy of Aerial Smuggling," Smithsonian National Air and Space Museum, https://airandspace.si.edu/stories/editorial/barry-seal-legacy-aerial-smuggling

[86] Quoted by Freedman, Eric, "Mobsters in the Vacationlands", https://greatlakesecho.org/2020/07/09/mobsters-in-the-vacationlands/

[87] https://iwrhs.org/history/introduction/

The Inland Route known to the Indians and fur traders, also included Round Lake (near Lake Michigan), and a small stream from Round Lake to Crooked Lake called Iduna Creek. The Inland Route was a highly desirable passage, due to the naturally protected inland waters and eliminating the need to take the treacherous journey around Waugoshance Point on lake Michigan. Therefore, navigation of the Great Lakes waters between, Petoskey and the mouth of the Cheboygan River, could be eliminated by taking the Inland Route.

In 1874, Mr. Frank Sammons of Cheboygan conceived the idea of transporting the mail via the Inland Waterway from Cheboygan to a point on the Crooked River (Alanson) where it could be taken via the State Road to Petoskey, then, to the railroad. In order to make his plan work, Mr. Sammons needed to remove sediment from the mouth of the Indian River at Burt Lake. He set out with a team of horses, two white men, and two Indians, then proceeded to plough and scrape the sand bar wide enough for the tug Maud Sammons (short name Maude S) to enter Burt lake with a full load of supplies and mail for the lumber camps established along the shores.

In 1876, the Bureau of Swamp Lands made an appropriation of $20,000 for the dredging of the Crooked River. Dredging began in June, later that same year, a tug piloted by Captain Andrews of Petoskey made the full trip from Conway to Cheboygan in 10.5 hours. Prior to the establishment of the railroads around the Inland Route, the only means to transport logs and finished products in the area was by using tugs between Conway and Cheboygan. With the advent of the railroads, the Inland Waterway went into a decline.

As tourists began to discover the attractions of the Inland Route, it became one of the busiest inland waterways in the country. At one point, up to 32 boats a day were traveling the route with tours lasting 2-3 hours up to an overnight stay at various hotels. The types of boats providing tours were; Side Wheelers, Paddle Wheelers, Naphtha Launches, and Steam Boats.

The first steamer on the Inland Water Route that did not require a paddle-wheel for propulsion was the Irene. Mr. Hamill who later operated the Steamer Topinabee, owned the Irene. The Irene's boiler operated on coal and wood. The Irene operated on the Inland Water Route from 1884 until 1915 hauling freight and passengers and was piloted by Capt. Fields for most of its existence. When taking passengers, a souvenir booklet was given as a reminder, there were at least two different types.

In 1880, the Inland Navigation Company was organized by Mr. Charles R. Smith of Cheboygan and three boats were running until 1883. Two prominent boats for the Inland Navigation Company were the side wheelers "City of Cheboygan" and the Northern Belle". These two boats would make trips from Conway to the Mullet Lake House. People wanting to make the trip to "The Island of Mackinac", would board the "Propeller Mary" to continue their journey. Many boats traveled the river at the time, as the river proved to be the best means of transportation. Mr. Frank Joslin better known as Captain Joslin first ran the Ida May a steamer tug that hauled logs. On Feb 7 1887 he had purchased this steamer from Jane Dagwell for $259. In 1893 Capt. Joslin piloted a new boat, the Oden, on her first trip down the river. This vessel was built expressly for the Inland Route.

In 1903 a steamboat traveled daily from Oden to Cheboygan during the navigation season.

While touring Conway, Oden, Ponshewaing, were attractions themselves, the most interesting part of the journey was the cruise down the Crooked River. Alanson from 1882 until 1901 had a 14 foot high wooden bridge known as the "High Bridge". At this point on the river, many steamers had to hinge back their smokestack to pass under the bridge. The Steamer Topinabee being a double decked steamer had to hinge back its Pilot House, and the smoke-stack was a telescoping design. In 1901 a Swing Bridge: replaced the High Bridge. From 1901 until the mid 1960's the swing bridge that had to be opened via a manual key placed into a gearing system. In the mid 1960's a hydraulic system was installed to actuate the gearing. The Topinabee was seventy two feet long and had a twelve feet beam providing for a very minimal clearance at the bridge opening, thus very slow accurate navigation was needed. The second bridge location across the Crooked River in Alanson is at the present day site of the M68 bridge. In 1903 a drawbridge was installed by the Grand Rapids Bridge Co. Careful navigation was also need at this bridge too. In 1937 the drawbridge was replaced by a cement bridge similar to the bridge of today. Further down river were many tight narrow bends in the river. Of particular interest were two corners called "Devils Elbow" and "Horse Shoe Bend". While touring Conway, Oden, Ponshewaing, were attractions themselves, the most interesting part of the journey was the cruise down the Crooked River. Alanson from 1882 until 1901 had a 14 foot high wooden bridge known as the "High Bridge". At this point on the river, many steamers had to hinge back their smokestack to pass under the bridge. The Steamer Topinabee being a double decked steamer had to hinge back its Pilot House, and the smoke-stack was a telescoping design. In 1901 a Swing Bridge: replaced the High Bridge. From 1901 until the mid 1960's the swing bridge that had to be opened via a manual key placed into a gearing system. In the mid 1960's a hydraulic system was installed to actuate the gearing. The Topinabee was seventy two feet long and had a twelve feet beam providing for a very minimal clearance at the bridge opening, thus very slow accurate navigation was needed. The second bridge location across the Crooked River in Alanson is at the present day site of the M68 bridge. In 1903 a drawbridge was installed by the Grand Rapids Bridge Co. Careful navigation was also need at this bridge too. In 1937 the drawbridge was replaced by a cement bridge similar to the bridge of today. Further down river were many tight narrow bends in the river. Of particular interest were two corners called "Devils Elbow" and "Horse Shoe Bend".

From 1876 until 1920, nearly 100 commercial water craft were in business on the Inland Waterway. The water craft included: Steam Tug Boats, Side-wheel Steamers, Stern Paddlewheel Steamers, Propeller driven Steamers, Naphtha Steamers, and Gas powered water craft.. Tug boats were primarily used to facilitate the transporting of supplies and logs. The steamers were primarily used for the transport of people to various places along the Inland Route. Some steamers were owned by a particular resort. Examples include: the Columbus Maid (1893) was operated by the Columbus Beach association (Indian River), the Argonaut Belle (1898) and The Pittsburg (1896-1905) were operated by the Argonaut Club (Burt Lake). The Buckeye Belle a resort steamship ran from 1905-1915 and was owned by the Dodge Resort.

[88] Harbor Springs: A Collection of Historical Sketches referenced in Petoskey News Review, December 17, 1987, page 2

[89] 1926 speakeasy list in Chicago

[Image of a vintage drink menu showing Champagnes, Sparkling Burgundy, Liqueurs and Cordials, Ports and Sherries, Cocktails (Short Drinks), and Long Drinks with prices]

[90] U.S. Bureau of Labor Statistics CPI inflation calculator.
https://www.bls.gov/data/inflation_calculator.htm

[91] July 2017 revenue report from the Nevada Gaming Control Board.
https://www.winkslots.com/blog/how-much-money-slot-machine-makes In that month, there were 38,434 slot machines in operation at the Strip's 40 locations. They earned $269,527,000.

[92] Rauch, William (November 1981). "Recalling Harbor Springs in the Era of Prohibition and Gambling". Harbor Light News.

[93] https://prohibition.themobmuseum.org/the-history/the-prohibition-underworld/bootleggers-and-bathtub-gin/

[94] https://northernmichmashpreserve.weebly.com/winter-sports-parks.html

[95] Rauch, op. cit. "There seems to have been very little difficulty obtaining the cooperation of local authorities. The slots, poker, and bootlegging were viewed as relatively harmless pastimes which might introduce some revenues into the community. The State Police kept their hands off Harbor Springs for these two decades [1920s and 30s]."

[96] Northern Express, "Booze Flowed Freely Through", May 24, 2015.
https://www.northernexpress.com/news/feature/article-6925-booze-flowed-freely-through/

[97] Harbor Springs: A Collection of Historical Sketches referenced in Petoskey News Review,

December 17, 1987, page 1.

⁹⁸ The jail door is now in possession of the Harbor Springs Area Historical Society. The door was removed by Judy Landis because it impeded her access to bicycles stored in the basement.

⁹⁹ Hanging doors were not a new thing. One was unearthed in Pompeii, buried under 20-30' of ash and pumice in AD 79 when Mt. Vesuvius erupted.

Sliding door from Pompeii.

¹⁰⁰ In a late 2021 phone conversation with Wendy Morris, source of many of the photos in this book, she mentioned that a young woman had crawled several times from the basement to the garage. Thus, the transit could be made if not easily.

¹⁰¹ With the exception of a note in Rauch, op. cit. "Gerhart denies there were ever any tunnels save for the one from the old building to the new building. He claims the mysterious underground rooms were all just part of the kitchen facilities." Apparently, Slim had a poor memory. The tunnel starting at the southeast corner of the basement was on the opposite side of the basement from the kitchen, and led away from the kitchen. And why the concrete doors? Was wood in short supply?

However, Rauch is very likely correct that the lengths of the tunnels were gradually exaggerated. That a tunnel would extend all the way to the Ramona Park Casino would seem such a stretch of the imagination: Club Manitou and its tunnels were built several years before Slim acquired the Ramona. However, more practical lengths are not out of the question. Clearly, the north tunnel stretched the short distance to the garage. The east tunnel may have terminated somewhere near the lawn's retaining wall and near the road. That investigation is underway by the author.

Soil probing started March 19, 2022. A report from Lake Superior State University's geology department on August 18, 2023, confirmed the existence of one escape tunnel, but not the East tunnel. This may have been because the tunnel collapsed, was filled in, or is too deep to show up on the sonar calibrated to 1-3 meters. The report is copied verbatim below:

Ground Penetrating Radar Investigation of Possible Prohibition Era Tunnels at Club Manitou

Stephanie Georgevich, Dr. Paul Kelso   Lake Superior State University Geology Program

Introduction

Club Manitou in Harbor Springs, Michigan (Figure 1) was a legal nightclub that was in business from the 1920s to 1950s. During the 1920s, the basement of the same property was used to run a hidden speakeasy during Prohibition. According to stories told by patrons at the time, tunnels were built so workers and alcohol could be moved discretely to and from the basement. The one tunnel still accessible today was used to move supplies into the kitchen of the nightclub from a storage building. This and other rumored tunnels could also be used if the establishment was raided, and gang members and patrons needed to escape. Club Manitou stands today as a residential property. The objective of this study was to locate any tunnels leading away from the house.

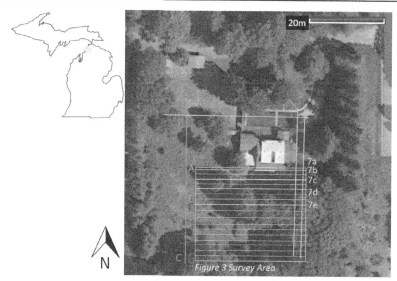

Figure 1: Map of the Club Manitou property in Harbor Springs, MI. After preliminary scans, it was determined that the south side of the house was the main area of interest. The area outlined in purple is shown in Figure 3. Grey lines are all data collected. Green and red lines more closely examined in Figures 4 and 5. Blue line more closely examined in Figure 6. Yellow lines are more closely examined in Figure 7.

Methodology:

A ground penetrating radar (GPR) study was conducted at the Club Manitou property (Figures 1 and 2) to investigate the possibility of other tunnels. Our pilot study employed 100MHz and 250MHz antennas and determined that the 250MHz antenna had the clearest reflections at the greatest depth.

Figure 2: LSSU geology students Stephanie Georgevich and Travis Smith collecting GPR data at the former Club Manitou.

Thus, all data presented below was collected with the 250MHz antenna. Individual GPR profiles were collected on the north, east and west sides of the old Club Manitou. For the detailed survey area (Figure 3, area outlined in purple in Figure 1), data was collected along 17 parallel lines, with each line being 30 meters long spaced 1.5 meters apart and parallel to the south wall of Club Manitou. The GPR data was compiled in GFP edit and processed in EKKO Project.

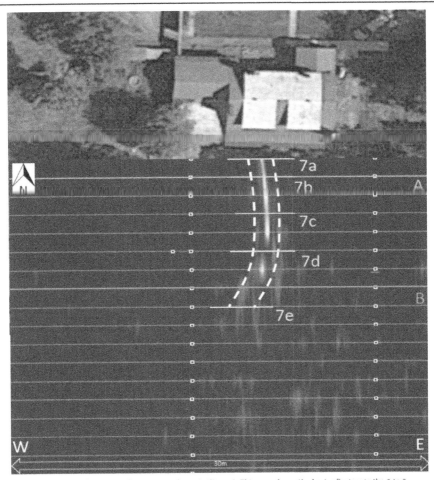

Figure 3: Map view of GPR data of survey area shown in Figure 1. This map shows the best reflectors in the 1 to 3 meter depth. Dashed yellow line showing location and direction of tunnel. The tunnel may end past Line B or continue to a depth not resolved with this GPR study. Boxes on lines are used to align and orient individual data lines. Yellow lines labeled 7a-7e show where the strongest reflections were found.

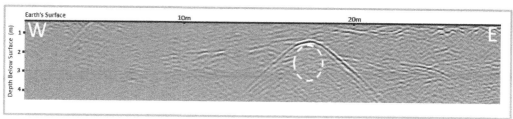

Figure 4 – Line A – Cross-sectional view. The dashed yellow line shows likely tunnel. This shows clear reflections of the tunnel leaving the house at approximately 1.25m depth.

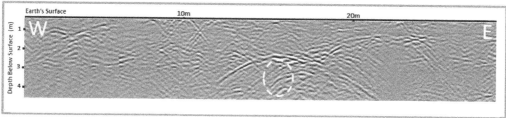

Figure 5 – Line B – Cross-sectional view. The dashed yellow line shows likely tunnel. Moving further from the house, the reflections become less pronounced and increases in depth.

Results

The lines on the south side of the house (Figure 3) show an reflection leading away from the house towards the southwest (Figure 3, 4, 5, and 7). The reflection occurs at about a depth of approximately 1.25 meters near the Club Manitou south wall (Figure 4) and increases to 2 to 2.5 meters by approximately 12 meters from Club Manitou (Figure 5). Beyond 12 meters from the wall this reflection is no longer observed possibly because the tunnel goes deeper than the observed GPR reflections or the tunnel may have collapsed or becomes gradually filled in. The lines on the north, west, and east sides of the house only show small diffraction parabolas that are probably tree roots and utility lines based on their reflection quality and depth and locations relative to know utilities and trees (Figure 6). The results of this GPR study are consistent with the stories that there was a tunnel leading from the Club Manitou speakeasy basement to the south.

Conclusion

Clear reflections in the subsurface heading away from the south side of the house are likely a prohibition era escape tunnel that leaves the basement and becomes gradually deeper the further it moves away from the house.

[103] Tim Offenhauser lives in a house to the east of Club Manitou.

[104] Struble, Chris, conversation with author on March 19, 2022 at Club Manitou grounds.

[105] Email from Beth Wemigwase of Harbor Springs Area Historic Association to authors on January 18, 2023: "We had a gentleman come in to see the exhibit today and he has a fascinating history with

the club. His name is Tim Hayner and he used to be part of the house band for Club Ponytail from roughly 1965-66. The band was called both the 'Nightwalkers' and 'The Other Kind.' He apparently at one time had a key to the old basement in Club Manitou and remembers walking the tunnels, including one where he could hear M-119 and cars driving by above him."

106 Christophe Struble email to author, November 25, 2022: "I recently had two very credible guests on a History Tour I was leading and afterwards they told me about a house near Harbor Springs they had been shown by a realtor in the '80's as potential buyers. They both recounted that they had gone down at least 5 or 6 sequential staircases that led them deeper and deeper until they figured they had to be 'at least as far down as the Harbor Springs airport. They began to get worried because of all of the water at that depth and insisted that they turn around and head back towards the 'old speakeasy basement'. When I asked where the house was located, they replied 'just off of Pleasant View [sic.] road'.".

107 Wiles, op. cit., draft copy, citing Gerhart's interview with William Rausch in the The Harbor Light, 1981.

108 Clock, Bob, "Club Manitou Opened as 'Stork Club of the North'", Petoskey News Review, March 19, 1969, page 52.

109 https://opencorporates.com/companies/us_oh/134733

110 https://www.lawrencechs.com/museum/collections/shenango-china-collection/

111 https://www.ncr.com/about/history

112 Idem.

113 https://www.ebay.com/itm/164223354484

114 Idem.

115 Petoskey News Review, December 17, 1987, page 2. "Friends remember club owner."

116 Idem. Whether Henie actually owned a mink farm is subject to debate. Neighbors Emery and Helen Chase reported that she did, while the daughter of the Omar Broder-Larsen, Amie Siekmann, who also owned a mink farm on Mink Road, reported to the authors in 2022 that she did not. It may well be that Henie was a spokesperson for the Norwegian fur interests and not an actual owner. Omar and Sonje had met in Washington D.C. in the late 1930s to represent the Norwegian fur industry at some meeting. Slim may likely have been embellishing the guest list. He had a way with stories; ask the judges he appeared before.

Henie did visit Detroit for an Ice Review in March of 1937. She may have made her way to Harbor Springs then as well for some Norge ambience. While the skiing in Michigan is modest, it was in existence from 1928 when the Petoskey Rotary Club started operation of the town tow at the Petoskey Winter Sports Park. Omar Broder-Larsen did not open his farm until the early 1940s.

117 Harker, Brian C., 1997, Early Musical Development of Louis Armstrong, 1921–1928, unpublished

PhD Dissertation, Columbia University referenced at https://en.wikipedia.org/wiki/Swing_music

[118] Idem.

[119] Shore, Michael; Dick Clark (1985). The History of American Bandstand. New York: Ballantine Books. p. 54, quoted in https://en.wikipedia.org/wiki/Jitterbug

[120] https://squiresandcorrie.com/manufacturers_watling_history.php

[121] https://retroslotsonline.blogspot.com/

[122] Vadukul, Alex, "Ghosts of New York's Glamorous Past Haunt an Empty Pub", New York Times, September 25, 2022, https://www.nytimes.com/2022/09/25/style/stork-club-closed.html

[123] Idem.

[124] Idem.

[125] https://en.wikipedia.org/wiki/Canadian_Club

[126] https://www.wpwines.com/canadian-club-whiskey-bottled-1930-driven-cork

[127] https://ip.com/blog/how-popular-inventions-came-to-life-who-invented-the-air-conditioner/

[128] "Poor Francois Vatel. His passions for perfecting a 2000-person banquet in honor of King Louis XIV led to Vatel taking his own life. After not sleeping for almost 12 nights in preparation of the party and some trouble with celebratory fireworks in a foggy sky, Vatel was so overwhelmed by news of a delay in his fish delivery that he ran into the sword given to him by the royal court. In a somewhat comical twist, immediately after Vatel's suicide, the fish delivery started rushing in. This story became infamous among aristocrats and royalty of the time."
https://www.mentalfloss.com/article/60130/8-celebrity-chefs-yesteryear

François Vatel

Killed himself over a delivery of fish

The suicide of François Vatel by E. Zier. Clejo / wikimedia / 2011 / Public Domain

[129] https://www.nytimes.com/2014/04/04/nyregion/roger-fessaguet-a-wizard-of-haute-cuisine-dies-at-82.html

[130] Anna Kinkaid, "90 Years of Excellence: The History of the American Culinary Federation." https://wearechefs.com/%ef%bb%bf90-years-of-excellence-acf-history/

[131] Rauch, William (November 1981). "Recalling Harbor Springs in the Era of Prohibition and Gambling". Harbor Light News. https://en.m.wikipedia.org/wiki/Club_Manitou_of_Harbor_Springs

[132] Doyle, Annie, "Historian: Charlevoix gambling win was significant for Ernest Hemingway," February 6, 2020. Petoskey News-Review. https://www.petoskeynews.com/story/news/local/charlevoix/2020/02/06/historian-charlevoix-gambling-win-was-significant-for-ernest-hemingway/43686059/ Ernest Hemingway parlayed his last $6 into $59 at the Colonial Club in July 1920, helping to avoid having to take a job at the cement plant where Bay Harbor is now.

[133] Rausch, op. cit.

[134] Wiles, Rick, "The Infamous Club Manitou: Northern Michigan's Favorite 'Speakeasy'" Mackinac

Journal, December 2013, page 14.

[135] Russell M. Magnaghi, "Prohibition in the Upper Peninsula," The History Press, 2017.

[136] Van Winkle, Claire, "The Grand Hotel Mackinac Island: Sagas of Ancient Native Chiefs, Frozen Shipwrecks, and Ancient Ballroom Dances," October 8, 2018. https://storiedhotels.com/hotels/the-storied-grand-hotel-mackinac-island-sagas-of-ancient-native-american-chiefs-frozen-shipwrecks-and-ancient-ballroom-dances/

[137] Van Winkle, Claire, op. cit.

[138] Russell M. Magnaghi, "Mackinaw City at the Heart of Northern Michigan Rum Running," August 31, 2018. https://www.mackinawcity.com/mackinaw-city-at-the-heart-of-northern-michigan-rum-running/

[139] Kavieff, op. cit., location 1363 of 2421.

[140] The Free Library, "Graceland: a ballroom & it's builder: one of Michigan's most famous dance halls was located near the quiet community of Lupton. Built by a man with ties to Detroit's notorious Purple Gang, the Graceland's rustic charm drew patrons from miles around until the night it went up in smoke." Retrieved Nov 28 2021 from https://www.thefreelibrary.com/Graceland%3a+a+ballroom+%26+it%27s+builder%3a+one+of+Michigan%27s+most+famous...-a0240992476

[141] Knapp, op. cit., page 172.

[142] Charlevoix Courier clipping supplied to Judith Landis by Richard Wiles.

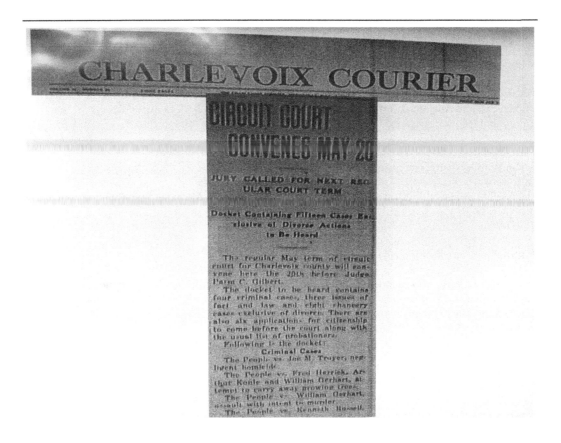

[143] Lansing State Journal, January 15, 1935, page 1 referenced in Knapp, op. cit., page 172.

[144] Wiles, op.cit., page 14.

[145] Ancestry.com. Indiana, U.S., Marriages, 1810-2001 [database on-line]. Provo, UT, USA: Ancestry.com Operations, Inc., 2014. Original data: Indiana, Marriages, 1810-2001. Salt Lake City, Utah: FamilySearch, 2013. Page 63.

[146] "U.S., School Yearbooks, 1880-2012"; School Name: Northern High School; Year: 1926. Source Information: Ancestry.com. U.S., School Yearbooks, 1900-1999 [database on-line]. Lehi, UT, USA: Ancestry.com Operations, Inc., 2010. Original data: Various school yearbooks from across the United States.

[147] https://www.thepalmersociety.org/662-2/about-the-palmer-society/alice-freeman-palmer/

[148] Kavieff, op. cit.

[149] Burke, Kathleen, "How the DC-3 Revolutionized Air Travel," Smithsonian Magazine, April 2013. https://www.smithsonianmag.com/history/how-the-dc-3-revolutionized-air-travel-5444300/

[150] https://en.wikipedia.org/wiki/Transcontinental_flight

[151] http://www.migenweb.org/emmet/military/wwii.htm

[152] https://en.wikipedia.org/wiki/Club_Manitou_of_Harbor_Springs

[153] https://polona.pl/archive?uid=115804723&cid=116099488 referenced at https://en.wikipedia.org/wiki/Walkie-talkie#cite_note-4

[154] Petoskey News-Review, December 28, 2017 at https://www.petoskeynews.com/story/news/local/2017/12/29/reviewing-the-news/44842529/

[155] Idem.

[156] Weber, Timothy, "Crime pays: the role of prohibition and rum running along US 112 in the transformation of the Michigan State Police." 2005: Eastern Michigan University Honors Thesis. Page, Page 9.
https://commons.emich.edu/cgi/viewcontent.cgi?referer=&httpsredir=1&article=1005&context=honors

[157] Ibid., pages 11-12.

[158] State Trooper magazine, June 1929, cited in Ibid., page 23.

[159] See https://en.wikipedia.org/wiki/Federal_Reserve#Check_clearing_system

[160] https://www.atlantafed.org/-/media/documents/research/publications/economic-review/2008/vol93no4_quinn_roberds.pdf

[161] Charleston Sunday Gazette-Mail, August 28, 1960, page 46.
https://www.newspapers.com/clip/15277131/sunday-gazette-mail-aug-28-1960/

[162] Idem.

[163] https://law.justia.com/cases/federal/district-courts/FSupp/275/443/1458851/

[164] Kavieff, op. cit., location 1837 of 2421.

[165] Idem.

[166] Idem.

[167] Dearborn Historical Museum. https://thedhm.com/rowdysouthend/photos/

[168] Knapp, op. cit., page 197.

[169] https://www.slideshare.net/alexcoyhis/alex-coyhis-prohibition

[170] Warnes, Kathy, Ecorse along the Detroit River, quoting herself on website https://ecorsealongthedetroitriver.weebly.com/the-detroit-river-the-poster-highway-for-prohibition.html

[171] Kovanis, Georgea, "DEA seized 4 million deadly doses of fentanyl in Michigan, Ohio from May to September, agency says" Detroit Free Press, October 6, 2022, based on October 5, 2022 press conference, reprinted at https://www.usatoday.com/story/news/nation/2022/10/06/dea-seizes-4-million-deadly-doses-fentanyl/8194862001/

[172] Cox, Rev. Dr. Donna, "The Superpower of Singing: Music and the Struggle Against Slavery", https://www.nps.gov/articles/000/the-superpower-of-singing-music-and-the-struggle-against-slavery.htm

[173] Lowndes County, Mississippi Largest Slaveholders from 1860 Slave Census Schedules and Surname Matches for African Americans on 1870 Census. Transcribed by Tom Blake, October 2001 at https://sites.rootsweb.com/~ajac/mslowndes.htm

[174] "The United States considered the Chickasaw one of the Five Civilized Tribes of the Southeast, as they adopted numerous practices of European Americans. Resisting European-American settlers encroaching on their territory, they were forced by the U.S. government to sell their traditional lands in the 1832 Treaty of Pontotoc Creek and move to Indian Territory (Oklahoma) during the era of Indian removal in the 1830s." https://en.wikipedia.org/wiki/Chickasaw

[175] Holt, Lauren, "History of Slavery and Plantations in Mississippi" Preserve Marshall County and Holly Springs, Inc.

"Most enslaved persons in Mississippi worked to cultivate and harvest cotton on large plantations. "Field slaves," as they were called, worked from sunrise to sunset, often stopping only at mid-day for a short meal. Abe Kelley remembered that he and others "had to git up at three in the morning, then we carried our breakfast to the field…When we was working far from the house, we carried our dinner, too." Field labor was physically exhausting and left enslaved people little free time. As Frances
Fluker, a woman enslaved in Marshall County recollected, "at night we was all tired and went to bed 'cause we had to be up by daybreak—children and all." In the fields, overseers supervised the work and were often violent and cruel—Aaron Jones and Belle Caruthers remember
that enslaved persons were punished for displeasing overseers by being whipped, beaten, or "locked in the gin house." …

"Enslaved persons were subject to a number of laws that restricted their mobility and education, in large part because slaveowners and other whites were afraid of mass rebellion against their authority. Between 1826 and 1860, there were at least four attempted slave uprisings in Mississippi, though none was successful. In order to prevent activity that could lead to insurrection, enslaved people were required to have a 'pass' or be accompanied by a white 'monitor' when traveling more than one mile away from their residences. Since church meetings were some of the only times that groups of enslaved people were allowed to congregate freely, they became an important place not only for fellowship, but also for sharing information or making plans away from owners and overseers. …

"Enslaved persons were also prohibited from having contact with free blacks and were not permitted

to learn to read or write. Although it
was difficult and dangerous, some enslaved persons did learn, many "by trickery," as George Washington Albright remembers. Belle
Caruthers recalls that the white child she took care of "had Alphabet blocks to play with, and I learned my letters while she learned hers."
When Caruthers was discovered studying a spelling book, her owner "struck [her] with his muddy boot." Though the consequences for learning were often severe, literacy was powerful as both a tool and a symbol in enslaved communities. When Caruthers discovered she was able to spell out the words in a hymnal, she remembers, "I wasso happy...that I ran around telling all the other slaves."

[176] Lowry, William and William McCardie, A History of Mississippi: From the Discovery of the Great River by Hernando DeSoto, Including the Earliest Settlement Made by the French Under Iberville, to the Death of Jefferson Davis, 1891: AMS Press. pg. 527.

[177] https://en.wikipedia.org/w/index.php?title=Jackie_Wilson&oldid=1005810959

[178] Ford was absorbing almost as much labor arriving in Detroit during the Roaring Twenties, but was himself an ardent racist.

From Ronnie Schreiber, "How Henry Ford, Who Published Rascist Diatribes Against Jazz, Helped Popularize the Sound of Jazz and R&B" January, 2020, https://www.thetruthaboutcars.com/2020/01/how-henry-ford-who-published-racist-diatribes-against-jazz-helped-popularize-the-sound-of-jazz-and-rb/ :

"One of African-Americans' great cultural contributions to America and the world, jazz music, was also seen by Ford and Liebold as a Jewish plot*. Jewish Jazz – Moron Music – Becomes Our National Music, was published in the August 6, 1921 issue of the Dearborn Independent. Recorded music had been around since Edison's 1877 wax-cylinder phonograph, and the "modern" Victrola that played Emile Berliner's flat recordings was introduced in 1906. However, though the phonograph was a great success, in the 1920s much of what was considered popular music was still being sold as sheet music, and much of that originated from music publishing firms in New York City's "Tin Pan Alley," where many of the composers, lyricists, and publishers were from Jewish backgrounds.

"From The International Jew:

'Many people have wondered whence come the waves upon waves of musical slush that invade decent parlors and set the young people of this generation imitating the drivel of morons... Popular Music is a Jewish monopoly. Jazz is a Jewish creation. The mush, the slush, the sly suggestion, the abandoned sensuousness of sliding notes, are of Jewish origin.

'Monkey talk, jungle squeals, grunts and squeaks and gasps suggestive of cave love are camouflaged by a few feverish notes and admitted to homes where the thing itself, unaided by the piano, would be stamped out in horror. Girls and boys a little while ago were inquiring who paid Mrs. Rip Van Winkle's rent while Mr. Rip Van Winkle was away. In decent parlors the fluttering music sheets disclosed expressions taken directly from the cesspools of modern capitals, to be made the daily slang, the thoughtlessly hummed remarks of high school boys and girls.'

And you thought jazz was about improvising on a musical theme."

179 Map attribution unknown. The Great Migration — which took place from 1916 to 1970 — saw 6 million African Americans move from the South to the North and West. It eclipsed the Gold Rush and the flight from the Dust Bowl in terms of population movement within the U.S., according to Allyson Hobbs, a Stanford University historian. Before this period, 90 percent of Black Americans lived in the South, and after, just 53 percent did according to Hobbs.

180 https://www.findagrave.com/memorial/221154954/berry-gordy

181 https://www.history-of-rock.com/motown_records.htm

182 https://www.findagrave.com/memorial/40676238/bertha-ida-gordy

183 Posner, Gerald, 'Motown', Jan. 12, 2003, https://www.nytimes.com/2003/01/12/books/chapters/motown.html

184 https://www.adampwhite.com/westgrandblog/bertha-gordy

185 https://engineering-channel.com/electric-guitar-history/

186 https://www.mozartproject.org/how-did-the-electric-guitar-changed-music

187 "Vital Statistics of the United States: 1980–2003". Table 1-1. Live births, birth rates, and fertility rates, by race: United States, 1909–2003. Centers for Disease Control and Prevention/National Center for Health Statistics. June 6, 2019.

188 Idem.

189 https://en.wikipedia.org/wiki/Top_40

190 https://en.wikipedia.org/wiki/Music_radio

191 Idem.

192 Idem.

193 https://en.wikipedia.org/wiki/Transistor_radio

194 https://en.wikipedia.org/wiki/Jackie_Wilson

196 Idem.

197 Idem.

198 https://en.wikipedia.org/wiki/Berry_Gordy

199 In 1960, Gordy officially incorporated his company, Motown Records including Tamla Records under the Motown Record Corporation name.

200 Idem.

201 This date is uncertain. The sale may have been as early as 1959 or as late as 1962. The 1961 date is chosen as it allows time for the Douglases to learn that the Michigan Liquor Control Board will not grant them a liquor license and to pivot to the idea of a teen night club.

202 Gitlin, Todd, The Sixties: Years of Hope, Days of Rage, Bantam 1993. Preface, page 9.

203 "Man Of The Year: John F. Kennedy, A Way with the People" Time Magazine, January 5, 1962. https://content.time.com/time/subscriber/article/0,33009,874369-11,00.html

204 https://en.wikipedia.org/wiki/June_1962

205 https://en.wikipedia.org/wiki/June_1962

206 https://www.encyclopedia.com/history/encyclopedias-almanacs-transcripts-and-maps/race-riots-1960s

207 https://en.wikipedia.org/wiki/January_1962

208 Kulwicki, Cara, "Top-5 Motown Singles" https://thecurvature.wordpress.com/2012/07/13/top-5-motown-singles-1962/

209 https://en.wikipedia.org/wiki/The_Beatles

210 Wiles, Rick, "The Club Ponytail: Northern Michigan's famous teen nightclub." Mackinac Journal, February/March 2014, page 12.

211 Club Ponytail Part 6 of 8 medley on Youtube. Channel "Atwoods History" https://youtu.be/m7FaTHnvozE?list=PLrlh_muSfPT9jVotSTotComT9wJyLepri&t=256

212 Club Ponytail Part 6 of 8 medley on Youtube. Channel "Atwoods History" https://youtu.be/o-TLuIGpi14?list=PLrlh_muSfPT9jVotSTotComT9wJyLepri&t=94

213 Idem.

214 https://en.wikipedia.org/wiki/Club_Manitou_of_Harbor_Springs#The_Beachboys-Roy_Orbison

215 https://en.wikipedia.org/wiki/Billboard_Year-End_Hot_100_singles_of_1962

216 Griswold, Deirdre, "Revolutionary youth held first protest of Vietnam War", August 13, 2012, https://www.workers.org/2012/08/3117/

217 https://en.wikipedia.org/wiki/Billboard_Year-End_Hot_100_singles_of_1963

218 Public Domain, https://commons.wikimedia.org/

[219] Public Domain, https://commons.wikimedia.org/w/index.php?curid=3765015

[220] Murphy, James B. Becoming the Beach Boys: 1961-1963. Pages 304-305.

[221] https://michiganrockandrolllegends.com/index.php/mrrl-hall-of-fame/345-kingtones

[222] http://www.thekingtones.com/samples/wishforangel.mp3

[223] http://www.thekingtones.com/

[224] https://en.wikipedia.org/wiki/Brian_Hyland

[225] https://en.wikipedia.org/wiki/Lou_Christie

[226] https://en.wikipedia.org/wiki/Johnny_and_the_Hurricanes

[227] https://www.velikovsky.info/bulletin-of-the-atomic-scientists/

[228] "Club Ponytail Part 3 of 8 medley" https://youtu.be/WiRDkIzgt-0?list=PLrlh_muSfPT9jVotSTotComT9wJyLepri

[229] https://en.wikipedia.org/wiki/Billboard_Year-End_Hot_100_singles_of_1963

[230] https://en.wikipedia.org/wiki/Billboard_Year-End_Hot_100_singles_of_1963

[231] https://en.wikipedia.org/wiki/The_Iguanas_(Michigan_band)

[232] Johnson, Gary, "Iguanas" June 1, 2018. https://michiganrockandrolllegends.com/index.php/mrrl-hall-of-fame/338-iguanas

[233] https://www.musixmatch.com/

[234] Wiles, Rick, "The Club Ponytail: Northern Michigan's famous teen nightclub." Mackinac Journal, February/March 2014, page 13.

[235] "Club Ponytail Part 1 of 8 medley" https://youtu.be/m7FaTHnvozE?list=PLrlh_muSfPT9jVotSTotComT9wJyLepri&t=159

[236] http://www.historylink.org/index.cfm?DisplayPage=output.cfm&file_id=5206. Released to the public domain.

[237] https://en.wikipedia.org/wiki/Billboard_Year-End_Hot_100_singles_of_1963

[238] This file is licensed under the Creative Commons Attribution-Share Alike 3.0 Unported license.

[239] Club Ponytail Part 6 of 8 medley on Youtube. Channel "Atwoods History"

https://www.youtube.com/channel/UCiRopnPYqdmFPkMwuLwyA_A Playlist: https://www.youtube.com/playlist?list=PLrlh_muSfPT9jVotSTotComT9wJyLepri

[240] Idem.

[241] Bishop, Chris, "The Chancellors" December 10, 2007. https://garagehangover.com/Chancellors/

[242] Idem.

[243] Idem.

[244] https://en.wikipedia.org/wiki/Sam_the_Sham

[245] Lindsay, James M., "The Twenty Best Vietnam Protest Songs" blog post on the Council on Foreign Relations, March 5, 2015. https://www.cfr.org/blog/twenty-best-vietnam-protest-songs

[246] Idem.
[247] https://en.wikipedia.org/wiki/Billboard_Year-End_Hot_100_singles_of_1967

[248] https://en.wikipedia.org/wiki/Vietnam_War

[249] https://en.wikipedia.org/wiki/Walter_Cronkite

[250] https://en.wikipedia.org/wiki/Billboard_Year-End_Hot_100_singles_of_1968

[251] https://en.wikipedia.org/wiki/MC5

[252] Idem.

[253] Idem.

[254] Songwriters: Nicholas Barry Chinn, Michael Chapman, Nicholas Chinn. musixmatch.com

[255] https://en.wikipedia.org/wiki/Jan_and_Dean

[256] Licensed under the Creative Commons Attribution 4.0 International license

[257] Tschmuck, Peter "The U.S. Recorded Music Market in the light of the Billboard Hot 100 – the 1960s" https://musicbusinessresearch.wordpress.com/2011/11/14/the-us-recorded-music-market-in-the-light-of-the-billboard-hot-100-%E2%80%93-the-1960s/

[258] Based on Billboard's Hottest Hot 100 Hits by Fred Bronson (4th Edition, 2007). https://www.listchallenges.com/the-top-100-songs-of-the-60s

[259] McCollum, Brian, "Detroit's 100 Greatest Songs extra: Greatest Detroit 1960s Songs" Detroit Free Press, August 15, 1016 https://www.freep.com/story/entertainment/music/2016/08/15/detroits-100-

greatest-songs-extra-greatest-detroit-1960s-songs/88698104/

[260] https://www.interlochen.org/about/history

[261] https://www.interlochen.org/about/history/timeline

[262] "The musical, which opened … on Oct. 12, 1971, turned the story of one of history's most notorious executions into a splashy spectacle. In doing so, it married rock and musical theater, ushering in Broadway's British invasion of the 1970s and 1980s and paving the way for shows like "Les Misérables" and "The Phantom of the Opera."

But the nearly 90-minute concept album came first in 1970, because, as Lloyd Webber recalled recently to The Telegraph, no producer wanted to put 'the worst idea in history" onstage."

https://www.nytimes.com/2021/10/12/theater/jesus-christ-superstar-50th-anniversary.html

[263] "10 now-defunct Detroit music venues'. Detroit Metro Times.
https://www.metrotimes.com/detroit/10-now-defunct-detroit-music-venues/Slideshow/29234883

[264] https://en.wikipedia.org/wiki/Vietnam_War

[265] Judith Landis notes.

[266] https://www.bbc.com/news/blogs-magazine-monitor-30250358

[267] https://en.wikipedia.org/wiki/Woodstock

[268] Claiborne, Lottie, "What We Talk About: The Body" in Coastal Connecticut Magazine, June 2014, pages 61-67 reprinted by Bebe Bardeaux, "In Lottie's Own Words: Farewell to a Burlesque Legend" March 2, 2020 https://www.bebebardot.com/post/in-lottie-s-own-words-farewell-to-a-burlesque-legend

[269] Greenwood Cemetery Genealogical http://www.gwood.us/research/genealogical-research/ referenced at https://www.findagrave.com/memorial/135637871/william-a-gerhart

Made in the USA
Middletown, DE
08 April 2024

52465528R10205